The Structured Vision
of Norman Mailer

The Structured Vision of Norman Mailer

by Barry H. Leeds

New York • New York University Press
London • University of London Press Limited
1969

This book is for my wife, Robin

Acknowledgments

I would like to express my deepest appreciation to Professor William Holmes, who aided and encouraged me immeasurably in the preparation of an earlier version of this book. I would also like to thank Professor Oscar Cargill, Mr. Granville Hicks, Mr. Scott Meredith, and Mr. Chris Kentera for the consideration they have shown me. Thanks are due my students, Anne Chapman and Joanne Rifenburg, for help in preparing the manuscript. Finally, this book would not have been possible without the constant help of my wife.

Permissions

Biographical Outline: Norman Mailer

1923 Born January 31, Long Branch, New Jersey; parents Isaac Barnett and Fanny (Schneider) Mailer.

1939 Graduated from Boys High School, Brooklyn, New York.

1943 Received B.A. degree, Harvard.

1944 Drafted into U.S. Army. Served as rifleman with 112th Cavalry out of San Antonio, Texas. Foreign service for eighteen months in Philippines and Japan.

1944 Married Beatrice Silverman; divorced 1951.

1946 Discharged from Army in May.

1954 Married Adele Morales; divorced 1962.

1962 Married Lady Jean Campbell; divorced 1963.

1963 Married Beverley Bentley.

Children:

> First marriage—Susan
> Second marriage—Danielle, Elizabeth
> Third marriage—Kate
> Fourth marriage—Michael, Stephen

Writings:

1948 *The Naked and the Dead*

1951 *Barbary Shore*

1955   *The Deer Park*
1958   "The White Negro" [1]
1959   *Advertisements for Myself*
1962   *Deaths for the Ladies and Other Disasters*
1963   *The Presidential Papers*
1965   *An American Dream*
1966   *Cannibals and Christians*
1967   *The Deer Park: A Play* [2]
        The Short Fiction of Norman Mailer
        Why Are We in Vietnam?
1968   *The Armies of the Night*
        Miami and the Siege of Chicago

Miscellaneous:

1941   *Story* Magazine's College Award
1953–1963   An Editor of *Dissent*
1956   Co-founder of *Village Voice*
1960   National Institute of Arts and Letters Grant in Literature
1968   Produced, directed, and starred in three movies: "Wild 90," "Beyond the Law," and "Maidstone."
1969   National Book Award in arts and letters for 1968 (for *The Armies of the Night*).

        Pulitzer Prize in general nonfiction for 1968 (for *The Armies of the Night*).

[1] Dates given here are for first publication in book form. Dates used in my text for "The White Negro" and *An American Dream* deal more precisely with time of writing and first appearance of the work in print. The bibliography and the footnotes (especially the notes to the introduction) make this clear.

[2] This play ran for 127 performances in an off-Broadway production beginning January 31, 1967.

Contents

The Structured Vision
of Norman Mailer

Introduction

This is a critical study of all of Norman Mailer's major work to date, organized around the thesis that there is a definite line of development to be traced between *The Naked and the Dead* (1948) and *The Armies of the Night* (1968). A study of two particular elements in the work, narrative voice and concern with social issues, reveals that Mailer has grown enormously in the sophistication of his thematic concerns and his effectiveness in presenting them to the reader. At the same time, questions are raised (and some answers hazarded) as to why Mailer has not been totally successful in achieving the degree of fictional control to write the massively significant work which he himself and his readers have expected of him.

The five novels are treated first, in chronological order. *The Naked and the Dead* and *An American Dream* (1964)[1] receive greatest attention because it is my contention that they represent the two significant poles in the development of Mailer's fictional art at the time of this writing.

Two major themes loom large in all of Mailer's fiction: that of social ills and that of the plight of the individual in contemporary society. Each of the novels proceeds simultaneously on two levels, social and individual. It will be shown that Mailer's earliest work grows out of the tradition of social criticism of the thirties: that he is most clearly influenced in *The Naked and the Dead* (in both subject matter and mechanics) by Dos Passos, Farrell, and Steinbeck, with the significant distinction that Mailer invests less hope in the individual common man than do these writers.

By the time he wrote *An American Dream,* Mailer had shifted from a position of total despair at the plight of the individual, to one of very carefully qualified hope. The problem of individual alienation as presented in *An American Dream* is integrally connected to Mailer's personal conception of American existentialism, as it is most clearly set forth in the essay "The White Negro" (1957).[2] It should be emphasized that this study deals with existentialism only as Mailer sees it. No attempt has been made to study or define the existentialism of other writers, European or American. Positions intermediate between those of despair and mitigated hope in regard to the human condition are evident in *Barbary Shore* (1951) and *The Deer Park* (1955). A comparison of the latter novel to the stage version of *The Deer Park* (produced 1967) provides a clearer view of the shift in the author's developing vision.

As a perceptive and conscientious social critic in constant proximity to contemporary social issues in America, Mailer remains cynical and pessimistic in his fiction (although the most recent nonfiction works show some sense of possible hope for America's future). The major line of development on this level lies in the aesthetic form by which the material is presented. After the clearly derivative *The Naked and the Dead*,[2] the increasingly original perceptions of America's social ills presented by Mailer are paralleled by the progressive development of a highly personal narrative voice. Therefore, in tracing the two major thematic concerns throughout the fiction, this study deals as well with the changing narrative stance and the intricate metaphorical patterns which grow out of it. It is my contention that these reach their most effective fictional form in *An American Dream.*

Point of view has been, at Mailer's own admission, a constant problem to him after *The Naked and the Dead.* (All four novels succeeding that have been written in the first person.) The second and third chapters, dealing with *Barbary Shore* and *The Deer Park,* discuss this problem and show how Mailer attempted to divorce himself from the direct influence of other novelists while still devoting himself to the two major themes introduced in *The Naked and the Dead.* References to essays and fictional fragments written between 1955 and 1964 further help to explore the problem of novelistic form and to introduce the emerging system of metaphor by which Mailer made his narrative voice a uniquely personal one. Comparison of the two versions of *The Deer Park,* through emphasizing the differences in conception of two major characters from the earlier version to the later, introduces the central thesis that Mailer's later vision is conditioned by some hope for the individual.

Chapter 4, through a close critical reading of *An American Dream,* attempts to show that this novel is the direct result, formally, metaphorically, and thematically, of the linear development suggested in the earlier chapters. By showing how the elements of subject matter and artistic form are here united integrally in a more highly original fictional statement than Mailer has yet produced, the chapter places greater emphasis on the central thesis that a peculiarly American existentialism which governs the vision of *An American Dream* is the most significant thematic outgrowth of Mailer's fictional development since *The Naked and the Dead;* and that in this existentialism is an implicit hope for the salvation of the individual.

Why Are We in Vietnam? (1967) presents particular problems. Despite the fact that it has been well received by some reviewers, it seems to represent a retrogression rather than an advance in the artistic development which has hitherto been seen in Mailer's fiction. Although it presents thematic concerns and metaphorical patterns similar to those of the earlier novels (especially *An American Dream*) and thus fits easily into a treatment of the canon, the fifth novel lacks the controlled integration of form and subject which make *An American Dream* effective.

The Armies of the Night (1968) and, less strikingly, *Miami and the Siege of Chicago* (1968) represent a new prose form for Mailer, in which we are presented with the novelist in a new role: not as journalist, but as narrator/participant in a nonfiction novel. The significance of these books may be more clearly understood in terms of their development out of Mailer's previous work, both fiction and nonfiction. These books do not pretend to be objectively rendered history. Structured like novels, they recount historical events through the subjective and metaphorically rich voice of the central character who experiences them: Mailer himself. Three lines of development converge here: Mailer's fiction, his previous nonfiction works, and his flamboyant public image.

At the outset of his career, Mailer can be seen to fit neatly into the American literary continuum, in that *The Naked and the Dead* clearly grows out of the social novels of the thirties. Mailer's concern with the shabbiness of the American dream, which is to inform all of his subsequent work, is introduced here. His parallel concern with the condition of the individual represents Mailer's most significant departure from the influence of earlier writers: the hopeless alienation of the individual characters in *The Naked and the Dead* informs the blackness of Mailer's vision of postwar America, and looks ahead to his more explicit concern in the works which follow with the problems confronting the individual in that society. Through the ambitious failure of *Barbary Shore* and the varying successes of the other novels, Mailer progressively refines both his understanding of what is wrong in American society, and his capacity to render these criticisms within the novel form through a credible and effective narrative character.

With *Advertisements for Myself* (1959), Mailer simultaneously begins to develop a parallel non-fiction prose voice, tied at many points to the metaphors and themes of his fiction and rooted in his sense of himself as a public personage. Much material pertinent to an understanding of Mailer's novels which appears in *Advertisements for Myself* and the succeeding non-fiction books, *The Presidential Papers* (1963) and *Cannibals and Christians* (1966), is dealt with in the first five chapters of this study. Chapter 6 briefly treats Mailer's poetry and begins to consider the problem of the man's controversial public image as it bears upon his work and the critical reception of it. In Chapter 7 a study of the first three non-fiction works (with some emphasis on "The White Negro") attempts to show that the personal essayistic style developed in these books forms a major part of the basis for Mailer's step into a new form in *The Armies of the Night*. The final chapter, dealing primarily with *The Armies of the Night* and peripherally with *Miami and the Siege of Chicago,* ties together the central lines of development posited in this study, and shows that *The Armies of the Night* is no freak success artistically, but rather the logical culmination of Mailer's personal concerns with the individual and American society, and his increasing control over narrative prose, as they have developed over two decades. The chapter closes with some guarded prognoses for Mailer's future as an artist.

One final suggestion to the reader is in order. The popularly adverse reaction to *An American Dream* may prompt you to avoid the chapter dealing with that novel. But I cannot overemphasize my feeling that an open-minded understanding of Mailer's intentions in *An American Dream* is the key to an understanding of Mailer's mind and art as they operate in the more warmly-received books which follow. Even a hurried or partial reading of this book should include the *American Dream* chapter.

Notes

1 *An American Dream* was first published in serial form in the first eight issues (January through August) of *Esquire* in 1964. Since it is my intention to be as precise as possible in tracing the often rapid development of Mailer's ideas, and since the novel was presented to a large reading audience in substantially final form in 1964, this is the date I use in referring to the novel in my text. *An American Dream* was subsequently published in hardcover by Dial Press in 1965, and in paperback by Dell in 1966. Subsequent footnotes make this clear.

2 Mailer, in *Advertisements for Myself,* gives 1957 as the year in which "The White Negro" was written, and it is therefore the date I use in my text. The essay was first published in 1958 by City Lights Book Shop in San Francisco. Since the most readily available text of "The White Negro" is in *Advertisements for Myself,* all references to the essay will be to that edition.

3 The structure of which is strikingly similar to that of Dos Passos' *USA* trilogy. Mailer himself admits this influence.

1

*T*he *N*aked and the *D*ead

In "The White Negro," Mailer writes:

The Second World War presented a mirror to the human condition which blinded anyone who looked into it . . . one was then obliged also to see that no matter how crippled and perverted an image of man was the society he had created, it was nonetheless his creation, his collective creation (at least his collective creation from the past) and if society was so murderous, then who could ignore the most hideous of questions about his own nature? [1]

The Naked and the Dead, drawing its subject matter directly from that war, proceeds on the two levels of concern suggested by the quotation: the sickness of society and the flawed nature of the individual which engenders and perpetuates that sickness. Mailer's vision of American society as it is represented in the American army is one of abject pessimism. In conjunction with his treatment of

9

individual soldiers and officers it more closely approaches despair than any novel he has written since.

Perhaps the most impressive thing about Mailer's performance in *The Naked and the Dead* is the structural effectiveness of the novel. The control of such a massive weight of material is not often within the ability of so young an author. It should be noted, however, that the structural success here proceeds naturally out of a happy choice of subject and setting, and out of extensive emulation of established writers, rather than from overwhelming precocity. The novel is, in fact, a rather naive product at many points. It is the recognition of his own limitations, and the establishment of certain guidelines within which his developing talent could operate without overextension, that enabled Mailer to execute a valid and comprehensible artistic statement.

The first of these limitations is that of subject matter. It was natural that a recent veteran should write of the war, and particularly of the Pacific theatre, in which he had served. But it would seem that the choice of this area over the European conflict represented to Mailer a greater decision than is immediately apparent. In *Advertisements for Myself,* speaking of the short novel "A Calculus at Heaven," which is the obvious precursor of *The Naked and the Dead,* he says:

> I may as well confess that by December 8th or 9th of 1941 . . . I was worrying darkly whether it would be more likely that a great war novel would be written about Europe or the Pacific, and the longer I thought, the less doubt there was in my mind. Europe was the place.
>
> So if a year later, in this short novel, I chose to write about the Pacific war, it was not because I was

in love with the tropics but because . . . it was and is easier to write a war novel about the Pacific—you don't have to have a feeling about the culture of Europe and the collision of America upon it. To try a major novel about the last war in Europe without a sense of the past is to fail in the worst way—as an overambitious and opportunistic slick.[2]

As will be seen later, Mailer returned, after almost twenty years, to his concern with the collision between European and American culture, in *An American Dream*. But at this point he resisted the temptation to attempt too much. He carried his self-imposed structural limitation further by setting the entire action of the novel on the island of Anopopei, tracing from landing to victory the history of a single, relatively minor campaign. Thus, although he incorporates well-spaced and accurate passages dealing with military tactics on the command level, these are not confused by a commitment to deal with the rest of the theatre, and thus with massive reams of historical documentation.

The concentration upon one infantry platoon from which to draw major characters is one of the most overused devices of war novels and grade B movies. The fortuitous makeup of the platoon, whose geographical and racial representation spans every area and ethnic group, may justly be considered clumsy. But the device is necessary to structural control, and criticism of it may be mitigated by the fact that here it is not the self-conscious establishment of a miniature melting-pot society as it is in hack novels and simplistic wartime movies. Instead, once provided with the method of introducing his characters, Mailer uses their various backgrounds to build a broad condemnation of American society and politics.

Certain obvious parallels may be drawn, here, be-

tween several of Mailer's characters and those of writers
he had read and admired at Harvard. In *Advertisements
for Myself,* he tells us that:

> Before I was seventeen I had formed the desire to be
> a major writer. . . . I read and reread *Studs Lonigan,
> U.S.A.,* and *The Grapes of Wrath.* Later I would add
> Wolfe and Hemingway and Faulkner and to a small
> measure, Fitzgerald; but Farrell, Dos Passos and Stein-
> beck were the novel for me in that sixty days before
> I turned seventeen.[3]

The influence of Farrell may be seen in Gallagher, the
Irishman from the Boston slums, who has many superficial similarities to Studs Lonigan. But while Gallagher,
like Lonigan, is represented as a mass of inarticulate
frustrations and hatreds, and while Mailer, like Farrell,
deals in a sort of economic determinism which lays much
of the blame at the feet of society, the emphasis has shifted
drastically. From Farrell, Mailer has inherited and accepted
the doctrine that poverty and ignorance and local political
corruption are self-perpetuating, and that they are destructive to the common man caught up in them. But
where Studs is a sympathetic character, and ultimately one
of some stature, Gallagher can evoke in us little more than
a grudging pity. Certainly neither is a man of particular
morality. The childhood Jew-baiting scenes in Farrell's
trilogy are, if anything, more brutal than the parallel
scene in the Gallagher flashback, for example. What
mitigates reader sympathy for Gallagher, and throws some
blame upon the individual as well as society for the hatred
and brutality which make up Gallagher's world vision, is
the man's own self-indulgent, aggressive stupidity. Further,
he is portrayed with no saving virtues. Unlike such men
as Croft, Martinez or Goldstein, who for widely different

and often selfish reasons act with courage or perseverence
to the ultimate good of their immediate society, the platoon, Gallagher is craven in his hatred. It would seem to
be one of Mailer's theses that no matter what the environ-
ment, only a particular type of man responds entirely to
the corrupt manipulation of machine politics and pro-
fessional bigots.

There is more than one side to the responsibility of the
individual here. It is significant that while Gallagher
represents in purest form the considerable bastions of anti-
Semitism in the Army and in America in the forties, he
has a despicable opposite number in Roth, the soft, whining, intellectually pretentious graduate of C.C.N.Y.; and
even in the relatively admirable Goldstein, whose paranoia when confronted with anti-Semitism is justified but
unbecoming. Despite the corruption of society, each individual has a certain latitude within which to establish a
viable system of personal morality if he so chooses. In this
novel, few achieve one, though the attempts of such men
as Red, Martinez, and even Lieutenant Hearn are important. It will be seen that it is the vision of personal
moral failure as much as that of social failure which makes
Mailer's so very pessimistic a statement.

In this one sense, he has gone beyond another of his
teachers, Steinbeck, whose powerful but idealized portraits of common men victimized by economic depression
(especially in such novels as *The Grapes of Wrath, In
Dubious Battle* and *Of Mice and Men*) have parallels in
the depression experiences of Ridges and Red. But where
Steinbeck's novels climax so often in the pathetic, almost
tragic destruction of a noble proletarian, they end characteristically on a note of hope. After the Preacher's death
there is still Tom Joad to take up the position of representative for social justice; in the clumsier and more
patently propagandistic ending to *In Dubious Battle,* the

pattern is still more obvious; and after Lennie's death there is still George to remember their dream and to question what changes are necessary so that such a dream need not be impossible. Steinbeck's works are optimistic because they throw total responsibility upon society, and society can be changed. What cannot be changed by legislation or revolution is the character of the common man, the primary resource upon which Steinbeck relies for his hope, and of which Mailer almost despairs.

To Steinbeck, ignorance and a stage version of inarticulacy are the things of which nobility and pathos are made. Tom Joad's parting speech to his mother represents perhaps the peak of effectiveness to which Steinbeck could bring these qualities. But to Mailer there is nothing noble about ignorance, which thrives upon and aggravates stupidity and hatred. His version of the Steinbeck "Okie" is Oscar Ridges, a stolid farmboy so beaten down by generations of poverty and blind religious acceptance of what misfortunes an incomprehensible God consistently showers upon him, that he is more bovine than human. Another direction is taken by Croft, a man who started with ignorance, and when he early learned enough to be cynical, fed every experience he had into a comprehensive, absolute hatred. He loves to kill gratuitously, and the massive scope of his hatred makes him a fascinating figure, more important to Mailer's treatment of the individual than any enlisted man besides Red Valsen. The latter, too, brings to Anopopei the credentials of a stock Steinbeck character. A coal miner at fourteen, subsequently a hobo/truck driver/dishwasher, Red has developed and clung to one basic value: to remain a loner. The considerable pain thrust upon him by the Depression and by other men have not created in him the passivity of a Ridges, nor the aggressive hatred of Croft. Concerned with preserving his own insular world, he reacts only to what threatens it.

The most obvious influence upon *The Naked and the Dead*, however, is that of Dos Passos. Maxwell Geismar, writing in *The Saturday Review* at the time of the novel's appearance, remarked that "Mr. Mailer uses some of the technical devices which John Dos Passos initiated in the American novel, while there is also an influence of tone." [4] Although the qualified comparison drawn by Geismar is to *Three Soldiers,* its far smaller scope and the relative lack of sophistication of plot and character development make it less like Mailer's novel than is *USA*.

Much that has been said of Steinbeck's proletarian characters can be applied to those of Dos Passos as well. Joe Williams, for example, is a totally sympathetic character whose consistent misfortunes are brought about by the social structure and by the treachery of others (such as his faithless wife, Del). Throughout, he remains ignorant to the point of opacity, thereby generating further misfortunes. But he never becomes evil, and rarely reacts with more than an apologetic slang euphemism. It is not with such a highly idealized and false portrait as Joe that Dos Passos can claim importance in an artistic (as distinct from a topically political) sense. Among his characters, it is the more socially mobile, such as Richard Ellsworth Savage or Eveline Hutchins, who are conducive to the far more sophisticated view of American society for which the trilogy is valuable.

The structure of *USA* is all-important here. Dos Passos had used an episodic structure in *Three Soldiers,* but that employed in *USA* not only presents in effective juxtaposition the experiences of characters from a widely divergent social and cultural context, but also adds elements of painful satire by means of several devices which then represented a major breakthrough in fictional form. *The Camera Eye,* the newsreels, and the short biographical sketches highlight the irony in the main episodes they adjoin. (For example, passages relating Joe Williams' victimization by bureaucratic governmental organizations are often followed by self-satisfied news releases from such organizations.) The effective scope of Dos Passos' social statement is extended so as to be almost unlimited, for no event or attitude or person is immune from *The Camera Eye,* newsreel, or biography.

Mailer seems to have lifted the basic structural concept of *The Naked and the Dead* directly from *USA,* with an important distinction. While he has not limited the scope of society that he can portray and attack, he has limited the arena within which the actual action, the main plot line, takes place. He follows, in a sense, a personal set of dramatic unities. In *USA,* the basic plot line is made up of the lives of the main characters, while the interlaced devices discussed above are used for authorial comment on wider concerns. In Mailer's novel, the plot is scrupulously limited to the happenings on Anopopei. *The Time Machine,* a dramatically effective mechanical device which must have been suggested by those used by Dos Passos, presents detailed flash-backs to the reader, of the previous life of each major character. With effective timing, Mailer introduces these "offstage" events at points where they will bear most directly upon the present action. Another device used periodically by Mailer is the *Chorus,* by which in a highly stylized manner he is able effectively to introduce the opinions of many enlisted men on a single topic (such as the faithlessness of women) within a short space.

Where Dos Passos relies heavily upon his three devices for the broad social scope that he wishes to represent, Mailer has provided himself, by his choice of setting and situation, with a natural hierarchical structure in the military chain of command. Thus, while *The Time Machine* is used to portray the home of a Midwestern businessman, the slums of Boston, or Harvard Yard, it is the presence on Anopopei of men who have experienced these places, which justifies Mailer's detailed treatment of them, and obviates the possibility of their introduction seeming stilted. Every element of American society dealt with becomes integral to the novel as a whole, not merely because it seems to fit into a re-creation in retrospect of that society, but because it is drawn from the life of a character in whom the reader has come to believe. For example, Martinez' desperate concern with the racial inferiority he feels as a Mexican-American is demonstrated by his actions in regard to other infantrymen, then further explored through a *Time Machine* sequence of his childhood. The two episodes integrally substantiate one another.

Rather than limit himself to the experiences of the enlisted man, Mailer seeks a broader scope of social experience by dealing as well with the upper strata of military society (which often coincides here with the upper strata of civilian society). It has been noted above that Mailer has executed the necessary campaign effectively, even to the point of providing a map of the island. This is a relatively simple and mechanical task. What is not simple nor mechanical is the manner in which he is able to create a believable general out of whose character the major action of the campaign proceeds.

General Cummings is an effective military man of considerable intelligence. He is presented in primarily rational terms, and the things he believes, in his emotional and highly informed logic, are frightening. He is reactionary, and believes that Hitler was right in foretelling a long ascendancy for the reactionaries. Coldly and logically he persists in sharpening and maintaining the class distinctions existing between officers and enlisted men, because he knows that effective command is made up of resentment and fear from below. Although he has certain very real neurotic traits, he rarely indulges them, but at times they have an immediate effect on the direction the novel's action takes. One of his indulgences is to provide himself with an intellectual companion by choosing Lieutenant Hearn as his aide.

Traditionally, second lieutenants are in an untenable position, pressured both from above and below. In Hearn's case the situation is immeasurably aggravated by his personal makeup. Product of a Midwestern prep school and Harvard, he is an upper class liberal who doesn't like people very much. As an officer, he is forced into daily contact with stupid bigots who outrank him. As a man who prides himself on a certain moral consistency (which shows itself in a dangerously self-indulgent freedom of speech) he manages to derive considerable discomfort from his co-officers' loud stupidity without managing to stay safely silent; and at the same time manages to speak out with no moral victory. In his relations with the General, he brings about a situation through minor rebellions which results in an unnecessary major humiliation. His relations with the enlisted men are distant if not hostile, but he finds himself, as a liberal, taking their part in his talks with General Cummings.

Hearn is a crucial structural device, bridging the gap between the enlisted men and their commanders. It is significant that during the first half of the novel, he spends most of his time in the reader's view, talking to the General. In the latter half, up to his pointedly anticlimactic death, he is the commander of the platoon about which the book revolves. But as a character, Hearn is rather empty. He comes off as less real, as well as less sympathetic, than most of the other characters. If only because Hearn's vacuity would appear more interesting as an intentional part of the pessimistic view of wartime and postwar

America posited by Mailer, I prefer to believe that the deficiencies in the Lieutenant's character are not accidental. In a gallery of well-drawn characters, it is difficult to believe that so pivotal a figure as Hearn would have slipped away from Mailer's control. Rather, it would seem a logical part of the statement this novel makes, that an intelligent and outspoken man who is ineffectual with and resented by both the upper and lower classes, and who is ultimately killed to no purpose, might be exactly the representative of liberalism that Mailer wished to show.

Such an intention on Mailer's part seems substantiated by General Cummings' confident prophecy that the world, and America in particular, is destined to undergo a long era in which the reactionaries will reign. But what crushes all hope for liberal ascendancy in American politics is Mailer's view of the common man. Mailer's enlisted men are not idealized representatives of the lower classes who make up the basis of Steinbeck's optimism for America. Nor are they the carefully documented representatives of diverse ethnic groups who are brought together in such war novels as Leon Uris' *Battle Cry* to point up with a maudlin, neo-Crane pride the brotherhood of men under fire. Rather, with as intense a liberal leaning as Steinbeck and as vivid a feeling for the realities of combat as any ex-riflemen writing, Mailer establishes a gallery of men in whose reality the reader believes, and destroys them all, leaving a message of despair. Lieutenant Hearn, the self-styled liberal, is killed by direct pressure of the hatred of the lower classes as it reposes in Croft, but not before he has recognized in himself a corresponding disgust for the men; and, more disturbing, a desire for power parallel to that of General Cummings. Both Hearn and Cummings make up part of Mailer's comprehensive despair at the plight of the individual. Not only is Hearn destroyed, but even Cummings, who survives and wins the campaign, recognizes personal failure at the novel's end:

> The men resisted him, resisted change, with maddening inertia. No matter how you pushed them, they always gave ground sullenly, regrouped once the pressure was off. You could work on them, you could trick them, but there were times now when he doubted basically whether he could change them, really mold them. And it might be the same again in the Philippines. With all his enemies at Army, he did not have much chance of gaining an added star before the Philippines, and with that would go all chance of an Army command before the war ended.
>
> Time was going by, and with it, opportunity. . . . He was getting older, and he would be bypassed. When the war with Russia came he would not be important enough, not close enough to the seats of power, to take the big step, the big leap. Perhaps after this war he might be smarter to take a fling at the State Department. His brother-in-law certainly would do him no harm.[5]

Cummings' sense of failure grows out of his final recognition that men cannot be controlled as he thought they could. Yet this refusal to be molded by leaders is not seen by Mailer as a proud reaffirmation of the human spirit. The sullen unwillingness with which the men respond to command is a totally negative quality, and not at all a noble one. The enlisted men who survive the Anopopei campaign are destroyed as surely as are those who die in it. They are dehumanized and beaten by the island and by the evil within their companions.

Certain of the characters serve only to fill out the spectrum of American culture represented, and to provide sounding boards for the more central ones. These may be

dismissed quickly: Brown, the classic middle-class sales-
man, who believes in the Horatio Alger myth, but is
totally cynical about women's fidelity; Stanley, the syco-
phant, who is frantically driven to achieve army promo-
tions and material possessions in civilian life, at the
expense of integrity and sound sleep; Wilson, whose ob-
session with sensual pleasure grows to disgust rather than
amuse the reader, by the time of his death. No sympathy
is shown either of these extremes by Mailer. The men
driven to achievement by the Protestant ethic are viewed
with scorn, but so is the irresponsible pleasure-oriented
country boy.

More central to the particular statements on flaws in
the makeup of American culture and the American character are Martinez, Goldstein and Roth, Gallagher, Ridges,
Croft and Red. Throughout the novel, the men are related to one another in a complex and comprehensive
series of relationships. These proceed out of the enormous
complex of neuroses which characterize each man. Momentary alliances are formed and broken constantly. For
example, Martinez' value as a scout puts him in a position
of favor with Croft. Brown, ambitious for promotion,
plays upon Martinez' personal insecurity, flattering him in
the hope of being mentioned favorably to Croft. Goldstein and Martinez are momentarily united by their shared
fears of rejection, though none of their basic values are at
all similar.

Of all the characters, Martinez is perhaps the most
obviously and understandably neurotic, and the most sympathetically presented. A product of the Mexican slums in
Texas, Martinez is an outsider who desperately wants
acceptance. Existing on the periphery of a white man's
society, he has received less from America than any other
man in the platoon. Yet, ironically, it is he who gives most
of himself, in his yearning after the American dream.

Throughout his youth, Martinez has accepted his inferior position with external passivity, with the result that he has become a mass of insecurities. The slightest hint of acceptance melts him, while the smallest rejection throws him into a panic. In Australia, British subjects can always get a shilling or two from him by calling him Yank, a name which embarrasses and thrills him. When Brown casually refers to him as a Texan, he is proud and fearful:

> Martinez was warmed by the name. . . . He liked to think of himself as a Texan, but he had never dared to use the title. Somewhere, deep in his mind, a fear had clotted; there was the memory of all the tall white men with the slow voices and the cold eyes. He was afraid of the look they might assume if he were to say, Martinez is a Texan. Now his pleasure was chilled, and he felt uneasy. I'm a better noncom than Brown, he assured himself, but he was still uncomfortable. Brown had a kind of assurance which Martinez had never known; something in him always withered when he talked to such men. Martinez had the suppressed malice, the contempt, and the anxiety of a servant who knows he is superior to his master.[6]

Martinez is a very frightened and yet a very brave man. After his menial assignments as houseboy to officers in the peacetime army, he has been presented with the opportunity, as he sees it, to gain recognition and acceptance through courage and competence. He is the scout of the platoon, constantly exposed to greater danger than anyone else, and he does his job well, with a fierce pride in his ability, and in the sergeant's stripes it has earned him. The price he has paid for this pittance of recognition is exorbitant. His nerves are shattered. Any loud noise frightens him, he cannot sleep or eat normally, and it is only with a sheer effort of will that he continues to function. But he is so committed to what he sees as his one path to success, and to the paradoxical loyalty he feels to a country that has treated him so shabbily, that he continues to seek out dangerous assignments:

> And another part of his mind had a quiet pride that he was the man upon whom the safety of the others depended. This was a sustaining force which carried him through dangers his will and body would have resisted . . . there was a part of his mind that drove him to do things he feared and detested. His pride with being a sergeant was the core about which nearly all his actions and thoughts were bound. Nobody see in the darkness like Martinez, he said to himself. . . . His feet were sore and his back and shoulders ached, but they were ills with which he no longer concerned himself; he was leading his squad, and that was sufficient in itself.[7]

Martinez lives by a code of desperate courage, and it has almost destroyed him. Yet he is by no means a totally admirable character. Not only are his motives held up as neurotic and his achievements viewed as foolish and ironical in light of the country in whose name he does them, but his ambitions are nebulous and shoddy. He is a sensitive man, but not an intelligent one, and his vague notions of success revolve about a vision of sexual vindictiveness. The *time machine* episode dealing with Martinez juxtaposes with enormous irony the passive exterior and the submerged, vindictive yearnings within him, as well as the futility of his efforts to satisfy himself:

> Fort Riley is big and green and the barracks are of red brick. The officers live in pretty little houses with gardens. Martinez is orderly for Lieutenant Bradford.
> Julio, will you do a good job on my boots today?
> Yes, Sir.

The Lieutenant takes a drink. Want one, Martinez?

Thank you, Sir.

I want you to do a real good job on the house today.

Yes, Sir, I do that.

The Lieutenant winks. Don't do anything I wouldn't do.

No, Sir.

The Lieutenant and his wife leave. Ah think yore the best boy we eveh had, Hooley, Mrs. Bradford says.

Thank you, Ma'am.

•   •   •

The blonde prostitutes to whom he makes love. Oh, what a roll you got, Joolie. . . . Gi' it to me, again.

I do that. (I screw Mrs. Lieutenant Bradford now. I screw Peggy Reilly and Alice Stewart, I will be hero.)

•   •   •

Martinez makes sergeant. Little Mexican boys also breathe the American fables. If they cannot be aviators or financiers or officers they can still be heroes. No need to stumble over pebbles and search the Texas sky. Any man jack can be a hero.

Only that does not make you White Protestant, firm and aloof.[8]

Sex is a serious and important concern to Mailer, and it plays a large part in the development of many of the characters. To Martinez, it is an instrument of vengeance, a leveling force. It is also an opiate to the lower classes. Both Martinez and Wilson have pursued indiscriminate promiscuity as an escape from poverty and boredom. The results of their irresponsibility are an illegitimate child whom Martinez deserted and an advanced case of venereal disease in Wilson. Other examples of sex in the novel are no more healthy. To Red it is something to be pursued without involvement, because comfort in another person can trap a man. For Croft it is another building block in the structure of his hatred for other people. His wife has been unfaithful and he trusts no woman. Sex for Hearn has had more sophisticated trappings in the New York publishing world, but it is still an empty thing, motivated by a desire to control. In General Cummings, sex is, in the first year of his marriage, a passionate conflict, symptomatic of his voracious ambition. When his marriage becomes an open conflict, the General becomes coldly asexual, with the exception of certain vague homosexual tendencies which contribute to the complex tension between him and Hearn. To the men as a group, sex and women are viewed cynically almost without exception, and a chorus is devoted to their mutterings on the topic.

In addition to the formal choruses of opinion on such topics as women, rotation or million-dollar-wounds, almost every man has an individual conversation with almost every other man in the platoon, sometime during the course of the novel. These interactions serve not merely to develop the characters involved but to make certain statements, by juxtaposition, on the social strata involved. For example, the conversation between Brown and Martinez (cited above) leads to an internal reaction in the latter which exposes the extent of his insecurity. At the same time, there is irony in Brown's statement to Martinez, which consists of sentimental nonsense about wanting to be received home in pride by his country. Brown, a miniature Babbitt, is the lesser man, but it is he who has received a share of the Horatio Alger rewards, while Martinez will always be emptyhanded.

The men's reactions to each other are conditioned by

a complex system of personal neuroses, ambitions, and anxieties. They are petty, scheming, oversensitive to slights. More often than not, they act like schoolgirls, and despite the massive incongruity of their jealousies, angers and shifting alliances in the face of suffering and impending death, Mailer's portraits seem disturbingly complete and accurate.

Each man is linked to several of the others by particular complementary needs or shared assumptions, but these are very tenuous and each man is ultimately isolated. Certain of these temporary liaisons are of particular interest. One obvious parallel exists between Martinez and the two Jews, Roth and Goldstein, as members of minority groups. The parallel is, in fact, a superficial one, although the vivid portrayal of particular instances of racial prejudice both on Anopopei and in the *time machine* sequence is not the least of Mailer's thrusts at American values. Not only is Martinez separated from the Jews by a complete absence of shared assumptions and values, but Goldstein and Roth are almost as far apart from each other. The conversation between Goldstein and Martinez about America is rife with irony, because the two men think they are communicating, when they really are not. While Goldstein rambles on about the typical bourgeois ambitions of New York Jewry, Martinez translates these in terms of his own experience. When Goldstein talks of his plans to open a small shop of his own and move to a suburb, Martinez thinks hungrily of his childhood memory of a rich brothel-keeper flashing a roll of bills. Yet while each pursues his separate visions, the two men are alike in their ingenuous acceptance of the American dream. Goldstein remarks:

> "I really believe in being honest and sincere in business; all the really big men got where they are through decency."

Martinez nodded. He wondered how big a room a very rich man needed to hold his money. Images of rich clothing, of shoeshines and hand-painted ties, a succession of tall blonde women with hard cold grace and brittle charm languished in his head. "A rich man do anything he damn well feel like it," Martinez said with admiration.

"Well, if I were rich I'd like to be charitable. And . . . what I want is to be well off, and have a nice house, some security. . . . Do you know New York?"

"No."

"Anyway, there's a suburb I'd like to live in," Goldstein said, nodding his head. "It's really a fine place, and nice people in it, cultured, refined. I wouldn't like my son to grow up the way I did."

Martinez nodded sagely. . . . "America's a good country," he said sincerely. He had a glow of righteous patriotism for a moment; half-remembered was his image of a schoolroom and the children singing 'My Country 'Tis of Thee.' For the first time in many years he thought of being an aviator, and felt a confused desire. "I learn to read good in school," he said. "The teacher thought I was smart."

"I'm sure she did," Goldstein said with conviction." [9]

The conversation helps also to characterize Goldstein, a man like a puppy dog:

Goldstein was feeling rather happy. He had never been particularly close to Martinez before, but they had been chatting for several hours and their confidences were becoming intimate. Goldstein was always satisfied if he could be friendly with someone; his ingenuous nature was always trusting. One of the main reasons for his wretchedness in the platoon was that his friendships never seemed to last. Men with whom he would have long amiable conversations would wound him or disregard him the next day, and he never understood it. To Goldstein men were friends or they weren't friends; he could not comprehend any variations or disloyalties. He was unhappy because he felt continually betrayed.

Yet he never became completely disheartened. Essentially he was an active man, a positive man. If his feelings were bruised, if another friend had proved himself undependable, Goldstein would nurse his pains, but almost always he would recover and sally out again.[10]

The most striking element in Goldstein's character is the fact that he is an effectual man. He has achieved part of his dream already, through hard work. Unable to afford college, he has put himself through a course in welding, and his small shop is within reach after the war. He has come willingly to war, despite his employer's protestations that he should be granted an occupational deferment. A physically strong man, he cheerfully accepts more than his share of the work assigned. Mailer calls Goldstein a "positive man," but it is questionable whether his greatest strength lies in his active nature. Rather, his capacity to emerge relatively more intact than others from the campaign seems to rest upon a sort of passive resilience. It is upon this that his developing friendship with Ridges seems to rest, and it is in terms of Ridges and of Roth that Goldstein's strengths may most clearly be defined.

Roth and Goldstein are as different as two men can be. Yet they are complementary figures, making up in sum Mailer's portrait of the New York Jew. Roth is a despicable man, whining, self-pitying, lazy; weak but not particularly kind or gentle; oversensitive to slights but not sensitive to the needs of others. Even his one act of apparent kindness, fondling a crippled bird he discovers

in the jungle, is described in terms of pity for himself.
Both his motives and his actions in the bird episode are
disgusting. He lisps baby talk to it, makes "little kissing
sounds," and basks in the attention it draws from the other
men. Croft's gratuitous killing of the bird is somewhat
understandable. (The further ramifications of Croft's act
will be discussed later.)

Roth is the most ineffectual man in the platoon and
the most dishonest to himself. In a beautifully conceived
scene on guard duty, Roth is shown to be governed by a
mass of conflicting and debilitating fears. Imagining he
hears a noise, he cannot decide whether to fire the machine
gun. Then he is unable to remember whether it is cocked,
but is too afraid of making a noise to pull the bolt back.
He considers throwing a grenade, but is so weak from
fear that he feels he may throw short and thus be killed.
He throws the safety catch on his rifle, and is so frightened
by the audible click that he does nothing more. Afraid
to awaken any of the men, he broods over his undeserved
plight until he falls asleep, endangering everyone's life.
Because Roth has overslept his stint, his relief accuses him
of having fallen asleep, and he retires to his blankets in
massive self-pity at being so unjustly chastised.

Strangely, since he is so much the weeping, beaten-
down Jew of stereotype, Roth does not practice his faith,
and in fact wishes to divorce himself from it as much as
possible. Although he is quite willing to admit that much
of his trouble may have come from being born a Jew, he
is annoyed when Goldstein launches a tirade against anti-
Semites. Roth is torn, in fact, between the temptation to
absolve himself of certain failures by crying anti-Semite,
and the desire to play the agnostic intellectual. He prides
himself on being a graduate of C.C.N.Y., but says nothing
particularly intelligent at any point, and has been singularly unsuccessful in civilian life, diploma notwithstanding.

Roth is proud that his parents were "modern," and scornfully sees Goldstein as "an old grandfather full of mutterings and curses, certain he would die a violent death." [11] The observation is well taken, for Goldstein does come from the pain-sodden, orthodox background. It is Goldstein's grandfather, in fact, who in the *time machine* sequence presents the most valid definition of what a Jew is. Mumbling half to himself, half to the boy Goldstein, the grandfather, lost in the mazes of archaic and useless Talmudic lore, makes an important statement:

> I think a Jew is a Jew because he suffers. Olla Juden suffer.
>   Why?
> So we will deserve the Messiah? The old man no longer knows. It makes us better and worse than the goyim, he thinks. But the child must always be given an answer. He rouses himself, concentrates and says without certainty, It is so we will last. He speaks again, wholly lucid for a moment. We are a harried people, beset by oppressors. We must always journey from disaster to disaster, and it makes us stronger and weaker than other men, makes us love and hate the other Juden more than other men. We have suffered so much that we know how to endure. We will always endure.[12]

But it is Goldstein rather than Roth who is more adaptable to the "modern" world. And it is Goldstein who survives, while Roth dies the "violent death" he snickered at Goldstein for brooding over. There are further ironies evident here. Goldstein has been speaking of some possible future pogrom, and to a postwar reading audience his concern would appear justifiable. Also, Roth's violent death proceeds not out of accident, but directly out of his character, aided slightly by the goadings of the anti-Semite Gallagher. Weaker than anyone else on the climb up Mount Anaka, but not decisive enough to refuse to continue, Roth feebly attempts to step across a gap in the trail while Gallagher curses and goads him, and plunges to his death.

Goldstein is far from a totally admirable character. Yet certain of his deficiencies, such as his inability to strike back at others, ultimately aid his survival as a whole human being. Despite the fact that Mailer is careful to present enough concrete examples [13] of anti-Semitism towards Goldstein to show that Goldstein's preoccupation with it is not mere paranoia, the man's silent, passive suffering under injustice fits well with his grandfather's definition. Throughout the novel, Ridges and Goldstein have not been thrown together. But on the long march they are part of the same four-man work party, cutting trail through the jungle. Because Roth and Minetta are weaker and unable to do their share of the work, Ridges and Goldstein shoulder most of it, and in the almost pleasant rhythms of labor they begin to establish a comraderie. Later, after Wilson is wounded, Ridges and Goldstein are selected as part of a four-man party to carry him back. The work is backbreaking, and eventually the other two men drop out and the two friends continue doggedly, even after Wilson dies, only to lose the body in crossing the rapids, when they are almost at their destination.

Ridges, we have said, is an unimaginative, ignorant, farm boy, characterized by a consistently uncomplaining capacity to endure labor and suffering. He is, in effect, a Jew. The Christian God he worships is an Old Testament deity who dispenses pain, crop failure and uncertainty which must be accepted. Within his faith he is able to endure untold hardship, although at times his willingness to do so makes him more a beast of burden than a man. Between Ridges and Goldstein, then, there grows a real bond, and if there is any minor pleasant note at the novel's end, it lies in the indication that Goldstein has found a real friend at last.

But it is only the man passive by nature who can emerge relatively unchanged from the Anopopei campaign. The values with which the men arrived on the island, whether informed by selfish cynicism or by a naive acceptance of the American dream, are enough to damn American society. The trek up Mount Anaka will be seen to eliminate the possibility for real hope on the individual level, by throwing into frightening focus the futility of individual courage or determination.

The division between the enlisted men and the officers in the structure of the novel is considerable in that the primary thematic concerns dealt with through development of the platoon's members are the sexual, and the immediate results of social corruption, such as personal bigotry. Broader political and cultural issues are dealt with almost exclusively through the officers' experiences, and particularly in several long conversations between Hearn and Cummings. But the sheer fact of their location on an island subjects both officers and men to certain of the same experiences, such as oppressive heat, torrential rain, and the risk of death in combat. Out of these shared dangers and discomforts grow certain unarticulated universal ramifications, and in the experiences of General Cummings and several of the enlisted men there seems to emerge some pattern, some theory of fate.

The role of fate in the action of this novel is not central to Mailer's statements on the nature of war, human character, and American society. It is, however, integral to the development of certain characters, and to one of the final plot reversals. Further, it may be noted as an early indication of the more systematically articulated view of fate in *An American Dream.*

Fate functions on two major levels in *The Naked and the Dead.* It is explored as an intellectual problem in the minds of two decidedly unintellectual characters, Croft and Red. In the first half of the novel, then, it is dealt with as a part of the human condition as seen by the individual. Later, not explicitly stated, but rendered in the action, fate manipulates the outcome of the campaign, thereby affecting each individual. The most direct recipient of the irony generated is General Cummings, and the agent of fate is, most ironically, Major Dalleson.

Important to both Croft's and Red's uncomfortable intuitions about fate is the death of an otherwise minor character, Hennessey. In the first chapter, crammed as it is with a rather clumsy exposition of a number of characters, Croft is established as a man who rides the tide of fate:

> He entered everything with as much skill and preparation as he could bring to it, but he knew that things finally would hang on his luck. This he welcomed. He had a deep unspoken belief that whatever made things happen was on his side. . . .[14]

Therefore, Croft's prophecy about the cautious Hennessey is invested with a portentous effect:

> Then, as Croft watched, Hennessey pulled his left trouser out of his legging, rolled it up to expose his knee, and with a great deal of care rubbed a little spittle over the irritated red spot on his knee. Croft gazed at the white flesh with its blond hairs, noticed the pains with which Hennessey replaced his trouser in the legging, and felt an odd excitement as if the motions were important. That boy is too careful, Croft told himself.

And then with a passionate certainty he thought, "Hennessey's going to get killed today." He felt like laughing to release the ferment in him. This time he was sure.[15]

Although the intuition is immediately undercut in Croft's mind by his recognition that such premonitions have not always proved correct, it is nonetheless invested with some significance:

> You figure you're getting a little too smart for your-self, he thought. His disgust came because he felt he could not trust such emotions, rather than from any conviction that they had no meaning at all.[16]

Red, in his initial appearance, is characterized in juxtaposition to Hennessey. Standing alone on deck the night before the assault, Red thinks mockingly of Hennessey's concern, on another occasion, with his life belt. Hennessey's stated ethic is to be prepared:

> "Listen," Hennessey had boasted, "I ain't taking any chances. What if this boat should get hit? I ain't going into the water unprepared." [17]

Red, on the other hand, is characterized by an isolated fatalism, and by a series of negations and rejections:

> He understood it all, knew he could do nothing about it any longer, and was not even tempted. What was the use? He sighed and the acuteness of his mood slipped out with his breath. There were some things you could never fix. It was too mixed-up. A man had to get out by himself or he became like Hennessey worrying over every gimcrack in his life.
>   He wanted none of it. He'd do no man harm if

he could help it, and he'd take no crap. He never had, he told himself proudly.

For a long time he remained staring at the water. He had never found anything. All he knew was what he didn't like. . . . All through his body he had the sense of every second sliding past, racing toward the approaching morning. This was the last time he would be alone for months, and he savored the sensation. He had always been a loner.[18]

When Hennessey does become the platoon's first casualty, because of his own frenetic attempts to move from a relatively secure position to one he feels will be safer, the reactions of Croft and Red are dramatically different. Red fearfully senses the presence of some malignant governing force:

What bothered Red was the memory of the night they had sat on deck during the air raid when Hennessey had inflated his life belt. It gave Red a moment of awe and panic as if someone, *something,* had been watching over their shoulder that night and laughing. There was a pattern where there shouldn't be one.[19]

But Croft is seized by an overwhelming sense of power, in this reaffirmation of his own infallibility:

But Croft brooded over the event all day. . . . Hennessey's death had opened to Croft vistas of such omnipotence that he was afraid to consider it directly. All day the fact hovered about his head, tantalizing him with odd dreams and portents of power.[20]

Hennessey's death has several other reverberations of lesser import, later in the novel. Gallagher, wandering on the beach with his dead wife's last letter in his pocket unopened, thinks hazily of Hennessey and of death in general. When, some time after Hennessey's death, mail arrives for him, it becomes the subject, for Mailer, not of poignance, but of a contemptuous irony directed at the superficiality of other men's sympathy:

> "Was Hennessey transferred from headquarters company?" he asked his assistant.
> "I don't know, name's familiar." The assistant thought a moment and then said, "Wait a minute, I remember, he was knocked off the day we came in." The assistant was pleased that he had recalled it when the mail clerk had forgotten.
>
> •   •   •
>
> The return address on the letters was "Mom and Dad, 12 Riverdale Avenue, Tacuchet, Indiana." The assistant read it to himself and thought for a moment of a rosy-cheeked man and woman with graying hair, the Mom and Pop of a thousand billboard ads for soft drinks and mouthwashes and toothpastes. "Gee, isn't that sad," he said.
> "Yeah, it sure is."
> "Makes you think," the assistant said.[21]

While it is obvious that Mailer realizes what slight significance death can have to men who deal with it in their everyday life, he presents nonetheless the usual spectrum of reactions: the emotional realization by Wilson that man is just so much carrion, the classic confrontation with the rotting corpse of a dead Japanese soldier that has its counterpart in war novels as far back as *The Red Badge of Courage.* But nowhere does the emphasis or lack of emphasis on the termination of a human life assume such importance as in the minds of Red and Croft. The knowledge of Hennessey's death plagues Red, brings sharply home to him a real sense of vulnerability, undermines his self-confidence. For Croft, it is the beginning of a compulsive movement toward power. Between these two men, one aggressively cruel, the other passive, stoical, fanatically resistant to external pressure, there arises a continual, accelerating conflict, which reaches its height on the long trek up Mount Anaka.

If there are gods who govern the larger affairs of the Anopopei campaign, the lesser decisions are carried out by decidedly inferior deities. It is a carefully placed bit of irony that the suggestion that Croft's platoon be deployed for their ultimately useless and abortive mission is made by the stupid, ineffectual Major Dalleson. It is emphasized that in a discussion of overall tactical policy, this is the only contribution made by Dalleson. It is Dalleson, again, who casually presents to General Cummings the possibility of assigning Lieutenant Hearn to lead the platoon, in the course of which assignment Hearn is killed. And finally, in a massive burst of irony, it is Dalleson who blunders with trepidation into an easy victory that wins the campaign, while General Cummings (whose tactical skill has generated the favorable situation which Dalleson encounters) is temporarily absent to request further support from upper levels. Consequently, what prestige Cummings might have milked the victory for is decidedly mitigated, and he is made to look foolish for the sound military logic by which he established the need for support. Dalleson, meanwhile, has succeeded in nothing but frightening himself by an exercise of power he feels inadequate for, and in alienating the general he worships. The irony extends to the reconnaissance platoon led by Croft, whose probing mission is ultimately purposeless in light of the victory. The death of Hearn, Roth, and Wilson, and the suffering of the other members is reduced to a position of no military significance whatsoever, and an obvious statement on the futility of the human condition is implicit.

Mount Anaka has remained always in the background of the campaign, a massive, distant representative of monolithic nature. But it is in the final portion of the book, when the platoon must climb it, that it becomes a force in its own right. As an exploratory measure upon which the decision to launch a daringly unorthodox attack may depend, General Cummings sends the platoon, led by Lieutenant Hearn, to scout the other side of the island. The full irony of the uselessness of the mission, and of the larger plan itself, is not made clear until the very end of the novel.

In the landing craft, immediately before they begin their march, the men have a clear view of Anaka:

> Far in the distance they could see Mount Anaka rising above the island. It arched coldly and remotely from the jungle beneath it, lofting itself massively into the low-hanging clouds of the sky. In the early drab twilight it looked like an immense old elephant erecting himself somberly on his front legs his haunches lost in the green bedding of his lair. The mountain seemed wise and powerful, and terrifying in its size. Gallagher stared at it in absorption, caught by a sense of beauty he could not express. The idea, the vision he always held of something finer and neater and more beautiful than the void in which he lived trembled now, pitched almost to a climax of words.[22]

If Gallagher, easily one of the most insensitive men in the platoon, reacts in this way, it is clear that the distant effect of the mountain is breathtaking. The perversion of this aesthetic appearance to one of unmitigated horror, and the metamorphosis of the men into plodding, cringing animals in the course of their battle with the mountain, are rendered more powerful by the initial view of Anaka. More central to Mailer's final statement on the position of the individual in the universal scheme are the reactions of Red and Croft, whose entirely different personal defeats will most clearly define the view of the human condition posited by the novel:

> Croft was moved as deeply, as fundamentally as caissons resettling in the river mud. The mountain attracted him, taunted and inflamed him with its size. He had never seen it so clearly before. . . . He stared at it now, examined its ridges, feeling an instinctive desire to climb the mountain and stand on its peak, to know that all its mighty weight was beneath his feet. His emotions were intense; he knew awe and hunger and the peculiar unique ecstasy he had felt after Hennessey was dead or when he had killed the Japanese prisoner. He gazed at it, almost hating the mountain, unconscious at first of the men about him. "That mountain's mighty old," he said at last.
>
> And Red felt only gloom, and a vague harass-ment. Croft's words bothered him subtly. He ex-amined the mountain with little emotion, almost in-difference. But when he looked away he was bothered by the fear all of the men in the platoon had felt at one time or another that day. Like the others, Red was wondering if this patrol would be the one where his luck ran out.[23]

Only three men are actually killed in the course of the mission: Wilson, Hearn, and Roth; and in the two latter cases more explicable causes than mere luck are involved. But in a very real sense, Red's luck does run out, as does that of Croft and every other man in the platoon (with the possible exceptions of Goldstein and Ridges). Every man is dehumanized to some extent by the debilitating efforts demanded by the climb. But Red, faced finally with a situation with which he cannot cope alone, is forced to relinquish all pride in his own strength as an individual. The combination of nature as represented by Anaka, and the Army as represented by Croft, have beaten him, and he admits it. For Croft, too, the mountain becomes the ultimate, unbeatable foe, and something in him breaks when he fails against it.

In the early stages of the mission, Hearn is in command, and the conflict between him and Croft throws into sharp focus the patterns of power established in the novel. Hearn, despite himself, is forced to realize that many of Cummings' cold-blooded views are valid. Not only does he recognize the distrust and consequent inertia of the enlisted men when faced with commands, but more disturbingly, he finds in himself a disdain for the men. Further, he is able to see his own desire for power, and the petty glee which the exercise of it brings. In a well-conceived scene, an obvious parallel is implied between Hearn and Cummings himself. When Croft kills the crippled bird which Roth has found, all the men are outraged. Red, conscious that he must confront Croft at some point in order to maintain his own code of self-respect, takes a stand. But before a fight can ensue, Hearn orders the two apart, and forces an apology to Roth, from Croft. Hearn is pleased with his own power to humiliate Croft, and disgusted by the pleasure. Red is relieved at being spared the showdown, and disgusted by the relief. Croft is homicidal, but unwilling to threaten the structure of military hierarchy (which he values highly) by overt defiance. It is not until after Croft's murder-by-omission of Hearn that the Red/Croft conflict becomes overt again, but the short period in which Hearn commands fulfills an important function in making clear the consistent corruption to be found in human nature at any level of the social, military or intellectual scale. The almost omnipotent intervention in the affairs of the two groundlings by Hearn is almost a carbon copy of the early scene in which General Cummings bails Hearn out of a confrontation with Lieutenant Colonel Conn. And the relief and self-disgust felt by Hearn on that occasion is pointedly similar to that of Red in the later scene.

Hearn's death is no accident, and it is more than circumstance which makes Martinez the instrument by which Croft effects it. After the encounter with the enemy in which Wilson is fatally wounded, Hearn wrestles with his own conscience, and comes to the conclusion that no matter how much he is personally driven to succeed in the mission (as a sort of inverted defiance toward Cummings) the responsible thing to do is to turn back. It is night, and in order to insure that he will obey his own decision in the morning, Hearn confides it to Croft. The latter persuades the Lieutenant to send a scout ahead, and to base the decision to continue or turn back on whether the enemy is present. Armed with Hearn's permission, the Sergeant delegates Martinez for the patrol, and admonishes him to report his findings only to Croft himself. Martinez does come upon a body of Japanese soldiers, and the manner in which the confrontation is rendered is fraught with philosophical overtones. With all of his skills of stealth heightened by his terror, "functioning more like an animal now than a man," [24] Martinez slips through the Japanese camp. The climax of the sequence comes when the terrified scout comes upon an enemy guard who, though unaware of his presence, poses an insurmountable threat. Martinez can neither retreat nor advance unless he kills the guard, and for a moment he cannot act:

> Martinez had a sense of unreality. What was to keep him from touching him, from greeting him? They were men. The entire structure of the war wavered

> in his brain for a moment, almost tottered, and then
> was restored by a returning wash of fear. If he touched
> him he would be killed. But it seemed unbelievable.[25]

He does, of course, kill the guard, skillfully and silently,
with his trench knife. But the quality of his hesitation as
Mailer renders it is significant. Even in Martinez' inarticulate reason, the primal basis of humanity holds a last,
momentary outpost. But it is a feeble bastion, and reason
has no place in war. Insofar as Martinez and the guard
are men, they are men irrevocably isolated by the hostility
and distrust inherent in the human condition. And they
are, in fact, barely human except in the negative aspects
of humanity. They are conceived more as animals. Mailer
has already described Martinez as functioning as an animal
and in the very act of murder for survival:

> The Jap thrashed in his arms like an unwilling animal
> being picked up by its master, and Martinez felt only
> a detached irritation. Why was he making so much
> trouble? [26]

Life and death have become merely indisputable facts,
physical laws robbed of all moral significance. In a very
real sense, Martinez has been thoroughly brutalized. The
fact that later in the novel he regains enough sensitivity
to feel guilt makes the juxtaposition of human mind and
animal instinct the more horrible, for man is robbed of
the amoral, guiltless instinct of the predator and the moral
choice of the human being, alike.

Martinez is not the only dehumanized character.
Throughout the march, animal imagery abounds. When
the exhausted men dully drag their bodies up a swift
stream, it is "with the motions of salmon laboring up-

stream for the spawning season." [27] Ridges at work cutting trail looks "like an animal fashioning its nest." [28] Under enemy fire, the men are seen "retreating pell-mell, sobbing like animals in anger and fear." [29] Seconds before Roth plunges to his death, Minetta soothingly calls encouragement to him, "talking to him as though he were an animal." [30] In an awful sense, it is only Croft's monolithic determination to conquer everything that is outside himself, and Red's passive but powerful desire to stand unconquered as an individual, that represent, almost to the end, the last remnants of human values and motivation in the platoon. And ultimately, both men are defeated.

When Croft receives Martinez' report on the enemy's presence ahead, he withholds it from Hearn, prompting the latter to order a further advance. Moments before he is killed, Hearn promises the men that if further enemy resistance is encountered, they will turn back. But when, a short distance further on, Hearn steps unsuspectingly from cover and is killed instantly by a machine gun bullet, Croft assumes command and feels no obligation to honor the promise of a dead man. The breakdown of the last humanitarian force as it reposed, somewhat soiled, in Hearn, has been accomplished. The liberal voice, no matter how questionable its motives or ineffective its vehicle, has been present in Hearn, has conflicted and interacted with the common man and with the policy-making powers. But the vectors of force from above and below, Cummings' vindicative power exerted through Major Dalleson as an instrument, and Croft's murderous resentment operating through Martinez, have proved far more than a match for Hearn. The death, and the circumstances which make it inevitable, are portentous as an authorial statement on the probable fate of liberalism in postwar America.

From this point, the disintegration of the men and the horror of their ordeal accelerate rapidly. Croft has been privately frustrated that the platoon was to advance through the pass, rather than climb the mountain. Now he is presented with a perfect situation. The enemy ahead obviate the further use of the pass; retreat is unthinkable to him; Mount Anaka is the only remaining alternative; and he is in a position of absolute power over the platoon, although he will later be forced to maintain it at gunpoint. The men grumble but obey, united in their hatred of Croft and their desire to turn back, but unable to act in unison.

Affected, as are all the men, by Roth's death, and suspicious of the truth about Hearn's, Red is further beaten down by the treachery of his own body. He is past thirty and his kidneys are sick, his appetite gone, his exhaustion complete. On one of the necessarily more frequent rest breaks, he senses his defeat:

> He had to face the truth. The Army had licked him. He had always gone along believing that if they pushed him around too much he would do something when the time came. And now. . . .[31]

In one last attempt to assert himself, he openly refuses Croft's order to move on. Croft levels his rifle at Red, and though the other men mutter in agreement with Red, none has the courage to act. Red, unarmed, faces the rifle for tense moments, but Croft's trump card is his demonstrated willingness to kill in cold blood, and no other man present is equal to it:

> Slowly the muzzle pointed toward Red. He found himself watching the expression on Croft's face.
> Suddenly he knew exactly what had happened to

Hearn, and the knowledge left him weak. Croft was going to shoot. He knew it.

•   •   •

It was worthless to temporize. Croft wanted to shoot him.

•   •   •

The muzzle made a tiny circular motion as if Croft were selecting a more exact aim. Red watched his finger on the trigger. When it began to tighten, he tensed suddenly. "Okay, Croft, you win." His voice croaked out weakly. He was making every effort to keep himself from trembling.

•   •   •

He was licked. That was all there was to it. At the base of his shame was an added guilt. He was glad it was over, glad the long contest with Croft was finished, and he could obey orders with submission, without feeling that he must resist. This was the extra humiliation, the crushing one. Could that be all, was that the end of all he had done in his life? Did it always come to laying down a load? [32]

Croft's immediate reaction after subduing the mutiny is a renewal of confidence in himself. But it lasts only briefly. The common man, no matter how fierce his pride, is no match for the pressures of society and of a natural universe that is indifferent but crushing in its insurmountable, massive passivity. At the same time, as Cummings has finally learned by the end of the novel, the sheer weight of sullen resistance generated by the mass of men will wear out the energy of any leader. Croft is doomed to fail because of this resistance, despite the fact that he has overcome its most overt expression in Red:

Even Croft was exhausted. He had the task of leading them . . . and he prostrated himself trying to pull them up the mountain. He felt not only the weight of his own body but the weight of all their bodies as effectively as if he had been pulling them in harness. They dragged him back, tugged at his shoulders and his heels. With all his physical exertion his mind fatigued him as greatly, for he was under the acute strain of gauging their limits.

There was another strain. The closer he came to the crest of the mountain the greater became his anxiety. Each new turn of the staircase demanded an excessive effort of will from him. He had been driving nearer and nearer the heart of this country for days, and it had a cumulative terror. All the vast alien stretches of land they had crossed had eroded his will, pitched him a little finer. It was an effort, almost palpable, to keep advancing over strange hills and up the flanks of an ancient resisting mountain.

• • •

The mission of the patrol, indeed even the mountain, hardly moved him now. He progressed out of some internal contest in himself as if to see which pole of his nature would be successful.

And at last he sensed that the top was near. . . . Each step he took closer to the summit left him more afraid. He might have quit before they reached it. But he never had the opportunity.[33]

What removes the choice of action from Croft's hands at this point is a retributive act by hitherto passive nature. Croft blunders onto a hornet's nest and accidentally smashes it. The pain of the hornets' stings drives the entire platoon, including Croft, far back down the mountain, screaming and discarding rifles and packs. When they finally come to their senses, it is obvious even to Croft that they can never climb back up.

Croft, Cummings and Red have all learned in different ways that one man alone cannot overcome the resistance
of nature and other men, cannot even remain passively
aloof and independent. Hearn, who counted more than
any other character upon the common man as a positive
force capable of constructive organization, has been betrayed and destroyed because both the common man and
those who manipulate him resented and feared his beliefs.
And when Red, searching for a new philosophy to replace
the one he has lost, explores in a primitive way the very
ideals Hearn represented, he finds . . . nothing:

> You carried it alone as long as you could, and
> then you weren't strong enough to take it any longer.
> You kept fighting everything, and everything broke
> you down, until in the end you were just a little
> goddam bolt holding on and squealing when the ma-
> chine went too fast.
> He had to depend on other men, he needed other
> men now, and he didn't know how to go about it.
> Deep within him were the first nebulae of an idea,
> but he could not phrase it. If they all stuck to-
> gether. . . .
> Aaah, fug. All they knew was to cut each other's
> throats. There were no answers, there wasn't even any
> pride a man could have at the end.[34]

Ultimately, then, men cannot help one another. But
can one man, unhindered by others and driven by a fierce
enough determination, be a match for a non-human foe?
The ultimate denial of even this possibility rests with, of
all people, Croft:

> He had failed, and it hurt him vitally. His frus-
> tration was loose again. He would never have another
> opportunity to climb it. And yet he was wondering

if he could have succeeded. Once more he was feeling
the anxiety and terror the mountain had roused on
the rock stairway. If he had gone alone, the fatigue of
the other men would not have slowed him but he
would not have had their company, and he realized
suddenly that he could not have gone without them.
The empty hills would have eroded any man's courage.

•   •   •

Croft kept looking at the mountain. He had lost
it, had missed some tantalizing revelation of himself.
Of himself and much more, Of life.
Everything.[35]

The human condition prescribes a movement toward self-
knowledge that often remains unfulfilled. When it is fulfilled, as in the cases of Red or Cummings, it results in
despair or at least the painful disillusionment of a Hearn.
With Croft's admitted failure, the last door is closed to a
significant human action in the novel, and the final statement is one of almost unmitigated blackness. Ultimately,
the destiny of the human race, and of American society
in particular, is left not with the stiff-necked individual,
nor with the military strongman or the intellectual.
Rather, it falls to the mediocre, placidly stupid, Rotary
type, as represented by Major Dalleson. The very last
scene in the novel shows him, pleased to be moored once
again in the reassuring monotony of bureaucratic detail,
filled with self-satisfied glee at one of his own few original
ideas: the use of a pin-up girl to illustrate the use of map
coordinates.

This final implicit statement on the ascendancy of
reactionary mediocrity in postwar America, in conjunction with the preoccupation in *The Naked and the Dead*
with the theme of the shabbiness of the American dream,
shows Mailer to be very much a social critic. The obvious

> his own as well as the outside, natural forces. The
> failure of these negative novels in portraying real
> characters stems from this refusal to see a purpose in
> man's efforts to endure.[36]

These charges, cloaked in an obvious subjectivity, stem
from Mailer's failure to subscribe to the particular form
of "protest" which Spicehandler feels is necessary to the
validity of a war novel. Yet it is in the very terms of this
condemnation that Mailer's particular achievement in *The
Naked and the Dead* may be finally defined. It is my
contention that Mailer learned from war something that
no earlier war had so clearly taught: the futility of the
human condition. War for Mailer is more than a subject
for fiction in itself: it is a concrete representation of
human weakness and of the society created by such weakness. If the protest in this novel were limited, as Spicehandler seems to suggest, only to a condemnation of the
American social structure, it would be understandable, for
Mailer's world is indeed "a world stripped of hope."
Within this hopelessness, however, is the germ of a protest.
Mailer's fiction is always, even at this point, about "man
who, in the final analysis, seeks redemption and who
desires to endure against all forces. . . ." In *The Naked
and the Dead* redemption is impossible (except on the
very limited level of the passive Goldstein and Ridges),
and even the endurance of such a man as Red, defined as
it is solely in terms of negatives, must crumble. Mailer
saw the plight of the individual in the postwar years
primarily in negative terms, but this does not mean that
he was willing to give up entirely on man's chances for
redemption, and to rest on the black vision of *The Naked
and the Dead* as his final statement. Other novels were to
follow, and although Mailer has maintained his cynicism
in regard to American society and to the evil and weakness

and self-admitted influences upon his work of Farrell, Steinbeck and Dos Passos place him at the beginning of his career within the literary continuum established by the social novels of the thirties. In the two decades following publication of *The Naked and the Dead*, Mailer was to move progressively further from the use of obviously derivative elements in his fiction; but he was to remain consistently critical of the ills of American society. Symptomatic of his proximity to immediately contemporary issues, and of his impending break from the direct influence of other writers, is Mailer's rejection of the conception of the common man held by the social writers of the Depression, in favor of a sophisticated and pessimistic vision of the human condition which is decidedly characteristic of postwar literary values. Yet it is this very element of concern with a more contemporary problem which draws vitriolic criticism of *The Naked and the Dead* from at least one critic writing as late as 1960. Daniel Spicehandler, in his dissertation, "The American War Novel," concludes his otherwise perceptive short treatment of Mailer's book with this condemnation:

> What has Mailer learned from war? What is the question asked, the theme expounded in *The Naked and the Dead?* . . . What right has an author to choose the topic of war and neither to protest it or learn something from it? . . . Mailer leaves the reader with no tragic sense. One would suppose that so brutal a description of war must result in a bitter protest. Instead, his war experience teaches nothing, "néant." The *nada* of the early Hemingway is at least clouded in a romantic idealism gone sour. Mailer's world is a world stripped of hope. The novel as a literary form is about man—sinful, murderous, inhuman and evil, mostly, but man who, in the final analysis, seeks redemption and who desires to endure against all forces,

within man, it will be shown how he progressed steadily toward the vision of possible hope for individual salvation that is *An American Dream.*

Notes

1 Norman Mailer, *Advertisements for Myself* (New York: G. P. Putnam's Sons, 1959), p. 336.
2 *Ibid.,* p. 28.
3 *Ibid.,* p. 27.
4 Reprinted in Maxwell Geismar, *American Moderns: From Rebellion to Conformity* (New York: Hill and Wang, 1966), p. 171. The parallel is mentioned by other critics as well, including Spicehandler and Scott, whose dissertations are referred to later in this book.
5 Norman Mailer, *The Naked and the Dead* (New York: Holt, Rinehart and Winston, 1948). Paperback edition published 1951 by Signet (New American Library of World Literature, New York), p. 556. All page references are to the Signet edition.
6 *Ibid.,* p. 360.
7 *Ibid.,* p. 114.
8 *Ibid.,* pp. 54-55.
9 *Ibid.,* p. 350.
10 *Ibid.,* p. 349.
11 *Ibid.,* p. 44.
12 *Ibid.,* p. 376.
13 For example, Croft unjustly blames Goldstein for not pulling his weight on a gun, and allowing it to be wrecked, when it was Wyman who was to blame.
14 *The Naked and the Dead,* p. 11.
15 *Ibid.,* p. 27.
16 *Ibid.*
17 *Ibid.,* p. 15.
18 *Ibid.,* p. 16.
19 *Ibid.,* p. 35.
20 *Ibid.*
21 *Ibid.,* p. 207.
22 *Ibid.,* p. 348.
23 *Ibid.,* pp. 348–49.
24 *Ibid.,* p. 456.
25 *Ibid.,* p. 462.

26 *Ibid.*, p. 463.
27 *Ibid.*, p. 364.
28 *Ibid.*, p. 368.
29 *Ibid.*, p. 398.
30 *Ibid.*, p. 517.
31 *Ibid.*, p. 540.
32 *Ibid.*, pp. 541–42.
33 *Ibid.*, pp. 544–45.
34 *Ibid.*, p. 548.
35 *Ibid.*, p. 552.
36 Daniel Spicehandler, "The American War Novel" (unpublished doctoral dissertation, Columbia University, New York, 1960), p. 208.

2

Barbary Shore

Barbary Shore (1951) is of more interest as a stage in Mailer's development than as an artistically effective work in itself. Certainly it fits easily into a treatment of the five novels, dealing as it does with the two basic issues with which Mailer always concerns himself: the state of American society and the problems of the individual in it. But the second novel, for several reasons, marks a faltering in Mailer's progress. This is not to say that it is a retrogression, for though it falls short of the artistic success of *The Naked and the Dead, Barbary Shore* represents a step in the direction of an increasingly nonderivative art.

Perhaps *Barbary Shore* can be better understood in light of the circumstances under which it was written, and of Mailer's own retrospective understanding of the book. In *Advertisements for Myself,* he tells of the several years following the publication of *The Naked and the Dead,* during which *Barbary Shore* was written:

Once it became obvious that *The Naked and the Dead* was going to be a best seller . . . a depression set in on me.

•   •   •

. . . I was blasted a considerable distance away from dead center by the size of its success. . . . My farewell to an average man's experience was too abrupt . . . there was nothing left in the first twenty-four years of my life to write about; one way or another, my life seemed to have been mined and melted into the long reaches of the book. And so I was prominent and empty, and I had to begin life again. . . .

•   •   •

Willy-nilly I had had existentialism forced upon me. I was free . . . I could seek to become what I chose to be, and if I failed . . . I would have nothing to excuse failure. I would fail because I had not been brave enough to succeed. So I was much too free. Success had been a lobotomy to my past, there seemed no power from the past which could help me in the present, and I had no choice but to force myself to step into the war of the enormous present . . . setting out by myself to cut a track through a new wild.

. . . I could as well have described the years which followed the appearance of *The Naked and the Dead* by saying that I traveled scared . . . ridden by the question . . . which I was forever asking of myself: had this first published novel been all of my talent? Or would my next book be better?

In a sense, I may have tried to evade the question by writing *Barbary Shore,* but there was no real choice. If my past had become empty as a theme, was I to write about Brooklyn streets, or my mother and father, or another war novel (*The Naked and the Dead Go to Japan*) was I to do the book of the return-

ing veteran when I had lived like a mole writing and
rewriting seven hundred pages in those fifteen months?
No, those were not real choices. I was drawn instead
to write about an imaginary future. . . . But *Barbary Shore* was really a book to emerge from the bom-
barded cellars of my unconscious, an agonized eye of
a novel which tried to find some amalgam of my new
experience and the larger horror of that world which
might be preparing to destroy itself. I was obviously
trying for something which was at the very end of my
reach, and then beyond it, and toward the end the
novel collapsed into a chapter of political speech and
never quite recovered. Yet, it could be that if my work
is alive one hundred years from now, *Barbary Shore*
will be considered the richest of my first three novels
for it has in its high fevers a kind of insane insight
into the psychic mysteries of Stalinists, secret policemen, narcissists, children, Lesbians, hysterics, revolu-
tionaries—it has an air which for me is the air of our
time, authority and nihilism stalking one another in
the orgiastic hollow of this century . . . and yet
much of my later writing cannot be understood without a glimpse of the odd shadow and theme-maddened
light *Barbary Shore* casts before it.[1]

There is much in what Mailer says to help us understand *Barbary Shore*. To begin with, there is a good deal
of Mailer himself in his protagonist/narrator, Mikey
Lovett. Like Mailer, Lovett is deprived of a past and
committed to the present, but in his case the situation is
more drastic, and therefore more symbolically significant.
For Lovett has literally no past: he is an amnesia victim,
a product of the war who is thrust with no emotional
connection whatever into a nightmarish postwar world.
The tone of the novel and of his personality is set in the
very first paragraph of the book:

Probably I was in the war. There is the mark of
a wound behind my ear, an oblong of unfertile flesh
where no hair grows. It is covered over now, and may
be disguised by even the clumsiest barber, but no barber can hide the scar on my back. For that a tailor
is more in order.

When I stare into the mirror I am returned a
face doubtless more handsome than the original, but
the straight nose, the modelled chin, and the smooth
cheeks are only evidence of a stranger's art.[2]

The reader is immediately presented with a wealth of
fairly standard symbolic leads. A classic product of the
war, Lovett has not merely been deprived of his past, but
literally, physically, scarred as well. His identity is irrecoverable because his face is not his own. He stares out at
a strange world from behind a mask which is *artificial,*
the "art of a stranger" at that. Although he has not
returned from war physically impotent (as does Sergius
in *The Deer Park* [3]) his scar is "unfertile flesh." Finally,
his preoccupation with the mirror will be echoed later in
a tendency to psychic narcissism.

Lovett, forced into a commitment to the present, is
the embodiment of Mailer's preoccupation with his own
existential situation at the time. Because of the admitted
paucity of external experience upon which Mailer could
draw, the novel is set in a vacuum of psychic experience,
within which the painfully obvious symbols of alienation
and emotional bankruptcy are garishly highlighted. Yet
the novel, in drawing its characters and locale from the
real world, in taking for its central message the very real
political problems of a real country, purports implicitly
to treat human life in realistic terms, and cannot therefore
be accepted simply in terms of allegory. It is in the attempt
to deal with such problems as alienation in bald symbolic

outline while simultaneously developing credible characters and also presenting a lengthy political diatribe, that
Mailer overreaches himself. The structure and tone of the
novel are inconsistent and ineffective because of a lack of
integration, and finally *Barbary Shore* is neither successful
allegory, successful fiction, nor successful polemic.

Mikey Lovett, armed with five hundred carefully
hoarded dollars and the desire to be a novelist, seeks the
opportunity to live, as Mailer did while writing *The
Naked and the Dead,* "like a mole." To this end, he is led
by an acquaintance to a shabby boarding house in Brooklyn Heights, where he becomes enmeshed in a nightmarish
set of relationships with the five other inhabitants of the
building.

Showing foresight similar to that he used in *The
Naked and the Dead,* Mailer limited himself, in the second
novel, to a narrow physical setting and a small number of
characters. But two elements of the conscious self-limita-
tion which helped make the first novel effective are absent
in the second. First, Mailer was admittedly unable to draw
his subject from an area he knew well from personal
experience. Although the sense of being cut off from the
past, the awareness of existential choice, and the involvement with contemporary politics are part of Mailer's
personal experience, they had not yet been thought through
when he wrote *Barbary Shore.* Consequently, deprived of
the benefit of unhurried retrospection, Mailer seems to
deliver these thematic preoccupations to the reader only
partially assimilated, with the result that the book is lumpy
in style, structure and resolution.

The second (and possibly more significant) departure
from the successful formula used in *The Naked and the
Dead* involves novelistic structure and narrative voice. The
clearly derivative qualities of the first novel in this regard
have been pointed out in the preceding chapter. Yet one

of the most striking characteristics of Mailer's fiction is the novelist's progression towards an increasingly individual art. *Barbary Shore,* no matter what its shortcomings, is a first step in this breaking away from previous influences. Abandoning the comfortable devices available to the omniscient third person narrator of his first novel, Mailer chose to write *Barbary Shore* in the first person. This decision was a necessary one. Feeling cut off from his past, Mailer could not express himself in the idiom and form of that past. The considerable difficulty he experienced in creating a credible first person voice which would fit his prose style becomes centrally important in understanding *The Deer Park* (in which it reaches a peak) and *An American Dream* (in which it is momentarily resolved). This is one area in which, as Mailer himself realizes, *Barbary Shore* casts light upon the work which follows it.

Mikey Lovett sets out, as did Mailer, "to begin life again . . . to force [himself] to step into the war of the enormous present . . . setting out by [himself] to cut a track through a new wild." [4] Although he remains essentially *alone,* he is not by himself for long. The series of intertwined relationships into which he is drawn begins with the landlady, Mrs. Guinevere. Mikey's initial conception of her is that given him before he has seen her, by Willie Dinsmore, the casual acquaintance who has occupied the room Lovett is to live in. He is the only character in the book besides the six inhabitants of the house, and after performing the function of introducing Mikey into the house, he leaves and does not reappear. He is so patently a device that even Mailer, through Mikey, remarks on it:

I suppose even a magic box must have its handle. Yet once the box is opened, I wonder if it is too unreasonable that the handle is then ignored. I am more concerned with the contents. If I begin with Willie Dinsmore, it is because he served as a handle; and I, who was to serve for so long as the sorcerer's apprentice, forgot him quickly.[5]

Dinsmore is a leftist playwright who sees the world in terms of a simplistic understanding of the class struggle. He is equally simplistic about people:

> Like so many writers he had very little interest in people, and if they could serve his didactic demands, a pigeonhole was all he required. I had been installed immediately in the one he undoubtedly labelled Postwar Problems.[6]

It is a measure of Mikey's naiveté (which is accentuated by his diminutive first name and the pronunciation of his second, "love it") that despite his recognition of Dinsmore's shortcomings as a character analyst, he accepts the man's simple evaluation of Guinevere: "Guinevere's a nymphomaniac." [7]

Sexuality is to play an important part in the relationship between Guinevere and Lovett, as it does with all the relationships in the book, but it is significant that these two never sleep together. Appearances are never proven true in this book. Between Dinsmore's statement and Guinevere's surprisingly attractive initial appearance, Lovett is caught in his first external involvement (a unilateral one at that):

> I was startled. Dinsmore had poorly prepared me. She was quite pretty, at least to my taste, pretty in a flamboyant, cootchy way, so that my first impression was of no more than a fabulous crop of red hair and a woman beneath, waggling her hips. Undeniably short

and stout, her limbs were nevertheless delicate, her
face was not heavy, and her waist, respectably narrow,
tapered inward from her broad shoulders in an ex-
aggeration which was piquing.[8]

And later, he thinks of her as:

A jewel. But set in brass. This morning she had
sported a house dress and covered it with a bathrobe.
. . . Yet there had been opera pumps on her feet, her
nails had been painted, her lipstick was fresh. She
was a house whose lawn was landscaped and whose
kitchen was on fire.
    The nymphomaniac. As I was about to fall asleep
for the first time in my new room, I realized that I
wanted to take Guinevere to bed.[9]

Mikey is, finally, the only resident of the house (except Guinevere's little daughter, Monina) who does not
take her to bed. In a series of vulgar, but knowledgeably
coy confrontations, she teases and refuses him, ultimately
proposing that he spy on the other boarders for her.
Lovett's indigant refusal places their subsequent dealings
on a cooler footing, but by this time he has become involved with the other boarders.
    McLeod, Lovett's next acquaintance, is perhaps the
most important character in the book. A wry, cynical man
who works in a department store, he describes himself as
a self-educated "Marxist-at-liberty," claims never to have
travelled beyond New Jersey, and leads a life of monastic
isolation:

In everything he did there were elements of such
order, demanding, monastic. He was unyielding and
sometimes forbidding. Dressed in the anonymous

clothing of a man who buys his garments as cheaply as possible. . . . And his room, clean as any cell could have been in our aged mansion. . . .[10]

He is ultimately revealed to be, first, Guinevere's husband, and second, a former high-ranking international communist operative sought by the American government.

McLeod is primarily significant in terms of Mikey. In their talks, as mutual distrust very gradually fades, McLeod assumes the role of tutor to Lovett's tyro.[11] It is through him that Mailer is able to introduce long passages of Marxist theory, but it is more important that after much confused vacillation Mikey's loyalties are directed entirely to McLeod. It is Mikey's progress toward understanding and embracing McLeod's theories (and finally of accepting the responsibility of carrying them on) which represents the central movement of the novel.

The two thematic levels of the novel, individual and social, are focused almost exclusively in Mikey's two major preoccupations: sexual communication and Marxism, respectively. The first part of the book deals primarily with the former, the last part with the latter; and it is the shift from one to the other on Mikey's part that embodies what resolution the novel offers.

Just as Guinevere and McLeod are not what they first appear, Leroy Hollingsworth, secret policeman [12] and grand inquisitor, presents a very deceptive first impression. Invited casually into Hollingsworth's room for a beer, Lovett finds it "unbelievably messed." In contrast, Hollingsworth himself is so neat that Lovett observes, "He seemed to have no relation to the room." [13] The fact is that Hollingsworth seems to have no relation to the situation and setting at all. He is described in terms of the Norman Rockwell vision of the typical American boy, and it is significant that at no point in the subsequent revelation of his true role is it suggested that his appearance or manner are falsely assumed:

> He was obviously from a small town; the talk about the weather, the accent, the politeness were unmistakable signs. The simple small-town boy come to the big city. . . .
>
> The features were in character. He had straight corn-colored hair with a part to the side, and a cowlick over one temple. His eyes were small and intensely blue and were remarked immediately, for his nose and mouth were without distinction. He was still freckled, which made me wonder at his age. I was to learn later that like myself he was at least in his middle twenties, but there must have been many people who thought him eighteen.
>
> . . . he was in considerable contrast to his room. It seemed wrong for him. I had a picture of the places in which he had slept through his boyhood: a bed, a Bible, and in the corner a baseball bat perhaps. As though in confirmation, the only decoration upon his wall was a phosphorescent cross printed on cardboard. It would glow when the lights were out.[14]

In light of Hollingsworth's later role in the novel, this description is significant. Mailer seems to be saying, as he does repeatedly in the later books, and as he did in *The Naked and the Dead,* that the primary threat of totalitarian takeover in this country lies in internal fascism. His choice of Hollingsworth, a blonde, blue-eyed boy/man whose features are "without distinction" suggests that secret policemen do not spring full blown from the ground, bearing fangs and truncheons, but appear naturally from the ranks of the populace when governmental policy re-

quires them. The physical characteristics of Hollingsworth
are in themselves slightly chilling, for they conform not
only to the American stereotype but to that of the Nazi
"master race" as well.

Hollingsworth is lacking in intellectual distinction as
well as physical. Though cunning in his tenacious hound-
ing of McLeod, he betrays no real understanding of political or moral issues, is aggressively anti-intellectual, and
sees both international and personal issues in terms of
black and white. His ultimate commitment is to expedience, and towards the book's end he is ready to desert his
country for personal gain. He is, finally, despicable because he is so unquestioning in his assurance that what
he does is right. This attitude is early demonstrated in his
attitude towards sex. In his sexual dealings with Guinevere, with Lannie (a female boarder who moves in after
Lovett), and with a waitress he picks up while drinking
with Mikey, he is vulgar and sadistic. In his first conversation with Lovett, he reveals an offensively lewd preoccupation with sex:

> "Do you know any good books I could read?"
> "What kind do you mean?"
> "Oh, you know."

> •   •   •

> "What kind of books do you want?" I asked again.
> "Well. . . ." He seemed hesitant. "In the Army there
> was an awful lot of literature that I liked. You know
> things with the facts of life in them. . . . I don't
> remember the titles, but there were you know things
> about American fellows and girls. The real stuff
> though. You know the way we feel."
> I mentioned several of the major novels which

had been written by Americans between the two wars.
This seemed to satisfy Hollingsworth.

•   •   •

"And there's lots of real things in them, isn't
there? I mean, you know, . . . *foolish* girls, and
boys who are willing to . . . to take a chance." He
grinned.
"You'll probably find some."
"I'm really surprised they print things like that.
I wonder if they should allow it. Atheistic things, and
the Bolshevists, I understand, write for them a lot."
"For what?"
"Oh, for them, you know."

•   •   •

"I've been in New York two months," he said
suddenly, "and do you know I haven't found any of
the evil quarters. . . ."

•   •   •

He leered at me suddenly. "I've had some interesting experiences with the lady downstairs. Mrs.
Guinevere. She's a fine lady." The leer was shocking.[15]

Even were he truly what he purports to be, a minor clerk
in a large Wall Street firm (a cover whose fitness for a
representative of reactionary interests is obvious), the
character of Hollingsworth would be a devastating indictment of the "average" American, with his stag-film view
of sex, his unquestioning dedication to the status quo, and
his comfortable Christianity, which demands nothing of
him but token commitment to outward show. The symbol
of this (a strikingly effective touch which prefigures Mailer's later preoccupation with "plastic" falsity in the American material culture) is the "phosphorescent cross printed
on cardboard," which "would glow in the darkness when

the lights were out." Even the universal symbol of selfless-
ness and brotherly love is, in Hollingsworth's world, a
shoddy, mass-produced ornament, perhaps as significant to
him, but certainly no more so than a hand-painted novelty
tie decorated with a phosphorescent nude. The cross, one
must assume, glows mute witness to every act of unfeeling
seduction and self-righteous persecution which its owner
perpetrates.

Enter Lannie, directly into Mikey's room, seeking
someone who can rent her a room. She, like Lovett, proceeds to become involved with the other residents. But it
is Mikey to whom she comes first, and he becomes immediately involved by finding Guinevere and interceding
on Lannie's behalf with the fiction that she is a friend of
his.

Lannie is somewhat mad, living within a nightmare
world of her own. She is tormented, inconsistent, railing,
nearly incomprehensible but often frighteningly perceptive in her visions of human brutality and betrayal. After
a brief sexual contact with Lovett, unsatisfactory to either
and conceived in terms of vainly attempted communication on his part, Lannie consciously and eagerly seeks
abasement at the hands of Hollingsworth in an episode
which is not presented to the reader but left to be inferred
from her later mutterings. Late in the novel, she is revealed suddenly as the aggressor in a sexual affair with
Guinevere. The sexual alliances in this novel are without
exception sordid, one-sided in motivation, and significant
primarily in terms of negation rather than affirmation.
There is no enjoyable sex, no sex for love, no real communication between sexual partners. Further, the several
revelations of previously accomplished sexual contact to
which neither the reader nor Lovett have been witness
(such as Lannie and Guinevere, Lannie and Hollingsworth, McLeod's role as Guinevere's husband) lend a

further sense of surreptitious mystery, making the sex seem more sordid and increasing the sense of intricate machinations beneath the surface.

It should be obvious at this point that Guinevere is a sort of hub about which the other characters revolve on the sexual level. This is not to say that she is in control of them except on occasion, but that she represents a pivotal point which they all touch at some time. Her name may assume some significance here. Although, as we are to discover, her last name is legally McLeod and her given name is Beverly, she is referred to always as Guinevere, and only occasionally as Mrs. Guinevere. She explains at one point to Mikey:

> "I'll tell you," she said, "I was born Beverly Guinevere, but when I was on the stage, I just used to call myself Guinevere, you know one name like Margo or Zorina. And I like it, I keep it, you know it's not like other names."
> "You were on the stage?"
> She nodded profoundly.
> "What plays?" I asked.
> "Oh, I was in burlesque, I was a *queen*. Boy, they used to go for me." [16] [My italics]

The symbolic value of the name Guinevere is underlined not only by her previous profession of burlesque "queen," but also by such devices as ". . . the hem of her purple velvet wrapper swished luxuriously along the floor." It is an indication of the sordid state of our times and our society as Mailer sees it, if Beverly Guinevere is to represent our royalty.

With very little difficulty, other Arthurian parallels fall into place. Guinevere's lover is Lannie, too close to Launcelot to be ignored as coincidence. And finally, who is to be Arthur? The role is assigned by Mailer, not to

McLeod the husband, but to *Leroy*, the king, Hollingsworth, inheritor of a new world where mediocrity, expedience, and narrow-minded ignorance rule. And if the
point is not yet clear enough, we have Guinevere's statement about Hollingsworth, whom she takes as a lover and
with whom she agrees to betray McLeod and seek a new
life: "Sometimes I think he's the son of a prince, now I
don't mean that exactly, but you know, a magnate, or
a . . . a potentate, and that he's living here in disguise." [17]

For Guinevere, sex is a marketable commodity. Not
only does she use it to play upon Lovett and the other
boarders, but she has made her living displaying herself
as a sexual object in the past. Her ambitions for the future
hinge upon a simple, cynical, and perhaps frighteningly
accurate conception of the American dream. Like many
ignorant, cynical people who feel they have seen much of
life, she feels she has something important to tell the
world. At one point she proposes to Lovett that he per-
form the necessary but mechanical (as she sees it) task of
writing up a semi-autobiographical love story which she
feels would be a sure financial success in Hollywood. The
story, presented in full by Mailer, is no more than a
particularly sordid soap opera, with the emphasis more on
lust than sentimentality.

Another of Guinevere's schemes is to make her daughter, Monina, a child star in Hollywood. To this end, she
attempts to keep the child a baby as long as possible; but
Monina, despite her lisping baby talk, is perhaps too much
her mother's daughter. At the age of three, she is all too
aware of her own sexuality, and attempts to gain male attention through a parody of striptease, revealing a body
which is "virtually a miniature of a girl of eighteen." [18]
Monina is a perverse child, strangely reminiscent of Hester
Prynne's daughter Pearl, in *The Scarlet Letter*. Not only

does she embody the sins of her mother and threaten to duplicate them, but she calls attention to certain of Guinevere's indiscretions by perversely parroting private and revealing exclamations she has heard from her mother. Again, it is Monina who, like Pearl, reveals to the reader the identity of her incognito father, McLeod.

If most of the human relationships in this novel are informed by a tawdry sex without love that underlines the distance our culture has travelled from the ostensible nobility of the Arthurian age, not all the characters are satisfied with (or unaware of) the lack of meaning in it. Unlike the other characters, Mikey Lovett is truly desirous of sex as a means of communication. In this aim, he is continually frustrated. The abortive encounters with Guinevere and Lannie will be seen later to acquire some symbolic import when, late in the book, it becomes clear what these characters represent. At this point, however, they serve the function of throwing the discouraged Mikey back into the isolation of his own mind. Repeatedly, he drags up visions from his murky past, some of which may be vague memories from before his accident, some merely fantasies. Several of these are sexual in nature, and one, presented early in the narrative, is of particular significance in understanding the nature of Mikey's character and quest:

> Across the blur of the past, I have a memory which returns over and over again, and I am almost certain it happened. Perhaps it was during a furlough from the Army, although that is not important. I knew a girl then who was in love with me and I very much in love with her. We spent a week in a tourist home at some seashore resort, and that week provided more happiness and more pain than I could have thought possible. For the girl love had always been difficult

. . . but I adored her so completely, so confidently, that my admiration seemed to accomplish everything. The room we shared burgeoned for her. She came to love her flesh, and from there it was but a step to loving mine. We lay beside each other for hours on end, brilliant with new knowledge. I had discovered magic to her and reaped the benefit; I could shine in the reflection of her face. . . . She blossomed in that week, and I was so proud of myself. We were very close. We fed upon one another. . . . We lived under the shadow of the war and perhaps that furnished its spice.

While I was with her I was very happy, but the moment I had to talk to someone else, an agony of shyness beset me. To order a meal from a waitress became a minor ordeal. . . .

•   •   •

When we parted, and I believe I never saw her again, she whispered a phrase not devoid of literary ambition, "Mikey, you know the room is the trap of the heart," and the extravagance of the words was not completely without meaning.

This is one of the few memories I possess, and I offer it for what explanation it may provide. If I lived in a close relation with the few people I knew in the rooming house and became progressively less capable of doing without them, there is after all a precedent. I was a dog on a chain, and the radius circumscribed a world in which I was able to provide for many of my wants and most of my needs.[19]

Mikey's alienation, then, is not merely a function of his amnesia or any other scar of war, though the former is certainly a symptom and a symbol of it. Nor is complete alienation a state which he chooses to embrace, for his

statement makes clear his need to relate to his fellow
boarders.

Other memories and fantasies, less explicit in significance, are related by Lovett periodically, and it is never
clear even to him which of them are rooted in actual history and which proceed from sheer subconscious inven-
tion. All are somewhat nightmarish, and one particularly
Kafkaesque scene, related in the first chapter, is worthy of
mention:

> I see a traveller. He is most certainly not myself.
> A plump middle-aged man, and I have the idea he
> has just finished a long trip. He has landed at an
> airfield or his train has pulled into a depot. It hardly
> matters which.
>
> He is in a hurry to return home . . . he hails a
> taxi . . . settles back comfortably in the rear seat.
>
> •   •   •
>
> The cab is taking the wrong route!
> What shall he do? It seems so simple to raise his
> hand and tap upon the glass, but he feels he dare not
> disturb the driver. Instead, he looks through the
> window once more.
>
> The man lives in this city, but he has never seen
> these streets. The architecture is strange, and the
> people are dressed in unfamiliar clothing. He looks
> at a sign, but it is printed in an alphabet he cannot
> read.
>
> His hand folds upon his heart to still its beating.
> It is a dream, he thinks, hugging his body in the rear
> of the cab. He is dreaming and the city is imaginary
> and the cab is imaginary. And on he goes.
>
> I shout at him. You are wrong, I cry, although
> he does not hear me; this city is the real city, the ma-
> terial city, and your vehicle is history. Those are the
> words I use, and then the image shatters.[20]

This passage is significant to Mikey's understanding of the events of the novel, as he relates them in retrospect. The realization that history is a vehicle, one which moves so rapidly as to make men strangers in their own world, is central to Mikey's movement towards understanding what the future demands of him. The plump, middle-aged traveller has been left behind by history, and in this respect he may be seen as representative of most men in this era of rapid and complex historical development. More particularly, considering the time the novel was written, he may be representative of the returning veterans of every country, who find that the society and ideals they fought for are really unfamiliar to them, no longer the clear-cut things they were represented as during the war. Mikey Lovett, understanding the nature of history, becomes the voice of these men, who themselves cannot comprehend and articulate.

In this role, Lovett is unhampered by ties to a life prior to the war, and the various clouded memories and visions he drags up serve to reinforce the universal nature of his jumbled experience. For example, he vaguely remembers himself as a faceless part of the American Army in Europe:

> I saw all the endless children who waited for our leavings on garbage lines, all the whores we abused, the peasants we cursed because they could not understand us and we were drunk. It almost comes back, the diarrhea, the trench foot, the boots we polished, the men who got killed. The machine stopped at last, but I stopped first, and lay on my cot that summer in a Paris which might be mythical, and counted the cracks in the wall. Empires had fallen, kingdoms been reshuffled, but that was over the horizon. I played a closet drama in which the machine would let me go
> . . . go where? [21]

Mikey's recognition of the fact that he has been a faceless component in a national machine renders more significant his literal loss of his face and his identity; and his separation from that machine is the first in a series of experiences and realizations which lead him ultimately to exercise his individual will.

Again, he imagines another, earlier past for himself:

> Could it not be possible that I was born in an old house in the center of a Midwestern city, the house going quietly to seed, while the distinction of being one of the oldest families became less important to everyone but ourselves? . . . Institutions altered, and with them, men, and there would be a new country club and insurance brokers who peopled it. My parents would talk about such things with distaste for they lived in the memory of an earlier world, illumined in the transitory splendor of a calendar sunset, and they would assure me that forty years ago the city was lovely, adorned by small quiet streets and brownstone stairways. . . . Spring mornings the men would walk to work, and on Sundays the entire family was in black, the quiet afternoons in the back yard annotated only by church bells.
>
> It is a sweet picture, but it is a false shore. The only brownstone houses I ever knew were in disrepair and skived by landlords. I was born into a world which would move forever faster, and if I had to create for myself a tropical isle, I could not render it perfect, for I would always find the darkening clouds of typhoon, and hear the surf lashing the shore. It was possible to engage in such a voyage, but only to return to the hard cot beneath the dirty window of my narrow room.
>
> So I lay there that evening while McLeod across the hall must also have stared at the ceiling, and I dreamed that I was in another room in a vast dormi-

tory for children, and while we slept a fire had begun in the cellar and was sweeping along the dry wood of the walls and through the deep vent of the staircase. Soon it would reach the great room in which we slept and sear a passage through the door, and we would awake to the sound of children's screams and hear our own voice.[22]

Perhaps because Lovett is not committed to any definite personal past, he belongs to any and all of them, and is as much a product of the serene Midwestern streets as of the shabby orphanage. He is a representative figure, grown to young manhood in all regions of America, responsible for the victories and brutalities of all American soldiers. Finally, he is the spokesman for all postwar cripples, a man of his generation, cut off irrevocably from the past.

The visions and dreams, memories and fantasies, related to us by Lovett are to continue periodically throughout the book. But by the middle of the narrative, he has begun to fall under the influence of McLeod, and consequently these passages become colored almost exclusively by Marxist theory and preoccupation with the history of the communist movement. Immediately after a talk with McLeod, Lovett returns to his room and imagines or remembers himself as a youthful, idealistic follower of Trotsky:

I was exhausted from the argument we had had, so pointless, so stereotyped, and so demanding upon me. I had not talked like that for how many years? And with the labor of parturition, a heartland of whole experience was separating itself to float toward the sea.

I was an adolescent again, and it was before the war, and I belonged to a small organization dedicated to a workers' revolution. . . . I was young then, and no dedication could match mine. . . . There was a great man who led us, and I read almost every word he had written, and listened with the passion of the noviate to each message he sent from the magical center in Mexico. Of all the students in the study group, none could have been more ardent than I, and for a winter and a spring, I lived more intensely in the past than I could ever in the present.

•   •   •

So the memory came down to the sea, and across my back scar tissue burned ever new circuits with its old pain. Things had altered this night. With a pain throbbing in my head I continued slowly home.[23]

Lovett's reaction to McLeod's disturbing political talk is significant. He resists the influence it has on him, attempts to regard it as "pointless." He is exhausted because the effort has been "demanding" upon him; and finally it must be obvious to the reader that concern with the social problems presented by the communist movement has not been pointless to him in the past, and that he wishes to retain his protective cloak of amnesia and unconcern. He is unable to do so, and it is no accident that he uses the phrase, "the labor of parturition," to describe the painful process of bringing to light this new memory. McLeod is not a mere gadfly to Lovett, but the midwife attending the painful birth of a new conception of self, a new social involvement, in the younger man.

Realization piles upon realization, as Mikey spends increasingly more time lying on his cot, which seems to function as an analyst's couch for his self-probings. He is too painfully honest with himself, too concerned with finding some truth and therefore some true conception of his own role in the world, to cling any longer to his blanket of darkness, and so he plumbs his mind ceaselessly. In a long

passage which occurs almost at the exact center of the
novel, he relates a series of thoughts which culminate in a
major breakthrough. He remembers an incident of the
war, in which, having crossed into the "enemy's country" as
part of the invading army, he shared with the rest of his
squad the willingly sold favors of a farmer's daughter.
The incident is related in terms of the utmost dehumanization:

> There was moonlight on the field, and I made love
> from the hip and looked across the meadow with open
> eyes, for I was also on guard. I never saw the girl.
> Above my head in magnification of myself the barrel
> of the machine gun pointed toward the trees, and
> once, hearing a noise, my fingers stole up to the trigger
> handle, and I was surprised to find it cold.
>
> My ration consumed, I went back to the hay and
> stretched out in a nervous half-sleep which consisted
> of love with artillery shells and sex of polished steel.
> By the next afternoon we were ten miles away. . . .
> There are times when I have the idea I was wounded
> in the action which followed.[24]

This episode marks the lowest point of dehumanization
to which Mikey Lovett had been brought by the war. Part
of a massive war machine, he had become himself mecha-
nized, "making love" mechanically without love or even
passionate hatred. He is shown as an appurtenance of his
machine gun, and it dwarfs him in its greater importance
and potence, as it rises "above my head in magnification
of myself." The impending victory over the enemy is
implicitly robbed of moral significance by the fact that the
bovine farm girl whose face he never sees responds to the
invaders without hatred, fear, or any other emotion. An
act which, were it accompanied by gratitude or passion,
might be romanticized into a reaffirmation of the basic

humanity of all people is instead shown as a matter of cold economic trade, and thus the insignificance of individual human emotion in the shadow of grinding international movement is made clear.

The fact that Lovett believes that he sustained his wounds in the action following the incident with the farm girl is symptomatic of the ultimate depth of dehumanization to which it brought him. The wounds may be real, physical ones, but the amnesia which accompanies them is obviously similar to the repression of memory experienced in cases of severe neurotic trauma. His ability to face the memory marks the turning point in a sort of auto-psycho-analysis in which he has been aided by McLeod's proddings, and from this point on, Lovett's mind moves progressively (though stumblingly) toward human commitment. Immediately, his thoughts move upward from that lowest point, touching again the intermediate plateaus to which we have already been introduced, the girl of the week-long idyll and Lannie:

> I may have thought of the girl at the seashore resort, perhaps I even carried a letter from her in my pocket. I know that after leaving Lannie, I brooded about that girl I would never see again, and as Lannie had recalled the farm girl to me so she could recall the other.[25]
>
> Where was that girl and what did she look like? I wanted her so badly I was almost ill.

But this time, in his painful reverie, Lovett comes to a crucial knowledge:

> Frustration put me on the rack, and with the frustration came something worse. For I would never meet that girl, and if I did I would not remember her and she would not recognize me. And if all these impos-

sibilities one by one were to be solved and the wheel
presented a double miracle for the same chip, then
undoubtedly the girl and I, having changed, would be
magical no more to each other. So that was done and
that was dead. There could be no solutions from the
past nor duplicates found in the present, and I could
have cried out in resentment against the implacability
of the logic . . . whatever I was to find could not
come from the past.[26]

Lovett's concern with the past has, finally, yielded up the
inner kernel of his personal alienation from humanity and
its problems. Having achieved this much, Lovett recognizes the limitations of the past, and for the first time becomes truly committed to the present as he has claimed to
be from the outset. The forward movement of his now un-
fettered mind will not let him rest, however, and his preoccupation with present issues is ultimately to lead him to
think of the future, and finally to assume the responsibility
of his own role in that future.

It is interesting to note that the farm girl episode,
so central to Lovett's switch in commitment from the past
to the future, is rendered in terms of the two primary
preoccupations which govern his mind throughout the
book: sex and international politics. In the wartime
episode, sex is shown to be not an act of self-definition or
even a temporary refuge from the dehumanizing regi-
mentation of war, but a final proof of the extent to which
the impersonal forces of national interest can stifle the
individual personality, rendering the act of love and pro-
creation a mere mechanical function.[27] The memory of the
seashore resort girl is recognized as an irrecoverable dream,
as pleasant but as insignificant to the present as the outmoded Midwestern city of Lovett's fantasy. Mikey dwells
no longer on that girl, nor does he attempt any further

sexual liaison with either Guinevere or Lannie. It is at this point, the structural center of the novel, that Lovett turns from the sexual preoccupation of the first half of the book, to the devotion to political issues which drives him thereafter.

Lying on his bed, Mikey reviews the present world situation and faces the fact that the Russian Revolution and the communist movement have changed nothing for mankind:

> The proletariat which crawled to glory beneath the belly of a Cossack's horse, the summer flies of Vyborg, I could see it all again, and know with the despair which follows fervor that nothing had changed, and social relations, economic relations, were still independent of man's will.
>
> Except for myself. I lived, and was it I alone, in relation to nothing? The world would revolve, and I who might exercise a will for so long as money lasted, exercised nothing dreamed away hours upon my bed.[28]

The knowledge that larger forces in the world rob men of their power to exercise individual will does not, this time, cause Lovett to despair. He has come some distance from the state of mind he held scarcely twenty-four hours earlier when the conversation with McLeod seemed "pointless" and the world situation without hope. Mikey has begun to enter into a sense of his own potential power, as a thinker, to exercise free will and influence the world. His novel, always in the far background of the plot, no longer seems the proper vehicle for his personal mission. He has begun to understand that he must define himself through his own actions, and in this respect he begins to embody certain values of postwar existentialism as Mailer saw it.[29]

Lovett has already begun to sense in what arena his will must be exercised, and it is no idle impulse that leads him again to seek out McLeod:

> Now, the silence about me became doubly oppressive. I started up and crossed the hall to McLeod's door, knocked upon it as if I could summon him to be present. There was no answer, and when I knocked again, the door gave before my fist, swung slowly open.
>
> My eyes were drawn immediately to the table which had been placed in the center of the room and was bracketed by two wooden chairs which stared blankly at one another across its empty surface. Adjacent to one of the chairs was set a floor lamp so arranged that it would shine into the eyes of whoever sat on the other side of the table. Everything else had been pushed to the side.
>
> Then I realised McLeod had vacated the room.[30]

McLeod, too, has returned to his past in one sense, by returning to the household of his wife. But this change has been precipitated not by a domestic reconciliation so much as by a new stage in the Hollingsworth situation. The secret policeman is ready to begin questioning in earnest, and McLeod's room will now function as interrogation chamber. In the long and closely spaced interviews which follow, McLeod is forced to relive his past, to admit his true identity as a high party official, and to agonize over the more brutal acts he has perpetrated in the name of his former cause.

At all of these interrogation sessions, both Mikey and Lannie are present, and because the latter figures as a sort of assistant persecutor, for reasons vastly different from Hollingsworth's, her motivations should be mentioned. From the beginning, her ravings have been colored by a consciousness of the class struggle. Entering her newly rented room for the first time,

> . . . she had gone to the window and was playing with the fastener on the middle sash. "It's like a finger," she said. "Look" and crooked her hand. "When they finished the house, there were no locks for the windows, and so the builder, a cruel capitalist who later built a house at Newport, cried at the top of his lungs, 'Cut off the fingers of the workmen, and nail them into place.' And this is a poor workingman's finger." She stroked it. "It's all that's left of him now, his finger and his thumb." [31]

And later, she tells Mikey:

> "The wall is so nice. I can make it anything I want. This afternoon when you left, I kept looking at it, and I decided it was Guernica, and I could hear the horses screaming." [32]

She lives in a world of strange visions, and she is unable to distinguish fantasy from reality, fiction from real experience. Mikey realizes this when she tells him the story of Wing Biddlebaum from Sherwood Anderson's *Winesburg, Ohio* as though it were part of her own past:

> "I knew only one man who was kinder than you, and he was a middle-aged man, a teacher in a little school in a small town, and he had beautiful hands, and he used to love to touch little boys with them because the little boys were so beautiful, only he never did dare; he would keep his hands in his pockets. They used to nickname him Wing, and they treated him dreadfully."
> "Why I read that," I blurted. "It's a story." [33]

From the beginning, it is clear to Mikey that Lannie is distracted, "not wholly aware of herself," but the extent of her madness becomes clearer in several garbled memories she expresses of time spent in a mental institution. For example:

> "You see, Mikey, they were always putting me on a bed, and then there were hands and the shock. I know what they were doing because each time they gave me the shock it would leave a little less of my brain, and they wanted to render me stupid as others render fat. They hated me, and they made a record of everything they took from my brain, and there was the girl in the corner with the eyeglasses who kept writing everything on the pad, and now it's in some green filing cabinet. They hated me, and I loved them for their sins." [34]

Despite her incoherence, Lannie is often frighteningly perceptive, rounding out the gallery of horrors presented by the novel with the nightmarish visions of human brutality she seems compelled to relate, such as an execution scene in a Nazi concentration camp.

In some ways, Lannie is at first similar to Lovett. Like him, she is rootless, cut off from her personal past by the cloudiness of her mind; and like him, she is compelled to recount visions in which the line between fantasy and memory is rarely clear. But unlike him, she finds it unnecessary to distinguish between the two, and thus is willing to live in her own world, rather than attempt to connect it with reality. She will be seen later to cling to the values of a static political past rather than change her outmoded values and move forward to the future as he ultimately does. In her loyalties within the boarding house, she takes a directly antithetical position to that of Lovett. Where Mikey has rejected the shabby sexuality of Guinevere, she embraces it; and where Lovett grows to disdain Hollingsworth and respect McLeod, she aids the government man in persecuting McLeod. The logic of these antithetical commitments becomes valid within the structure of the novel when certain patterns of allegory begin to emerge, with each of the characters seen as representative of a particular ideology.

I have suggested earlier that Hollingsworth represents the unquestioning, narrow-minded fascism of the postwar era, and that Lovett is the spokesman for a confused and naive postwar liberalism. As the novel progresses, it becomes clear that the politically sophisticated but worn-out McLeod is representative of the expedient prewar communist movement. Guinevere, defined as she is by vulgar, commercial sexuality, and committed to the grasping, materialistic values of a society whose capital is Hollywood, is all too representative of the majority of the population of that society. Mikey, in a confused groping after something to commit himself to, has attempted a union with Guinevere, only to find that what she offers is a false and shabby reward, a worthless tinsel mock-up of love which must be paid for with one's integrity.

If Hollingsworth and Lovett are the two possible versions of the new, postwar American, the choice open to America is a frightening one. For Hollingsworth is chosen by both Guinevere and Lannie, and the path he leads them down is a dead end, immoral, destructive, closed to anything that is good. McLeod's ultimate rejection of Hollingsworth in favor of Lovett, and the latter's decision to follow the guidance of the older man provide a hope which is frighteningly slender, for it is obvious that the power is with the Hollingsworths.

Why does Lannie reject Mikey but grasp eagerly what Guinevere offers? Why does she seek out Hollingsworth and oppose McLeod? The answer lies in what

Lannie herself comes to represent. Lannie has been deeply involved, in the past, with the communist movement, but she is now disillusioned by the amoral inhumanity of its policies. She embodies the views of the idealistic prewar American Left, who tried to rationalize and condone Soviet domestic and foreign policy in terms of conventional humanistic morality and, finally unable to do so, renounced it. She sees McLeod as the symbol of the worst expedience in the movement, and wishes to help destroy him in retribution for the death of a utopian dream. The idol and spokesman of that dream was Trotsky, and he (although his name is never used) is a crucial pivotal point in the loyalties and hatreds of Lannie, Lovett and McLeod, and of the three distinct segments of the Left they represent. We know already that Lovett followed Trotsky's teachings. (See quotation above, p. 74.) And at the point we meet him, Mikey has lost his passion because, we may assume, of the disillusioning events following the death of the Trotsky dream.

For Lannie, Trotsky was even more important than he was to Lovett, and his murder was the unforgivable sin which has prompted her renunciation of communism and her hatred of McLeod. Revealing herself clearly for the first time, she shouts at McLeod:

> "He was the man I loved, the only man I ever truly loved with heart and not with body, the man with the beard because he was a fool—a brilliant man and I loved his beard, and there was the mountain ax in his brain, and all the blood poured out, and he could not see the Mexican sun. Your people raised the ax, and the last blood of revolutionary mankind, his poor blood, ran into the carpet." [35]

The accusation is more valid than she realizes, for McLeod later admits that he has not merely been guilty of tacit consent but that he actually played a small part in the bureaucratic paperwork which led to the assassination. What is at issue is not McLeod's guilt as stated by Lannie, for his later admissions reveal still greater complicity in political murders. Rather, what is central to the political resolution of the novel is the difference in reaction between Lannie and Lovett.

Her illusions destroyed, Lannie is devoid of hope for the world, and rejects any possibility for the individual to change it. She is thus in direct contrast to Mikey, who at this point has begun once again to believe in the potential of his own will, and looks to McLeod for guidance. For this she derides him:

> "Oh, Mikey, I'm convinced. It's only you who is still the fool as I was once the fool, and you will not recognize that all these years, ever since the great man sat on his piles in the British Museum and let us think there was a world we could make, when all the time he was wrong, and we've been wrong, and there's no world to make for the world devours."
> "We still don't know," I muttered.[36]

In her militant hopelessness, Lannie does not feel it sufficient to renounce the communist movement. In addition, she embraces (figuratively) a reactionary ideology and (literally) its representatives, Guinevere and Hollingsworth. These alliances are somewhat perverse for an erstwhile idealist and the sexual unions which symbolize them are therefore also somewhat unnatural (lesbianism with Guinevere, brutal abasement at the hands of Hollingsworth).[37] Further, Lannie intentionally assumes the role of a passively adoring object of exploitation to each of these partners, thus fulfilling her belief that the will of the individual has no place in this world. This passivity is given symbolic depth by at least one of several metaphorical patterns which attach to her, that of the mirror.[38] Lannie tells Guinevere late in the book:

> "And that is why you love me, for I would be a mirror to you, and we escape only when we follow our mirror and let it lead us out of the forest. I can let you see your beauty, and so you will love me for I adore you and unlike the others want nothing but to lie in your arms, the mirror."
>
> Guinevere heard this with her lips parted, her eyes far away. Bliss animated every curve in her face. "Yes," she murmured, "yes," dropping her voice into a gentle reflective sigh. The nectar she tasted rolled in her mouth until she could have absorbed her tongue in the sentience of the moment. Unconsciously, she clasped her breast. If it had been possible she would have kissed herself upon the throat.[39]

This emphasis upon the mirror may suggest another, less obvious Arthurian parallel. Lannie is a submissive figure whose love is unrequited, and who is ultimately deserted. This situation, combined with her ambiguous sexual identity and the sound of her name, may suggest that Lannie performs a dual role in the Arthurian pattern: not merely that of Launcelot, but also that of Elaine, the Fair Maid of Astolat, particularly as represented by Tennyson in "The Lady of Shalott."

Another echo of the mirror motif occurs after the second and final episode of lovemaking between Lannie and Lovett, when she calls him Narcissus. The partial truth of that accusatory label, as well as the nature of the abortive sexual affair between the two, leads to a clearer distinction between their values.

The fact that Lannie and Lovett turn to one another at first, in an attempt to escape the pain of alienation, is no mere accident of proximity. Rather, it may be seen, on a less literal level, as the final attempt of the splintered forces of the prewar idealistic Left to reunite in some valid basis for common belief. It is a desperate attempt:

> I held her in my arms, gave her my body to which she could cling, and remotely without tenderness or desire or even incapacity I performed, riding through the darkness of my closed eyes while she sobbed beneath me in fathomless desperation.
>
> If it were love, it was also fear, and we might have huddled behind a rock while the night wind devoured the plain.
>
> "Save me," I heard her cry.[40]

And it is doomed to be a vain one as well, for neither can offer what the other needs. They are proceeding in opposite directions, drawing further apart as the novel progresses. This polarity is made obvious the second time they are together sexually. Groping for some feeling outside himself, Mikey attempts to convince himself that he loves Lannie:

> . . . with a pity I offered to her in preference to myself, I heard my voice say, "Don't you understand? I think I love you."
>
> •   •   •
>
> "Let me love you," I pleaded. "I want to, don't you understand?"
>
> •   •   •
>
> [She replies] "But I can't. I can't love you." She tried to push me away. "I don't like you. And you don't need me." [41]

Not out of desire, but in an attempt to convince both of them of the truth of what he has said, Lovett makes love once again to Lannie, and ". . . she lay beneath me stiffly and suffered it with a smile, her face calm and patient, sweet suffering Jesus upon the cross." [42] The reference to Christ occurs more than once in regard to Lannie.[43] Already she has spoken in terms reminiscent of Christ (see quotation above, p. 81: "They hated me and I loved them for their sins.") and this seems to be the basic characteristic of her commitment to Hollingsworth and Guinevere. Because Mikey is not sufficiently selfish, harsh and insensitive, she cannot be a martyr with him, and so she attacks him. When he repeats, with less assurance, that he loves her, she replies:

> "You can't love anybody, Mikey, for you're Narcissus, and the closer you come to the water the more you adore yourself until your nose touches, and then you're alone again."
> I did not want to believe this. "It's true," I said, "but it's . . . it's not true. It's not all true." [44]

Certainly, this is a partial truth, but it is no more than that. Mikey's self-involvement is one from which he hopes to escape. His involvement with his own mind is, finally, a constructive preoccupation, out of which will grow his new capacity to become involved again with mankind. Lannie is a rather perverse Christ surrogate, for in her determination to become the footstool of the most selfish reactionary elements, she cannot countenance a man who aspires to goodness and to the humanitarian ideals which have so disappointed her. In her next, unjust accusation, she even uses the terms and values of Guinevere and Hollingsworth. She tells Lovett, "You came to me because

I was easy, and you thought it would not cost you anything." [45]

Lannie's rejection of Lovett is mild, however, in comparison to her vitriolic attack on McLeod,[46] in which she consciously rejects all Christian mercy in favor of an insatiable vengeance:

> "I know," she cried, "that I could sit by and watch cutthroats club you to the grave and I would shout them on, for I know that you are wholly irredeemable. I was afraid. I thought that I might have pity, that most crippling of the sentiments, or that looking into your face, I would say, he had suffered, or—and this is what tormented me most—that in helping them [Hollingsworth's people] what did I help? But you have buried the revolution, and it is fitting that they who exist because of you, they who rise to eminence here because you destroyed the revolution there, should have the right to flay your bones. And I shall cheer them on. . . ." [47]

This attitude is not, however, to be her final evaluation of McLeod. As the interrogations proceed, much is confessed that justifies and reinforces her condemnation of the man. But soon, mitigating and even selfless actions in McLeod's career are revealed, and she frantically refuses to accept them as true, in her determination to cling tenaciously to the black and white system of moral values she has adopted. She is incapable of understanding the necessity for a dynamic rather than a static ethic within a history which itself is dynamic and outstrips old ideals. This is what Mikey learns from McLeod. But it is not until the very end that Lannie forgives McLeod, and by then it is too late for her to play a part in the future.

The actions, fears and fates of the inhabitants of the

rooming house are symptomatic of those of mankind in this postwar world. Guinevere, asked by Hollingsworth where they should flee together after deserting both Mc-Leod and the American government, replies, "Anywhere. To the ends of the earth. To Barbary—I like the sound of that." [48] And this is no idle choice, for having betrayed both personal and national loyalties, the two are stripped to their essential barbarism, with not even the flimsiest of pretensions to disguise their absolute self-interest. The title of the novel is echoed one further time, when Mc-Leod, prophesying the series of endless wars which must inevitably be brought about by present economic systems concludes:

> The war begins again with a new alignment of forces, and to the accompaniment of famine and civil war, the deterioration continues until we are faced with mankind in barbary.[49]

This, then, is the significance of Mailer's title. Mankind is on the shore of barbary, ready to plunge in. It is a fearsome and depressing vision.

Viewed as an allegory of the postwar world situation, the novel's tortuous plot and symbolism become clearer. Lovett is unable to return to the past or to be satisfied with the present, unable to remain alienated from mankind but unwilling to embrace the values of Guinevere, Lannie or Hollingsworth. Rejecting the vulgar materialism of American popular culture, the static idealism of the old line Left, and the methods and values of the hard Right, as they are respectively represented by those three characters, Lovett turns to McLeod, hoping by an understanding of the mistakes of the past and of the nature of history, to influence the future. From total self-involvement and a preoccupation with the superficial human contact to be found through loveless sex, he progresses to a profound involvement with mankind. The novel carries the prophecy of postwar American fascism introduced in *The Naked and the Dead* a step further, evincing an even darker view of American society. But Mikey Lovett, in his movement toward positive action, represents a step towards the positive character of Rojack in *An American Dream*. The final commitment which Lovett makes, in accepting the responsibility of carrying on McLeod's ideas where the older man leaves off, is brought about only at the very end of the novel, as a result of the series of formal interrogations carried out by Hollingsworth.

Once the series of formal interrogations begins, events proceed rapidly toward their resolution. Ready to unburden himself, McLeod responds with little hesitation to Hollingsworth's prodding. The personal history which unfolds shows McLeod's rapid rise in power and in the scope of his influence, from local to international affairs. This increase in power is paralleled by a progressive dehumanization, an increasing commitment to expedience at the expense of personal morality. The tacit acceptance of betrayal and assassination gives way to sins of commission: the physical murder by McLeod, first of an inconveniently idealistic young subordinate and then of a personal friend who becomes unable to accept the methods of the party. The degree of ruthlessness of these acts increases in direct proportion to McLeod's own disillusionment with communist policy, prompted by a stated belief (which Hollingsworth quotes): "It is better to carry through a blunder with all one's energy, than attempt to halt midway and retrace one's steps." [50] The culmination of this philosophy is reached in McLeod's role in the murder of Trotsky, as he painfully relates in a confession reserved for Lovett's ear alone:

". . . and it's when I think of the other one with the
ax in his gray hair, and your friend Miss Madison
who'll never be able to live past that moment, and
it wasn't the direct participation of myself in it, oh,
I have no concrete blood on my hands, I was just a
cog in that one and arranged a passport, and smelled
a little of what was to come, but you see I did nothing
and all the while I was managing my infinitesimal
part of the operation, working on it while I was at
the height of a crisis for it was the time of the pact,
and I no longer believed a minute in what had been
the external and objective reality of my life." He had
begun to mutter. "This detail taken care of and that.
I could have not known who it was for, and yet I
knew it was him out in Mexico, and on the dark sly I
was reading his works behind my barricaded door. I
knew," he shouted suddenly, "I knew. There's the
crime. No longer believing and I went ahead. I let
him be murdered you see." [51]

And shortly afterwards, in a decision further motivated
by the pact he mentions, McLeod leaves the Party. His
subsequent history is related in his first brief autobio-
graphical summary to Hollingsworth:

In 1941, left the Party. Subsequently worked as statis-
tician for American government bureau 1941–1942.
Under assumed name. Quit bureau in 1942. Since
worked at odd jobs under name of William McLeod.
That's all.[52]

It becomes apparent at this point that it is McLeod's
activity as a U.S. government employee and the circumstances under which that employment terminated which
are of primary interest to Hollingsworth. McLeod goes on
to elaborate:

". . . I worked in one of the endless ramifications of
the embryonic State Capitalism, a big place with
thousands of people and thousands of desks, and this
but the local branch, mind you."

He went on to describe with relish how the
various parts of the organism fitted together. . . .

•   •   •

Then, after years of regular and orderly process,
something happened. "I don't know, I can't tell you
what it was," McLeod said, "an object of some sort
or other, not too large I imagine, but it was gone,
and no one knew how."

The organism reeled from the shock and trem-
bled to its extremities. ". . . The displacement of that
little object displaced a great deal else. Cysts broke,
pus spread, the blood became infected and carried
the fever with it. You should have seen the giant
stagger. There were guards collected at every joint
and operations galore." [53]

Although McLeod denies it, Hollingsworth is convinced that he is in possession of the "little object," and it
becomes the central *object* [54] of both Hollingsworth's and
Guinevere's ambitions. In the hope of acquiring it for personal gain, Hollingsworth makes no official report of the
progress of his interrogations. He eventually offers Mc-
Leod a deal in which the latter is to be allowed to escape
in exchange for giving up the object. Hollingsworth en-
lists Guinevere in his cause, offering to take her away
with him in exchange for her aid in convincing her husband to come across. Guinevere's capacity for treachery
and greed surpasses that of Hollingsworth. She is intoxi-
cated by the dream that if they can deliver the little object to a foreign power, "They'd make us royalty." [55] But
like Hollingsworth, Guinevere is loyal only to her own
desires, and she soon proposes to McLeod that he sell "The

thingamajig" and flee with her, leaving Hollingsworth behind. McLeod has, at this point, been flirting momentarily with the temptation of making a last attempt at a reconciliation with Guinevere, of renouncing moral responsibility in favor of the anonymity of an average American family man. The crass bluntness of her offer makes this course impossible for him to accept, and it is finally to Mikey that McLeod passes on the object and the moral mission that goes with it, after the younger man has shown himself willing and worthy to accept them.

What, then, is the "little object"? The question is never resolved. It is so very secret that no one knows what it is, and this ambiguity magnifies its mysterious significance. In this age of atomic secrets and spy stories (which, in a sense, this novel is) it could indeed be a material object: a microfilmed blueprint, a formula, or even a crucial component part. Hollingsworth and Guinevere obviously believe that this is the case (to her, it is a "thingamajig") because both are so rooted in a simplistic system of materialistic values that they are incapable of conceiving abstractions.[56]

Close to the end of the novel, Hollingsworth, in the passage perhaps most representative of his opinions and character, self-righteously rejects those things most valued by McLeod and Lovett: theory, individuality, and the desire to influence the future:

> "We all have our different characters, and that's true. It's just that we mustn't be stubborn. You've been an unhappy man all your life, and you didn't want to admit it was your own fault. So you blame it on society, as you call it. That isn't necessary. You could have had a good time, you could still have a good time if you'd realize that everybody is like you, and so it's pointless to work for the future." His hand

strayed over the desk. He might have been caressing
the wood. "More modestly. We ain't equipped to deal
with big things. If this fellow came to see me and
asked my advice, I would take him aside and let him
know that if he gives up the pursuits of vanity, and
acts like everybody else, he'd get along better. Cause
we never know what's deep down inside us"—Hollingsworth tapped his chest—"and it plays tricks. I don't
give two cents for all your papers. A good-time
Charley, that's myself, and that's why I'm smarter than
the lot of you." His pale face had become flushed.
"You can shove theory," he said suddenly. "Respect
your father and mother." [57]

Hollingsworth is the corrupt and shoddy instrument
of McLeod's confession, and finally it becomes clear that
the secret policeman is being used by his victim, rather
than vice versa. McLeod, confused, weary and guilt-ridden,
finds it necessary to confess and reevaluate his life; and so
he speaks, nominally to Hollingsworth, actually to Mikey,
heedless of whether Hollingsworth can or will understand
the theoretical and moral issues involved. But Mikey
understands and profits from the experience of McLeod,
and as his conversion to these teachings becomes apparent
and his loyalty to McLeod deepens, it is Mikey alone to
whom the older man confides the greatest of his sins (the
Trotsky episode, see above p. 91) and his hopes and fears
for the future. Finally certain that the past is significant
only in what it can teach for the future, McLeod states:

> "One of the small benefits I can permit myself
> is to spend no time apologizing for my past. It is what
> it is, and in the time permitted me here, I should
> prefer to indulge in the only meaningful defense, to
> transmit the intellectual conclusions of my life, and
> thus to give dignity to my experience. I shall not treat

the past as personal history, and I will attempt to delineate what I believe to be the future, for it is only as ideas are transmitted to someone else that they attain existence."

Hollingsworth interrupted him. "You talk like a fellow who doesn't think he's going to live long."

"You misunderstand. I speak metaphorically." [58]

But this time McLeod has been quite literal in his meaning, for he knows now that he must die in order that his ideas may live, and it is to the mind of Mikey Lovett that he entrusts them for the future. The night after the final interrogation, in which he has agreed to surrender the object to Hollingsworth, McLeod instead leaves an envelope with Mikey, goes to confront Hollingsworth with his refusal and is killed by the latter. He thus serves as a decoy, enabling Lovett to escape just as the house is raided by government agents.

The role which Mikey must play in the future had been explained by McLeod. The hope for mankind is that both of the corrupt systems presently existing, Western Capitalism and Eastern Communism, fail, and that a new, just society be established. But for this to happen, it is essential

". . . that the socialist theorist will once again find language to reach the many.

"That there be theorists at such a time is of incalculable importance. . . . not too many of us will be alive. Yet there must be some to participate, for revolutions are the periods of history when individuals count most. . . . It is the need to study, it is the obligation to influence those few we may, and if some nucleus of us rides out of the storm, we shall advance to the front of any revolutionary wave, for we alone shall have the experience and the insight so

vital for the period. Then we shall be the only ones
capable of occupying the historical stage." [59]

Thus, what hope there remains for mankind resides
primarily in the individual intellectual theorist who can
teach his fellows. Finally, the future rests upon the
synthesis of the experience of McLeod and the youthful
dedication of Lovett. The parallels between them lay the
groundwork for their union at the novel's end. Both have
been dehumanized by involvement with international
forces and each has withdrawn from the world, cut himself
off from his past, attempted to avoid moral responsibility.
It is only with each other's support that the two men
each regain a sense of faith in humanity's future. Without
Lovett to pass the object and quest on to, McLeod might
easily have succumbed to Hollingsworth's or Guinevere's
temptations. Without McLeod to present an alternative,
the confused and groping Lovett might have listened to
Lannie when she said, "Come with us. There's no place
else to be." [60]

The extent of McLeod's renewal of faith in humanity's
future is made explicit in his will, contained in the
envelope which he gives Lovett before going to his death:

> To Michael [61] Lovett to whom, at the end of my life
> and for the first time within it, I find myself capable
> of the rudiments of selfless friendship, I bequeath in
> heritage the remnants of my socialist culture. [62]

Almost as an afterthought he had scrawled:

> And may he be alive to see the rising of the Phoenix. [63]

The commitment to humanity which McLeod instills in
Lovett, and which is exemplified by the feeling of selfless

friendship he expresses toward the younger man, forms the basis for some hope. It must be emphasized, however, that what McLeod teaches Mikey is not a rigid commitment to static systems or values, but a sense of the dynamic principle in human history. The loyalty he is to embrace is to mankind, but not to any country or political party or even any single political or economic theory. This is where Mikey, in his capacity to understand that history is a vehicle which allows for no stagnation but demands constant revision of one's ideas, is truly worthy of McLeod's trust. He is the man of the future, capable of carrying out the mission entrusted him, because unlike Lannie, he is able to realize that there is no static good and evil: that the movement of history renders these values either totally irrelevant or at best temporarily valid in relation to a specific context.[64]

The concluding passage of the novel makes evident the circumstances under which Lovett relates the story:

So the heritage passed on to me, poor hope, and the little object as well, and I went out into the world. If I fled down the alley which led from that rooming house, it was only to enter another, and then another. I am obliged to live waiting for the signs which tell me I must move on again.

Thus, time passes, and I work and I study, and I keep my eye on the door.

Meanwhile, vast armies mount themselves, the world revolves, the traveller clutches his breast. From out of the unyielding contradictions of labor stolen from men, the march to the endless war forces its pace. Perhaps, as the millions will be lost, others will be created, and I shall discover brothers where I thought none existed.

But for the present the storm approaches its

thunderhead, and it is apparent that the boat drifts blind, and the deaf shout warnings to one another until their voices are lost.[65]

The final sentence of the novel is a repetition of the final sentence of the first chapter. It is clear, then, that Lovett recounts the story in retrospect, some time after it has taken place, and is thus aware of the significance of his experiences even in his first chapter. This impression is reinforced by other information presented in the opening chapter:

> Now, in the time I write, when other men besides myself must contrive a name, a story, and the papers they carry, I wonder if I do not possess an advantage. For I have been doing it longer, and am less tantalized by the memory of better years. They must suffer, those others like myself. I wonder what fantasies bother them?
>
> •   •   •
>
> Night comes and I am alone with a candle. What has been fanciful is now concrete. Although the room in which I write has an electric circuit, it functions no longer. Time passes and I wait by the door, listening to the footsteps of roomers as they go out to work for the night. In fourteen hours they will be back.[66]

Mailer's statement that *Barbary Shore* is set in an "imaginary future" is understandable in light of this passage. It is clear that Lovett writes in a future governed by the repressive State Capitalism predicted by McLeod, a totalitarianism in whose fearful shadow men must contrive names and carry false papers. The crumbling system forces men to work a fourteen hour night shift and live in rooms where electricity is no longer available. In this society, Michael Lovett is an outlaw, recounting the events of the novel as he waits to disseminate his knowledge of political theory. Ironically, Lovett is, in a sense, a singularly credible narrator for this book, in that the interminable passages of Marxist theory which are its single greatest weakness are to be expected from the mind of an avowed theorist. Nonetheless, the book is difficult to read, involved in plot, often confused and confusing. Several overlapping but nonintegrated systems of symbology [67] add to the difficulty without ever emerging into a clarity which might add to the novel's effectiveness.

Finally, Mailer's own stated intention gives us a key to where he failed, when he describes *Barbary Shore* as "an agonized eye of a novel which tried to find some amalgam of my experience and the larger horror of that world which might be preparing to destroy itself." (See above, p. 55.) It must be concluded (and Mailer himself might concur) that the amalgam was at best a lumpy one, that he did indeed overreach himself, and that while his own psychic experience and the external reality of the world he describes each have a validity of their own, they are never smoothly blended within the novel.

In a comparison between Mailer's first two novels, it must be admitted that the political views with which both are colored are better expressed in *The Naked and the Dead,* where they are often implicit and almost always integrated with the characters and situations involved, than in *Barbary Shore,* where they are expressed primarily in lengthy, explicit, polemical passages. Despite its glaring weaknesses, however, *Barbary Shore* does show evidence of some thematic progress in the direction of Mailer's later views. The dehumanization experienced by both McLeod and Lovett because of their use as instruments of national military machinery is parallel to that dehumanization by war which Mailer showed in *The Naked and the Dead.* But where the first novel left such men as

Red Valsen permanently bludgeoned into submission by the system and no longer hopeful of the potential of the individual, *Barbary Shore* suggests that if men learn from their experience, no matter how sordid, there can be purpose in it, and hope. Where Lieutenant Hearn was fated to die a pointless death, Mikey Lovett is destined to devote his life to a positive cause; consequently, McLeod's life and death have not been purposeless. Where the first novel left the future in the hands of the Major Dallesons, *Barbary Shore* shows that it has been held by them and their successors, the Hollingsworths. But there is a new, distant future to look forward to for Mikey Lovett, in which they may be deposed, and if this is a flimsy vision of hope, it is better than none.

It is easy for critics and fans of Mailer alike to wish that *Barbary Shore* had never been published. But an informed reader could never wish that it had not been written. The novel shows Mailer at his worst: confused, lacking control and fictional discipline, often simply boring. Yet the discrepancy between his narrator and his own prose style became all too clear to Mailer through this book, and in those that followed it would narrow. The conscientious and fearful concern with America's cultural and political shortcomings and with the dangerous and lonely path open to the individual would be expressed more cogently and powerfully. Mailer's voice may be muted and sometimes unintelligible at this point, but it is not yet hushed.

Notes

1 *Advertisements for Myself*, pp. 91–94.
2 Norman Mailer, *Barbary Shore* (New York: Rinehart and Company, Inc., 1951). Paperback edition published 1953 by Signet

(New American Library of World Literature, New York), p. 5. All
page references are to the Signet edition.

3 It is worth noting that war is a central experience for the protagonists of each of the novels. Sergius of *The Deer Park* and
Rojack of *An American Dream* are each profoundly affected by
war experiences which they relate early in their stories. D. J. of
Why Are We in Vietnam? goes off to war at the end of his
narrative.

4 See quotation p. 54 above.

5 *Barbary Shore*, p. 7.

6 *Ibid.*, p. 9.

7 *Ibid.*, p. 11.

8 *Ibid.*, p. 12.

9 *Ibid.*, p. 15.

10 *Ibid.*, p. 26.

11 This relationship is echoed by the Sergius/Eitel situation in *The
Deer Park*.

12 This is the title by which Mailer refers to Hollingsworth in
Advertisements for Myself.

13 *Barbary Shore*, p. 29.

14 *Ibid.*

15 *Ibid.*, pp. 31–33.

16 *Ibid.*, p. 45.

17 *Ibid.*, p. 66.

18 *Ibid.*, p. 45.

19 *Ibid.*, pp. 34–35.

20 *Ibid.*, pp. 6–7.

21 *Ibid.*, p. 53.

22 *Ibid.*, pp. 61–62.

23 *Ibid.*, pp. 90–91.

24 *Ibid.*, pp. 114–115.

25 *Ibid.*, p. 115.

26 *Ibid.*

27 In this respect and others (notably the terror evoked by the state
spying on citizens) the novel is reminiscent of George Orwell's
1984 (published 1949).

28 *Barbary Shore*, p. 117.

29 Like Sergius in *The Deer Park*, Mikey Lovett wishes to exercise
his will actively, and therefore both protagonists go a step further
than the passive resistance of Red Valsen. But although the
conclusions of *Barbary Shore* and *The Deer Park* show Mikey
and Sergius looking to the future in the determination to forge
a new life, their success or failure in doing so is not a part of
either book. It is in *An American Dream* that Mailer presents a
protagonist who demonstrates the capacity to act positively and

existentially within the author's own highly individual conception of existentialism.

30 *Barbary Shore*, p. 117.

31 *Ibid.*, p. 75.

32 *Ibid.*, p. 98.

33 *Ibid.*, pp. 94–95.

34 *Ibid.*, p. 109.

35 *Ibid.*, p. 136.

36 *Ibid.*, p. 152.

37 The implication of a passage she writes and later shows to Mikey is that she has performed fellatio upon Hollingsworth. The act in itself is not considered perverse by Mailer in light of sexual attitudes clarified in the later works, but the passive acceptance of harsh, loveless sexual exploitation certainly is, and this is clearly such a case.

38 The others, which are somewhat confused, include her momentary function as a Christ figure (dealt with briefly below, p. 87), and her part in several symbolic father/child patterns, notably in relation to Lovett and to Trotsky.

39 *Barbary Shore*, p. 186.

40 *Ibid.*, p. 100.

41 *Ibid.*, p. 110.

42 *Ibid.*

43 The Christ imagery in the novel (as I have suggested above) is inconsistent and confusing. It applies most often to Lannie, but occasionally to McLeod, and even to Lovett (whose hand is raked by Lannie's nails at the novel's end).

44 *Barbary Shore*, p. 111.

45 *Ibid.*, p. 112.

46 The two are parallel, however, as though Lovett receives a portion of the hatred Lannie feels for McLeod and the communist movement, in proportion to his involvement with them. This is one of several parallels between Mikey and McLeod.

47 *Barbary Shore*, pp. 135–36.

48 *Ibid.*, p. 148.

49 *Ibid.*, p. 202.

50 *Ibid.*, p. 165.

51 *Ibid.*, pp. 175–176.

52 *Ibid.*, p. 129.

53 *Ibid.*, pp. 132–133.

54 The ambiguity of this word seems to reflect the ambiguity of the "little object's" nature. It may be a material object, but it may also be the abstract object of everyone's desire.

55 This statement echoes the earlier Arthurian pattern, and there is particular irony in that today's "royalty" achieve their position

not through courage and nobility, but through greed and treachery.

56 Early in the novel, Mailer has wryly shown Hollingsworth's inability to understand even a simple metaphor. McLeod has stated, figuratively, that "poison may only be met with poison," and Hollingsworth jots down on the list he keeps of subversive beliefs admitted by McLeod, "Advocates use of poison."

57 *Barbary Shore*, pp. 193–94.

58 *Ibid.*, p. 195.

59 *Ibid.*, p. 204.

60 *Ibid.*, p. 140.

61 There may be some significance in the fact that this is the first time Lovett has been addressed by his full first name, rather than the diminutive nickname, Mikey. Perhaps it is an indication that he has come to manhood.

62 The passing on of one's essence for the future is echoed clearly in *The Deer Park*. The idea of selfless commitment to another person looks ahead not only to Eitel/Sergius, but even to Rojack/Cherry of *An American Dream*.

63 *Barbary Shore*, p. 223.

64 In this sense, a parallel exists between *Barbary Shore* and Arthur Koestler's *Darkness at Noon* (1941). More specifically, McLeod is reminiscent of Koestler's Rubashov in that novel, in his revelation of a ruthless personal past, his final recognition that the future belongs to a new generation, and his willing acceptance of death after that realization.

65 *Barbary Shore*, p. 223.

66 *Ibid.*, pp. 6–7.

67 Such as those mentioned in footnotes 38 and 43.

3

The Deer Park

Toward the end of *The Deer Park,* Sergius O'Shaugnessy, after his first abortive attempt to write, remarks that:

> . . . I tried to write my novel about bullfighting, but it was not very good. It was inevitably imitative of that excellently exiguous mathematician, Mr. Ernest Hemingway, and I was learning that it is not creatively satisfying to repeat the work of a good writer.[1]

It would seem that Mailer himself learned this after the completion of *The Naked and the Dead,* a book which marks the eminently successful completion of a self-admitted apprenticeship. The work which follows the first novel is characterized without exception by the struggle to forge a highly personal art by which Mailer hoped to articulate his own very individual concerns. Since it is one of the aims of this study to clarify these concerns, it is very much in order to devote some space to the methods by which Mailer arrived at his present fictional idiom.

The path is littered with false starts and fragments, many of which have been printed and discussed by Mailer in *Advertisements for Myself*. But the work which lies at the heart of the interim struggle for an adequate form which occupies the almost two decades between *The Naked and the Dead* and *An American Dream* is *The Deer Park*. The work is of particular interest because it underwent a major revision after Mailer had once decided it was ready for publication, and because he has been unable to let it lie, reworking it over a period of years into a play of the same title, which was produced in New York City in January, 1967. It is always interesting to compare two forms of the same work, and in the case of *The Deer Park* such comparison is central to an understanding of Mailer's artistic development. Certain significant shifts in emphasis condition Mailer's current vision as opposed to that of a decade earlier, and these are reflected in basic differences between *The Deer Park* as novel and as play.[2]

Barbary Shore, as has been demonstrated, is a rather shaky step in the development of artistic vision between the first and the last novels. The most significant step forward it represents is that it is written in the first person, as are the three novels which follow it. The devices of structure and point of view learned from Dos Passos were effective in *The Naked and the Dead,* but if Mailer believed what Sergius was to learn about derivative work they may have represented a dead end. Nonetheless, an acceptable new form did not come easily. The first person presented problems which made *Barbary Shore* artistically ineffective, an admission of which is implicit in Mailer's discussion of the point of view problems he experienced in writing *The Deer Park:*

> For six years I had been writing novels in the first person; it was the only way I could begin a book,

even though the third person was more to my taste.
Worse, I seemed unable to create a narrator in the
first person who was not overdelicate, oversensitive,
and painfully tender, which was an odd portrait to
give, because I was not delicate, not physically. . . .
Yet the first person seemed to paralyze me, as if I had
a horror of creating a voice which could be in any
way bigger than myself. So I had become mired in a
false style for every narrator I tried.[3]

The pre-publication history of *The Deer Park* (N) is
extremely relevant to the development of Mailer's narrative stance. As the author himself relates it in *Advertisements for Myself,* Rinehart and Company, who had a
contract with Mailer for the book, were bound to accept
it or to pay him a large advance. After much grumbling
over the novel, which no one at Rinehart liked, Stanley
Rinehart rejected it shortly before publication and attempted to avoid paying the advance. The decision was
precipitated by the author's refusal to delete six lines in
which, without graphic obscenity, the sexual relations
between a young call girl and an old producer are implied,
rather than described. There is considerable irony in the
fact that the passage is not only devoid of any word which
might be considered obscene (strikingly so in comparison
to the graphic sexual description of Mailer's later fiction)
but is rather well executed in this very avoidance. After
rejections from six other publishers, the novel was accepted
without revision at G. P. Putnam. But the experience had
precipitated in Mailer an emotional realization of something he had previously known only on an intellectual
level:

. . . that my fine America which I had been at pains
to criticize for so many years was in fact a real country

which did real things and ugly things to the characters
of more people than just the characters of my books.[4]

In retrospect, Mailer sees the episode as a major milestone
in his own development:

> And so as the language of sentiment would have it,
> something broke in me, but I do not know if it was
> so much a loving heart, as a cyst of the weak, the
> unreal, and the needy, and I was finally open to my
> anger. I turned within my psyche, I can almost
> believe, for I felt something shift to murder in me. I
> finally had the simple sense to understand that if I
> wanted my work to travel further than others, the life
> of my talent depended on fighting a little more, and
> looking for help a little less. But I deny the sequence
> in putting it this way, for it took me years to come to
> this fine point. All I felt was that I was an outlaw, a
> psychic outlaw, and I liked it, I liked it a good night
> better than trying to be a gentleman. . . .[5]

The concepts of the psychic outlaw and of murder within
oneself inform much of Mailer's artistic vision in the later
fiction. But the importance of the experience just recounted is most immediately reflected in the changes
Mailer made in *The Deer Park*. After a few months away
from the book, he read the page proofs and was struck
by the fact that the style was unsatisfactory to him:

> . . . the book read as if it had been written by
> someone else. I was changed from the writer who had
> labored on that novel. . . . I could at last admit the
> style was wrong . . . that I had been strangling the
> life of my novel in a poetic prose which was too self-
> consciously attractive and formal, false to the life of
> my characters, especially false to the life of my nar-

rator who was the voice of my novel and so gave the
story its air. He had been a lieutenant in the Air
Force, he had been cool enough and hard enough to
work his way up from an orphan asylum, and to allow
him to write in a style which at its best sounded like
Nick Garraway in *The Great Gatsby* must of course
blur his character and leave the book unreal. Nick
was legitimate, out of fair family, the Midwest and
Princeton [6]—he would write as he did, his style was
himself. But the style of Sergius O'Shaugnessy, no
matter how good it became . . . was a style which
came out of nothing so much as my determination to
prove I could muster a fine style.[7]

The comparison to *The Great Gatsby* is not idly
chosen, for even the final version of *The Deer Park* (N)
bears a structural parallel to Fitzgerald's book, in that in
both cases the novel is as much about the narrator as
about the major character he describes. Nick and Sergius
develop as men through the experience of knowing Gatsby
and Eitel. Because Sergius was so important to the structure of *The Deer Park,* Mailer now felt it essential to
revise the narrative style of the novel. This took some
commitment to artistic integrity, since the people at
Putnam were anxious to publish the exact text rejected
by Rinehart in order to capitalize on the consequent
notoriety. Mailer made hundreds of small changes he felt
necessary, and found that:

> for the first time I was able to use the first person in
> a way where I could suggest some of the stubbornness
> and belligerence I also might have, I was able to color
> the empty reality of that first person with some real
> feeling of how I had always felt, which was to be
> outside, for Brooklyn where I grew up is not the

center of anything. I was able, then, to create an
adventurer whom I believed in, and as he came alive
for me, the other parts of the book which had been
stagnant for a year or more also came to life, and new
things began to happen to Eitel my director and to
Elena his mistress and their characters changed. . . .
Before, the story of Eitel had been told by O'Shaugnessy of the weak voice; now by a confident young
man: when the new narrator would remark that Eitel
was his best friend and so he tried not to find Elena too
attractive, the man and woman he was talking about
were larger than they had once been. I was no longer
telling about two nice people who fail at love because
the world is too large and too cruel for them; the new
O'Shaugnessy had moved me by degrees to the more
painful story of two people who are strong as well as
weak, corrupt as much as pure, and fail to grow
despite their bravery in a poor world, because they
are finally not brave enough, and so do more damage
to each other than to the unjust world outside them.
Which for me was exciting, for here and there *The
Deer Park* had the rare tenderness of tragedy. The
most powerful leverage in fiction comes from point of
view, and giving O'Shaugnessy courage gave passion
to the others.[8]

This, then, is what *The Deer Park* finally was about:
individuals in a "cruel," "poor" and "unjust" world. And
the novel proceeds on two major levels: the social, in
which the particular evils of American society are con-
demned; and the individual, in which the inability of
each character to escape from his own alienation through
love is traced.

Charles Eitel is the most striking and poignant
example of failure on both the societal and individual
levels. He begins well: at the novel's beginning he has
already refused to tell of his leftist associations before a

congressional committee, thereby sacrificing his fabulously successful career as a movie director. And he persists in this refusal for several years, until late in the novel when he capitulates. In his relationship with Elena, his mistress, he tries at first to create something meaningful between them, and ultimately yields to infidelity, as does she. Their final solution is a sullen, empty marriage, surrounded by the dubious security of Eitel's regained success and supplemented by his resumed affair with his ex-wife, the matinee goddess Lulu Meyers.

Sergius undergoes temptations parallel to those of Eitel. Coming to Desert D'Or with fourteen thousand dollars won in a poker game just before leaving the Air Force, he is perceptive enough to see that the movie capital *is* merely a rich, glittering desert. But he is too aimless and weak to reject its glamour at first. After suffering a minor breakdown precipitated by the emotional realization of the horror he has visited on other human beings in flying napalm bombing missions over Korea, he finds himself rootless and sexually impotent. The latter problem is alleviated by his affair with Lulu Meyers, who has been divorced from Eitel for some time. Yet Sergius, in his adolescent glee at sleeping with a universally desired woman, commits himself to a greater and more shameful impotence. He becomes a flunky to Lulu, straight man to the ludicrous vaudeville act of public appearances.

The first inklings of strength in Sergius are seen when he is offered $20,000 for the movie rights to a romanticized version of his life story, with the further implication that he may be starred in the movie. The situation is tempting in more than a financial way. Sergius loves Lulu, and as a wealthy actor would be acceptable as a husband for her. He recognizes, however, that such a role would be the end of him as a man:

> I could see myself as Mr. Meyers, a sort of fancy long-
> shoreman scared of his wife, always busy mixing
> drinks for Lulu and the guests.[9]

Sergius turns down the movie offer, but a crisis has not
yet been reached. He still has Lulu and some money. Soon,
a more difficult situation is presented him. On a trip to
Las Vegas with Lulu, he loses most of his remaining
money, and because of this and the increasingly intolerable
pressures of publicity for Lulu's new movie, the two
separate. Sergius moves from his beautifully artificial
ranchhouse to a furnished room, and gets a job washing
dishes. Here, lonely and exhausted, he is able to see the
contract offer in a much more tempting perspective, and
it is still open.

It is at this point that Sergius, wavering in his plans,
divested of what small external security and confidence
he had derived from the accoutrements of money, is
confronted by the most immediately frightening threat in
the novel. He is visited in his room by two powerfully
built and insulting government agents,[10] partially because
of his friendship with the blacklisted Eitel, ostensibly
because of a ludicrously inaccurate gossip column which
referred to him as a Marine Captain rather than an Air
Force Lieutenant. Fighting his own paralyzing fear, Sergius
manages to walk the thin line between a qualified and
face-saving defiance and a severe beating. The agents leave
with the warning not to leave town, and Sergius, weak
and shaken in the aftermath of his minor victory, is forced
to come to terms with himself. He realizes that:

> . . . if I did not watch out, I would be a patsy in the
> world, that was the worst thing which could happen
> to a graduate from the orphanage. Too many men
> and too much history seemed to add up to no more
> than the death of the patsies. And then of course I

knew no history, that too occurred to me, and if I was going to speak up to the rough world out there, it was time for me to open a book.

•   •   •

I began then to make those first painful efforts to acquire the most elusive habit of all, the mind of the writer. . . . I knew that finally one must do, simply do, for we act in total ignorance and yet in honest ignorance we must act. . . . So I wrote a few poor pages and gave them up and knew I would try again.

In the meantime I did not hear from the detectives, and slowly I came to decide that it was time for me to leave Desert D'Or, and if I was in real trouble with them, which I doubted, well that for that. I would go to Mexico. . . .[11]

The scene with the two agents is significant as a part of Mailer's social criticism in *The Deer Park,* for they are characters who belong in a totalitarian state and who are not supposed to exist in an ostensible democracy. And they are only small cogs in the fearsome machinery represented by the subversive-hunting committee which interrogates Eitel. The hypocrisy which Mailer sees in the simplistic American dream of freedom and plenty has as another of its symptoms the very existence of a golden desert of celluloid make-believe. Ultimately, Sergius has been able to reject the falsity of Desert D'Or and Lulu, and to reinforce his first act of defiance to the agents by his departure for Mexico.

What hope there is in the novel is invested in Sergius. But on both the individual and the societal levels it is a decidedly qualified hope. Sergius has been able to reject the false love of Lulu, the false profession of movie star, the false values of a tinsel society. But at the end of the novel he has still not found a positive commitment. He has tried to write but is not yet able to do so successfully. And he does not yet know himself, though he searches through an apprenticeship to a bullfighter and an affair with the bullfighter's girl. Like that of Red Valsen in *The Naked and the Dead,* his definition of self has been limited to negatives. He knows what he must defy and reject, but not what he must affirm and commit himself to. The social ills which Sergius sees continue to exist, and he, feeling unable to rectify them, leaves America. Perhaps the most pessimistic statement on the sickness of the American society, and its contagious quality for the individual, is implicit in Eitel's return to the superficial trappings of the American dream.

But Eitel is old and tired, and Sergius is still young. It seems implicit in the novel that Sergius is meant to carry on where Eitel left off. The men are linked throughout the novel, not only by friendship but also through their parallel sexual connection with Lulu. It is significant that a part of Eitel's having returned full circle is his resumption of the sexual relationship with Lulu. In the course of his circular movement through defiance and ultimate capitulation, Eitel has lost his capacity to make artistically honest movies; and in recognizing his loss, he leaves Sergius with a final word of advice in an imaginary conversation within his mind:

> "For you see," he confessed in his mind, "I have lost the final desire of the artist, the desire which tells us that when all else is lost, when love is lost and adventure, pride of self, and pity, there still remains that world we may create, more real to us, more real to others, than the mummery of what happens, passes, and is gone. "So, do try, Sergius," he thought, "try for that other world, the real world, where orphans burn orphans and nothing is more difficult to discover than a simple fact. And with the pride of the artist, you

must blow against the walls of every power that exists, the small trumpet of your defiance." [12]

The implication that Sergius carries on the spirit and work of Eitel becomes explicit in the play version of *The Deer Park,* where Sergius says, "And as he [Eitel] died, his spirit passed on to me, for to pass on one's spirit is the one small gift we are allowed in Hell. . . ." [13] But in the play, certain major shifts in emphasis condition and clarify Mailer's message, informed as it is by more than a decade of development. It should be stated immediately that it is impossible to determine at what point during the period between the publication of the novel and the production of the play any particular element of the later version was written. In *Advertisements for Myself,* published in 1959, Mailer stated that "Some time next year I plan to publish the play of *The Deer Park."* [14] He went on to state that the script was complete, and that the major problem lay in cutting enough material. Nonetheless, eight years passed before the play reached the stage, and many lines are so similar to passages in *An American Dream* (1964) that they must seem to have been interpolated much later than 1959 and perhaps after 1964. Because of this textual situation, it seems simplest to deal with *The Deer Park* (P) as an interim piece in which Mailer's position approaches that in *An American Dream,* without raising the issue of what material appeared first in the latter novel.

The major shift in emphasis apparent in *The Deer Park* (P) lies in the fact that Sergius, though still the narrator, is far less important as a character than he was in the novel. The major conflicts with which he was presented in the novel, that of the movie contract offer and the visit from the government men, are absent from the play. The result is to throw the character of Eitel into a position of far greater importance to the dramatic structure of the play. Further, Eitel seems a stronger, more positive character than he was in the novel. He is given lines which did not appear in the novel and which sometimes look forward to the statements of Stephen Richards Rojack, narrator of *An American Dream,* rather than back to the Eitel of the novel. For example, the play Eitel, speaking of his first night with Elena, says:

> . . . something flew in like a madman on wings. An angel. For the first time in my life I felt there were some sweet substance to be found in love, not power, but the sweetest thing I'd ever known—heaven. . . . it was as if God had touched me with a finger, and I didn't want to lose that sensation ever again.[15]

And later, speaking of their lost love to Elena, he says, "It wasn't all wasted, Elena. I never knew what it was all about, until I learned from you." [16] At the end of the play, Eitel dies, a major plot departure from the novel. And this death has the ring of tragedy about it. For although Eitel has failed at love and at defying the committee in the play, he dies raging at what he should have done with his life:

> Aiiiiihhhh, the clot of unborn rage at all I have not done and all that I will never do . . . it tears now at my heart, and I am going to die. . . .[17]

This is the portrait of a stronger man than the Eitel of the novel, who sinks passively into an empty life and sends Sergius off to replace him.

In *Advertisements for Myself,* Mailer admits that in the final version of *The Deer Park* (N), Sergius began to become a portrait of the author himself:

> I was now creating a man who was braver and stronger
> than me, and the more my new style succeeded, the
> more I was writing an implicit portrait of myself as
> well.[18]

In the interests of accuracy it must be stated that Mailer
goes on to add that such a development is undesirable.
Nonetheless, it seems reasonable that the strengthening of
the character of Eitel in the play, and the shifting of
dramatic structure (through cutting Sergius' major conflicts) to highlight Eitel further would imply a shift in
authorial identification to the older man. (*The Deer Park*
(N) was begun by Mailer before he was thirty, while the
play was first performed on his forty-fourth birthday.)
This is not to say that Eitel is always Mailer's spokesman,
but it is possible to see in the strengthened Eitel a step
toward the next narrator of an author approaching middle
age: Stephen Richards Rojack, a man in his early forties.

In *An American Dream,* Barney Oswald Kelly (a
man evil enough to speak with some assurance of these
things) states that with the current state of man's world,
earthly centers of evil may rival Hell:

> "God might be having a very bad war with troops
> defecting everywhere. Who knows? Hell by now
> might be no worse than Las Vegas or Versailles." [19]

It may be of some significance that both of these places
figure in *The Deer Park* (N). Las Vegas is the scene of
Sergius' disastrous gambling losses, and Versailles was the
site of the original deer park of Louis XV. In *The Deer
Park* (P) the relation to Hell is explicit. Sergius tells the
audience from the outset that he is in Hell, and all of the
action takes place within Sergius' mind, as is suggested by
Mailer in his "Note on the Production":

> . . . the attempt must be made to suggest that the set
> bears some relation to the inner space of Sergius
> O'Shaugnessy's memory, that the audience is in effect
> living within his mind.[20]

The play, then, more than the novel, is a vision of Hell.
But it is not until *An American Dream* that Mailer will
present a vision of heaven. Nonetheless, there is a movement toward hope in Mailer's vision. Even in Hell, there
is the possibility of being saved, but it depends on communicating emotionally with other human beings. Sergius
tells us:

> . . . to pass on one's spirit is the one small gift we
> are allowed in Hell, and if there are enough to care
> for us, we can enter your world again . . .[21]

But the clearest possibility of reaching a vision of heaven
lies in a true love between a man and a woman. In the
novel Eitel has no such vision. The closest he comes is to
recognize the need for bravery in love, in his theory of
the "buried nature" in each person (paraphrased by
Sergius):

> Yet if people were lucky and if they were brave, some-
> times they would find a mate with the same buried
> nature and that could make them happy and strong.
> At least relatively so.[22]

In order to see the distance between this modest and
carefully qualified view of love and that of the play Eitel,
one need only compare this passage to that quoted above
(p. 116) in which the first night with Elena is described
in religious terms.

The necessity for one to be brave in order to keep

love alive looms larger in each succeeding work of Mailer's. In *The Deer Park* (P) Elena points out Eitel's failure to him:

> . . . I would travel anywhere with him, with any man who was brave enough to keep my love alive, brave enough to live with my cruel and greedy blood. But it hasn't been that way.[23]

Neither the Sergius nor the Eitel of the novel, nor the Eitel of the play succeed in being brave enough to make love work, and thereby to be saved. But each of these characters is another step toward the man who will be brave enough, Stephen Richards Rojack.

Mailer tells us in *Advertisements for Myself* [24] that he originally planned *The Deer Park* (N) as the first in a massive eight-novel series which was to encompass almost every aspect of twentieth-century American life. Long before the novel was completed, he abandoned the larger project and structured *The Deer Park* as an independent work. But vestiges of the eight-volume supra-novel may be seen in three pieces published in *Advertisements for Myself*. "The Man Who Studied Yoga" is a short story which was to serve as the prologue to the eight volumes, introducing the major themes involved. The most immediately obvious connection to *The Deer Park* lies in several echoes of the name Sergius O'Shaugnessy. In the story there are references to a psychiatrist named Dr. Sergius, and to two men named O'Shaugnessy. The other two pieces are a "Prologue to a Long Novel," and "The Time of Her Time," from the same untitled and unfinished novel. These indicate that major characters in this novel were to include Sergius O'Shaugnessy and Marion Faye, a homosexual pimp who figured largely in *The Deer Park*.

"The Time of Her Time," which may stand alone as a short story, deals entirely and explicitly with the sexual relations of the narrator and a college girl. The piece introduces the concept of sex as armed conflict which will be carried further in *An American Dream*.

The narrator of "The Time of Her Time" is Sergius O'Shaugnessy, back from Mexico and conducting a bull-fighting school in a Greenwich Village loft. But the first person narrator of "Prologue to a Long Novel" seems to present a much more complex experiment in point of view:

> So, properly, I should introduce myself here, and indeed I would, if I were able, but my name eludes me and at present would slip by without meaning to you—I am virtually married to Time unless she has already divorced me . . . and so my name alters as Time turns away from me. . . .[25]

The mysterious, shifting identity suggested by this narrator is similar to that in "The Man Who Studied Yoga":

> I would introduce myself if it were not useless. The name I had last night will not be the same as the name I have tonight.[26]

The projected long novel, ultimately abandoned, carries with it some of the plans and concerns of the eight-volume work. From the fragments it appears that Mailer intended a complex, chronologically shifting structure based on some theory of time which is difficult to understand from the limited material available to us. What is of some greater relevance here is the introduction, in the "Prologue," of a theory central to Mailer's developing system of metaphor: the relationship between murder and cancer:

The tension to murder is as excruciating as the temptations to confess when on a torture rack. So long as one holds one's tongue the destruction of the body continues, the limbs and organs under question may be passing the last answer by which they can still recover, and if one is going to confess eventually it is wiser to do it soon, do it now, before the damage is irrevocable. So with the desire to murder. Each day we contain it a little of that murder is visited on our own bodies . . . who knows? this may indeed be the day when the first of the exploited cells takes the independent and mysterious flip from one life into another —from the social, purposive, impoverished and unspeakably depressing daily life of an obedient cell, to the other life, wildlife, the life of the weed or hired gun, rebel cell growing by its own laws. . . . Yes, to hold murder too long is to lose the body, hasten that irreversible instant when the first cell leaps upon the habit of stale intelligence and gives itself as volunteer to the uniformed cadres. . . .[27]

A poem entitled "Dead Ends," which was to appear in the untitled novel, states in part that:

> Cancer comes from
>   television
>   filter cigarettes
>   air conditioning
>   foam rubber
>   the smell of plastic
>   deodorant
>   wit that fails
>   antibiotics
>   the mirror, yes,
>   and all other attempts
>   of the sucker esprit
>   to get something
>   for no.[28]

Cancer, then, is the result of artificiality and falsity. It exists in society and in the individual. And it is not, for Mailer, always figurative. The cancer which comes from stifling one's true impulses is a literal disease. In fact, years later, in *Cannibals and Christians* (1966), Mailer could carry his extra-medical theory to the point where he says:

> If one were to take the patients in a hospital, give them guns and let them shoot on pedestrians down from hospital windows you may be sure you would find a few miraculous cures.[29]

The Eitel of the play version of *The Deer Park* dies with a "clot of unborn rage" tearing at his heart. But both Mailer and his spokesmen have been changing, and the stifling of oneself to the point of destruction is not the way to be taken in the next work. Speaking of the untitled novel discussed above, Mailer says, "I have begun to work up another hand, a new book which will be the proper book of an outlaw." [30] The novel of which he was speaking was never written in its projected form, but in a very real sense the book of the outlaw, of the man set outside society, does take form in *An American Dream*.

Notes

[1] Norman Mailer, *The Deer Park* (New York: G. P. Putnam's Sons, 1955). Paperback edition published 1957 by Signet (New American Library of World Literature, New York), p. 300. All page references are to the Signet edition.

[2] Except when obvious, the distinction between these two works will be designated by the symbols (N) and (P).

[3] *Advertisements for Myself*, p. 237.

[4] *Ibid.*, p. 233.

[5] *Ibid.*, p. 234.

[6] Mailer is mistaken: Nick went to Yale.

[7] *Advertisements for Myself*, p. 235.

[8] *Ibid.*, p. 237.

[9] *The Deer Park*, p. 123.

[10] The scene has parallels in the "secret policeman's" quizzing of McLeod in *Barbary Shore* and in Rojack's confrontation with the strongarm cops, Laznicki and O'Brien, in *An American Dream*.

[11] *The Deer Park*, p. 276.

[12] *Ibid.*, p. 318.

[13] Norman Mailer, *The Deer Park: A Play* (New York: Dell Publishing Company, 1967), p. 189.

[14] *Advertisements for Myself*, p. 442.

[15] *The Deer Park: A Play*, p. 74. *Cf.* Norman Mailer, *An American Dream* (New York: Dial Press, 1965). Paperback edition published 1966 by Dell Publishing Co., New York, p. 122. All page references are to the Dell edition.

[16] *The Deer Park: A Play*, p. 187. *Cf. An American Dream*, p. 123.

[17] *The Deer Park: A Play*, p. 188.

[18] *Advertisements for Myself*, p. 238.

[19] *An American Dream*, p. 221.

[20] *The Deer Park: A Play*, p. 33.

[21] *Ibid.*, p. 189.

[22] *The Deer Park*, p. 107.

[23] *The Deer Park: A Play*, pp. 185–186.

[24] *Advertisements for Myself*, p. 154.

[25] *Ibid.*, p. 512.

[26] *Ibid.*, p. 157.

[27] *Ibid.*, p. 517.

[28] *Ibid.*, p. 510. The poem is written by a homosexual who, as Mailer tells us (*Advertisements for Myself*, p. 504) "is obsessed with the thesis that men become homosexual in order to save themselves from cancer."

[29] Norman Mailer, *Cannibals and Christians* (New York: The Dial Press, 1966), p. 91.

[30] *Advertisements for Myself*, p. 248.

4

An American Dream

The eight-volume supra-novel of which *The Deer Park* was to have been the first volume was conceived as a comprehensive statement on every facet of American society. *An American Dream* touches on most elements of society within one volume, compactly but not simplistically. Although the scope of this novel would seem to imply that Mailer has discarded the careful mechanical limitations of subject matter and setting which we have observed in the earlier novels, certain elements of structure are employed which are reminiscent of the classical unities. The entire action takes place within a twenty-four hour period, in Manhattan, and much pertinent action is related in retrospective flashbacks. The central character and narrator, Stephen Richards Rojack, moves constantly through the city, facing one confrontation after another; and though he is not chained to one spot, the nature of these repeated conflicts as they complicate and clarify the position of the protagonist, are parallel to those experienced in *Samson Agonistes* or *Prometheus Unbound*.

Because of the significant Christian overtones in *An American Dream,* a more apt literary analogue may be found in *Pilgrim's Progress.*

Conflict is the stuff of which every scene in this novel is composed. The proposed untitled novel referred to in *Advertisements for Myself* was to have dealt centrally with a murder. *An American Dream* begins with one. Stephen Richards Rojack, television personality, Professor of Existential Psychology, ex-congressman, holder of the Distinguished Service Cross, strangles his wife, Deborah, in a violent struggle at her apartment. The remainder of the novel traces his perilous journey through a hostile world to the ultimate achievement of personal salvation.

A central contention of this chapter should be stated here. Rojack's movement through the world of this novel represents a pilgrimage in the strictest religious sense of that word. He is a man who moves from imminent damnation to a state of grace by intimately encountering evil in many forms. But Mailer's message, although similar in structure to *Pilgrim's Progress,* presents a far more sophisticated and frightening concept. For Rojack can survive to achieve grace only by giving himself first to the Devil. He needs the evil within himself in order to combat the evil besieging him in the world.

This is not to say that the more difficult choice is not made at every point. The way in which Rojack earns salvation is through a courage which is constantly tested, one which is nurtured further by each successively more difficult victory. The early confrontations are faced with considerable weakness and trepidation, and barely won. All of them are faced unwillingly. But toward the last, there is presented a growing sense of strength and of commitment to good, as the need for evil is supplanted by something stronger and more positive in nature. Ultimately, the massive holocaust which he has precipitated spews Rojack forth not unscathed, but purged of his evil, the only person involved not to be destroyed or defeated. Mailer's message is one of carefully qualified hope. From much evil, in an external world decidedly blacker than that of *The Naked and the Dead*, good can come, but only at great personal cost in torment and courage.

It must further be stated that the pilgrimage Rojack undertakes is marked by clearly defined steps, each represented by a personal confrontation with another human being, each of whom presents a particular kind of evil which Rojack must overcome. And each prepares him for the more difficult one to follow, by giving him something of him or herself, as if Rojack had drunk the other's psychic blood.

A brief plot summary may be in order here, in the way of a catalog of the conflicts which Rojack faces in the course of the novel. In the first few pages, the narrator relates the story of how he won his D.S.C. by the single-handed killing of four German soldiers in two machine gun emplacements during World War Two. The episode is related in somewhat mystical terms, and it is suggested by Rojack that he had been touched briefly by fate as represented by the full moon on that night. A full moon is again present on the night, some twenty years later, when the major action of the novel takes place. In those twenty intervening years, Rojack has found some nominal success as an intellectual figure and marginal socialite. But he is actually at the end of his psychic rope. Unable to do any productive work on a long-planned and neglected major book, deeply in debt and estranged from his wife, Rojack has lost his self-respect and is on the verge of despair. Speaking particularly of his dependence on Deborah, and of his consequent compulsion to visit her frequently at odd hours, he tells the reader, "Probably I did not have the strength to stand alone." [1]

Thus, recognizing his current condition, Rojack stands alone on the balcony of a friend's apartment after a late party and, staring at the full moon, feels a powerful compulsion to suicide. He goes so far as to step over the balustrade; then, wavering, he clambers in fear back to safety. The failure to obey his impulse to jump is invested with great significance by Rojack, and described in terms of the theory of cancer introduced in the previous chapter of this book. Because he has stifled a pure impulse to destruction, he has generated cancer within himself:

> Will you understand me if I say that at that moment I felt the other illness come to me, that I knew then if it took twenty years or forty for my death, that if I died from a revolt of the cells, a growth against the design of my organs, that this was the moment it all began, this was the hour when the cells took their leap? [2]

Frightened and sick, Rojack hurries from the building to visit Deborah. After a brutal exchange of insults, the two struggle and Rojack strangles his wife. The act of murder is described by Rojack in terms of a vision of some heavenly city, and in the aftermath he feels as though he has been reborn. The purifying outpour of hatred leaves him in a calm and surrealistic mood which he compares to the experience of taking peyote. In this state, he leaves his wife's body on the floor of her bedroom, enters the maid's room, and engages in an extensive sexual bout with her. Later, he hurls Deborah's body from the window, and proceeds to counterfeit a suicide.

Although his course of action is at no time premeditated, he reacts intelligently and cooly to the pressures which begin to assail him. Roberts, the chief investigating detective, presents an immediate and recurrent challenge. Ruta, the German maid, though unaware of the true cir-

cumstances of Deborah's death, must be instructed to with-
hold the nature of her earlier actions with Rojack.

Deborah's body, landing on Riverside Drive, has precipitated a minor traffic accident which has far-reaching
reverberations in the action. Eddie Gannucci, a Mafia
leader, is caught in one of the cars involved. With him is
his nephew Tony, and a blonde named Cherry who is to
figure prominently in Rojack's life.

In the first of several scenes at the police station, Rojack holds police suspicions at bay through boldness and
quick, logical answers, aided immeasurably by the fact
that the police, preoccupied by the capture of Eddie
Gannucci, have no time to work over him all night. Released temporarily, Rojack makes his way downtown to
the after-hours club, owned by Tony, where Cherry sings.
In a palpably alien and hostile atmosphere, Rojack finds
himself in a state of heightened psychic awareness and
confidence. The ultimate result is a tense confrontation
with an ex-prizefighter, Ike "Romeo" Romalozzo, through
which Rojack wins Cherry's favor. An intense, cryptic
communication between Cherry and Rojack leads her to
leave work early, defying Tony and quitting her job.

Shortly thereafter, the two arrive at a lower east side
tenement, where Cherry maintains a secret retreat. Several
revelations from Cherry precede their sexual union. Her
younger sister, new to New York as an aspiring artist, had
taken the apartment. When the sister's sexual affair with
Shago Martin, a famous Negro singer, worried Cherry, she
arranged a meeting and became herself involved with him.
The sister, on the rebound, had a brutal affair with a
nameless pimp, which ended in her suicide. In one of the
many patterns of retribution which recur throughout the
novel, Cherry had the man killed.

The graphically recounted sexual encounter between
Rojack and Cherry is sharply different from his earlier one

with Ruta. Here, a choice is made to commit oneself to love. A tender and powerful sense of positive human emotion is engendered, culminating in the only sleep Rojack experiences in the novel. Awaking after several hours of sleep to a new day, he leaves Cherry asleep and enters the hostile outer world again, fighting a consuming desire for alcohol with the self-imposed decision not to have a drink until he can return to Cherry that evening.

Returning to his apartment for the only time in the book, Rojack shaves and changes, then undergoes the ordeal of dealing by phone with Arthur, the producer of his television show, and Dr. Frederick Tharchman, the head of his department at the university. Both squirm to appear sympathetic, but both are firm in cancelling his connections with their institutions. The conversations are important in establishing with a few deft strokes the hypocrisy which governs mass media and institutions of higher education alike, and the insecurity which governs men of authority in them. But another element is introduced for the first time here, in the veiled suggestion by Dr. Tharchman that secret governmental agencies are investigating Deborah's death. The incipient revelation is immediately supported by a phone call from Gigot, a mentally disturbed friend of Deborah, who earnestly suggests that Deborah was not merely a spy, but a double agent, and then caps this with the fact that Ruta is the mistress of Deborah's millionaire father, Barney Oswald Kelly, and was used by Kelly to spy on his daughter's personal life.

Feeling compelled by some arbitrary inner force to walk rather than take a taxi, Rojack arrives late for his appointment with Detective Roberts at the station house. In the climactic struggle between them, Roberts puts all the pressure of the doubtful autopsy report upon Rojack, falsely stating the strength of the police suspicions in a final attempt to extract a confession. As at each such encounter, Rojack wavers inwardly but remains firm. The result is a strikingly sudden reversal, a major turning point in the novel's action. Roberts, though obviously not convinced of Rojack's innocence, informs him that all charges have been dropped and he is free of suspicion. The detective contributes to the growing air of intrigue by telling Rojack that strong but unidentified pressure from above has been exerted to expedite the closing of the case, and, strangely, the release of Eddie Gannucci as well. He is, in fact, impressed enough to voice the suspicion that Rojack is a CIA operative.

Leaving the station, Rojack pauses to arrange an appointment by phone with Barney Oswald Kelly, then returns to Cherry's tenement retreat. This time, their communication begins on the same highly tuned sexual level of their last meeting, then proceeds to tense revelation of the past. Rojack freely admits to Deborah's murder, and Cherry paints a frighteningly sordid picture of her early youth in a home without parents, in which her older brother and sister regularly engaged in incest. She goes on to tell of her life in Las Vegas as the mistress of an older man, a wealthy and influential businessman who was integrally connected with the Mafia. When prodded by Rojack, she reveals that her lover was Barney Kelly. Their painful conversation turns next to Shago Martin, and it is at the point where the tension between them begins once again to give way before trust, that Shago himself enters.

Shago is angry and frightened at the intensity of feeling apparent between Rojack and Cherry, though his own affair with her has ostensibly been ended already. Rojack faces Shago's threats and then the knife he draws, and after some talk beats the singer, throwing him down the stairs to the street. Then, carrying (at Cherry's suggestion)

Shago's forgotten umbrella, he goes off to meet Barney
Kelly.

The confrontation with Kelly in his Waldorf Towers
suite is the climactic one of the novel. At first, other people
are present: not surprisingly at this point, Eddie Gannucci
and Ruta; also Deidre, Deborah's young daughter, and a
cousin of Deborah's mother named Bess. But soon the two
antagonists are alone, and as they drink, Kelly reveals his
own incestuous attachment to Deborah, along with a complex tangle of sexual, financial and mystical dealings. Ultimately, the perverse intimacy established by Kelly's tale
breaks out into hatred. Rojack feels compelled to face
death by a walk around the penthouse parapet with Kelly
the sole witness, a walk Deborah is said to have attempted
on earlier occasions and one which echoes Rojack's flirta-
tion with suicide in the novel's first chapter. Aware that
Deborah's death was not suicide, Kelly attempts to push
Rojack over the edge with Shago Martin's umbrella,
thrusting as with a sword. Grasping the umbrella, Rojack
pulls himself back to safety and bludgeons Kelly once
across the face with the umbrella, then leaves the hotel.

The final drama is played out when Rojack arrives
at Cherry's building to find her badly beaten, and Roberts
present, along with an ambulance. Roberts tells him that
Shago Martin had been beaten to death two hours earlier,
and a moment before she dies, Cherry whispers to Rojack
that her beating was administered in mistaken revenge by
a friend of Shago.

The epilogue finds Rojack, after a brief perception
of death and madness, both of which have brushed him
repeatedly throughout the novel, setting out on a drive to
South America. Various involved patterns of plot, theme
and imagery have been presented throughout Rojack's first
person narrative, and all are resolved or knotted together
by the story's end. One of the most important patterns to

be considered is the interlocking system of sexual involve-
ments by which the major characters are linked.

In his essay, "Some Children of the Goddess," written
before *An American Dream* and reprinted in *Cannibals
and Christians,* Mailer discusses such a system in James
Baldwin's *Another Country:*

> . . . There is a chain of fornication which is all but
> complete. . . . With the exception of Rufus Scott,
> who does not go to bed with his sister, everybody
> else in the book is connected by their skin to another
> character who is connected to still another. . . . All
> the sex in the book is displaced, whites with blacks,
> men with men, women with homosexuals; the sex is
> funky to suffocation, rich but claustrophobic, sensual
> but airless. Baldwin understands the existential abyss
> of love. In a world of Negroes and whites, nuclear
> fallout, marijuana, bennies, inversion, insomnia, and
> tapering off with beer at four in the morning, one
> no longer just falls in love—one has to take a brave
> leap over the wall of one's impacted rage and coward-
> ice. And nobody makes it, not quite. . . . They can-
> not find the juice to break out of their hatred into
> the other country of love.[3]

In *An American Dream,* Mailer presents a series of characters as promiscuously connected to one another sexually as
those who people Baldwin's book. But while the sexual
world of Mailer's characters is as dark as those in *Another
Country,* it is finally in the realm of sexual love that Mailer
presents his statement of hope for salvation; for Rojack
and Cherry *are* ultimately able to take the "brave leap over
the wall of . . . impacted rage and cowardice." The
significance of their breakthrough cannot, however, be
fully appreciated without first understanding the sexual
patterns in which the other characters figure.

The most consistent pattern of parallel sexual involve-
ments is that between Rojack and Barney Oswald Kelly.
Both men have had sexual relationships with Deborah,
Ruta, and Cherry, and in his confrontation with Kelly,
Rojack becomes aware of a sense of brutal sexual connec-
tion between the two men themselves:

> His body gave off the radiation of a fire, there was
> heat between us now the way there had been heat
> between Ruta and me in Deborah's hall; suddenly I
> knew what it had been like between Cherry and him,
> not so far from Ruta and me, no, not so far, and knew
> what a hot burning two-backed beast, and I could
> hear what he offered now: bring Ruta forth, three of
> us to pitch and tear and squat and lick, swill and
> grovel on that Lucchese bed, fuck until our eyes were
> out, bury the ghost of Deborah by gorging on her
> corpse, for this had been the bed, yes, this Lucchese
> had been the bed where he went out with Deborah
> to the tar pits of the moon. Now, he had a call to bury
> her raw. Desire came off Kelly to jump the murderer
> of his beast, and unfamiliar desire stirred in me, echo
> of that desire to eat with Ruta on Deborah's corpse.[4]

This is a lust spawned of hatred, as Rojack realizes in the
passage shortly preceding that quoted above:

> . . . a breath, an odium, came up over my face as if
> finally I had blundered through a barrier. Kelly was
> near to that violence Deborah used to give off, that
> hurricane rising from a swamp, that offer of carnage,
> of cannibals, the viscera came from him to me like
> suffocation. I was going to be dead in another minute;
> all Deborah's wrath passed now through him, he was
> agent to her fury and death set about me like a ringing
> of echoes in ether, red light and green. I waited for
> Kelly to attack—he came that close—I had only to close

my eyes and he would go to the fire, pick up a poker—
his stopped-up violence filled the room.[5]

It is implicit that a similarity exists between two men
who have lived intimately with the same woman, and that
the recognition of oneself in another can lead to hatred.
For Mailer's characters, the violent expression of such
hatred can have overtly sexual overtones. A parallel situation has erupted earlier, in the fight with Shago Martin,
and the two conflicts are linked tangibly by the umbrella,
an object of highly symbolic import here. Before discuss-
ing the homosexual overtones of the Shago episode, and
the major ramifications of that conflict within Mailer's
existential vision, it is necessary to clarify Mailer's position
in regard to homosexuality and anal intercourse. In the
play version of *The Deer Park,* Eitel responds to a sexual
proposition from Marion Faye with this speech:

> I'd never let a man touch me. I think that's the end
> of . . . change. It's what all the people who run the
> machine want us to be. Queer. Queer as cockroaches.
> Once you want it from behind, there's nothing to do
> but run. Thanks a lot, Angel, but I don't want to
> swish.[6]

Mailer's protagonists, then, reject overt homosexual activity because there is something cowardly about it. But anal
intercourse with women is not proscribed. Rather, it falls,
in Mailer's system, somewhere between the cowardice of
homosexuality and the bravery that must accompany a
real heterosexual love such as that between Rojack and
Cherry.

The two major instances of heterosexual anal intercourse in Mailer's fiction are the Ruta passage in *An
American Dream,* and the final sexual bout in "The Time

of Her Time." In both, the act is characterized by brutal force and hostility, although the result is pleasure. Even lust, on the male side, is dampened by cool calculation, and the terms used in description suggest a battle:

> . . . anger traveled from her body into mine, the avenger came to attention, cold and furious . . . and I was ready, not with any joy nor softness nor warmth nor care, but I was ready finally to take her tonight, I was going to beat new Time out of her if beat her I must. . . . And so I took her with a cold calculation, the rhythms of my body corresponding to no more than a metronome in my mind. . . . I worked on her like a riveter, knowing her resistances were made of steel, I threw her a fuck the equivalent of a fifteen-round fight, I wearied her. . . . I sprinted, I paced, I lay low, eyes all closed, under sexual water, like a submarine listening for the distant sound of her ship's motors, hoping to steal up close and trick her rhythms away.

●   ●   ●

> . . . I turned her over suddenly on her belly, my avenger wild with the mania of the madman, and giving her no chance, holding her prone against the mattress with the strength of my weight, I drove into the seat of all stubbornness, tight as a vise, and I wounded her, I knew it, she thrashed beneath me like a trapped little animal, making not a sound, but fierce not to allow me this last of the liberties, and yet caught, forced to give up millimeter by millimeter the bridal ground of her symbolic and therefore real vagina. So I made it, I made it all the way—it took ten minutes and maybe more, but as the avenger rode down to his hilt and tunneled the threshold of sexual home all those inches closer into the bypass of the womb, she gave at last a little cry of farewell. . . .[7]

This is, then, an invasion, carried out with cold strategy and implemented by physical force. This is the arena where the hostility/lust offered by Marion Faye and Barney Kelly, but rejected by Eitel and Rojack, can be carried out, in a parody of the sexual act between real lovers. It is acceptable to Mailer's code, but not, by any means, admirable, for it is a sterile act both biologically and emotionally. The "avenger" travels into "the bypass of the womb" and because he has chosen to bypass even the possibility of impregnation, the act is rendered ugly and insignificant. The central antithesis between the sterility of Rojack's sexual relations with Ruta and the fertility of those he shares with Cherry is important to an understanding of Rojack's development and of Mailer's message.

"The Time of Her Time" shares with the Ruta episode certain basic characteristics, which show that Mailer's own view is consistent, and not limited to the experience as seen by Rojack. In the latter passage there is, again, a sense of combat and the female unwillingness to allow what Ruta calls *verboten*, resulting finally in a sort of virtuoso success by the male. But Rojack's experience with Ruta introduces a number of other thematic ramifications. Where "The Time" is concerned almost entirely with the psychological makeup of the two characters and the conflict between male and female, the later passage is firmly tied into a complex web of themes and plot relationships.

This, the second link in the chain of three sexual relationships which create in Rojack a parallelism to Kelly, introduces a carefully articulated polarity between good and evil, God and the Devil, represented respectively by the vagina and the anus:

> . . . a host of the Devil's best gifts were coming to me, mendacity, guile, a fine-edged cupidity for the

stroke which steals, the wit to trick authority. I felt like a thief, a great thief. And like a thief returning to church, I seesawed up from that bank of pleasures up to her deserted warehouse, that empty tomb. But it was more ready now. Those flaccid walls had come together—back of my closed eyes I could see one poor flower growing in a gallery—what love she still possessed might have been in a flower. Like a thief I was out of church again and dropping down for more of that pirate's gold.

So that was how I finally made love to her, a minute for one, a minute for the other, a raid on the Devil and a trip back to the Lord . . . I was drunk with my choice . . . and then I was traveling up again that crucial few centimeters of distance from the end to the beginning, I was again in the place where the child is made. . . .

•   •   •

. . . I was gone like a bat and shaking hands with the Devil once more. . . . I was leaping back and forth in separate runs for separate strokes, bringing spoils and secrets up to the Lord from the red mills, bearing messages of defeat back from that sad womb, and then I chose—ah, but there was time to change—I chose her cunt. It was no graveyard now, no warehouse, no, more like a chapel now, a modest decent place, but its walls were snug, its odor was green, there was a sweetness in the chapel, a muted reverential sweetness in those walls of stone. "That is what prison will be like for you," said a last effort on my inner tongue. "Stay here!" came a command from inside of me; except that I could feel the Devil's meal beneath, its fires were lifting through the floor . . . I was up above a choice which would take me on one wind or another, and I had to give myself, I could not hold back. . . . I had one of those splittings of a second where the senses fly out and there in that instant the itch reached

into me and I jammed up her ass and came as if I'd
been flung across the room. . . . And with my eyes
closed, I felt low sullen waters wash about a dead
tree on a midnight pond. I had come to the Devil a
fraction too late, and nothing had been there to receive me. But I had a vision immediately after of a
huge city in the desert, in some desert, was it a place
on the moon? For the colors had the unreal pastel of
a plastic and the main street was flaming with light
at five A.M. A million light bulbs lit the scene.[8]

A number of metaphorical patterns are introduced in this
passage which will be seen to develop in complexity and
significance as the novel progresses. The question of good
and evil, of belonging to God or the Devil, is one with
which Rojack is obsessed throughout the story. He constantly wonders whether he himself or Deborah were the
evil partner, and discusses a parallel situation at length
with Cherry, that of herself and Shago. It is necessary to
recognize that there is a uniquely religious quality about
the conflicts within Rojack.

The immediate situation must be emphasized. This
man has left his wife's warm corpse scant yards away to
engage in this sexual conflict, and it must be recognized
as much more, therefore, than a physical act. It represents
a major turning point in his life, the first of many decisions to be faced during the next twenty-four hours. Before leaving Deborah's room, Rojack has come to no decision on whether to confess or attempt to cover up his
crime. A long prison sentence conducive to serious writing
has momentarily appealed to him, in fact, and he has come
close to giving himself up. It is clear to him that if he is
detected in an attempt to falsify the circumstances of
death, he will be executed.

The choice available to him within Ruta's body is
made clear. The vagina is a peaceful retreat, which he

consciously sees as a preview of prison. But he does not choose that direction. The reasons are several. He has become aware that too much evil remains bequeathed to him from Deborah, as a consequence of his act of murder: "I was doomed if I thought to do my work in jail, for her curse would be upon me." [9] Whether this evil is internal, or externally generated, Rojack senses that it must be propitiated or expiated before he can have peace. But the irrevocable commitment which he makes when he chooses Ruta's anus, and therefore the way of the Devil, comes about largely because of what he assimilates from her spiritual makeup. He has said (see quotation above, p. 137) that while within the Devil's orifice, "a host of the Devil's best gifts were coming to me, mendacity, guile . . . the wit to trick authority . . . ," and these are the very qualities he requires for his next confrontation, that with the police. His decision, then, is made, not when he picks up the phone and reports a suicide, but when he gives himself, through Ruta, to the Devil.

But there is good still within Rojack. He thinks, with momentary regret, of the sterility of his choice: "I had a thought then of what had been left in her. It was perishing in the kitchens of the Devil. Was its curse on me?" [10] And before the police arrive, he takes Ruta again, this time leaving that part of himself in her vagina, although the brief black lust by which the act is motivated detracts from its significance. Nonetheless, the good and evil within Rojack remain in conflict, and the pattern for the rest of the novel has been established by this first of many choices.

Rojack's decision to defy Shago Martin, even when the latter flourishes a knife, is central to the development of the protagonist's strength. It has been suggested earlier that this conflict is sexual in tone. The physical position from which Rojack beats Shago, and the words of abuse

used by the latter are too suggestive of homosexual contact to be ignored:

> And with that he walked over to me, put his fingers
> on my chest, gave a disdainful push, "Up your ass,
> Mother Fuck," and turned around, leaving the scent
> of marijuana on my clothes. The pressure back of my
> neck let go of itself and I was a brain full of blood,
> the light went red, it was red. I took him from behind,
> my arms around his waist, hefted him in the air, and
> slammed him to the floor so hard his legs went, and
> we ended with Shago in a sitting position, and me
> behind him on my knees, my arms choking the air
> from his chest as I lifted him up and smashed him
> down again. "Let me go, I'll kill you, bugger," he
> cried out, and there was a moment when I could have
> done that, I had the choice to let him go, let him
> stand up, we would fight, but I had a fear of what I
> heard in his voice. . . .[11]

The expressions "up your ass" and "bugger" are almost
always used figuratively, but this does not obviate the
possibility of some literal reverberation, particularly when
it is strengthened by the refusal of Rojack to relinquish
his aggressive position of control, from behind. The
sexuality of the encounter becomes consciously apparent
to Rojack immediately afterwards, and this frightens and
enrages him still further:

> Shago looked up at me from the ground and said,
> "Up your ass."
>   I almost kicked in his head. Close as that. Instead
> I picked him up, opened the door, manhandled him
> to the hall. There he put up resistance, and when I
> got a whiff of his odor which had something of defeat
> in it, and a smell of full nearness *as if we'd been in*
> *bed for an hour*—[my italics] well, it was too close: I

> threw him down the stairs. Some hard-lodged boulder
> of fear I had always felt with Negroes was in the bump-
> ing, elbow-busting and crash of sound as he went
> barreling down, my terror going with him. . . .[12]

Even the "fear I had always felt with Negroes" has a sexual
basis, if we are to apply Mailer's often-stated (in his remarks preceding "The White Negro," for example) [13]
thesis that the white American male is jealous and afraid
of the supposedly superior sexual capacity of the Negro
male. And the classic triangle situation which has precipitated the fight makes such fear concretely applicable
to Rojack at this point.

The beating of Shago does not show Rojack in an
unmitigatedly good light: his rage is prompted at least in
part by fear, and his earlier ability to face Shago in fair
challenge wavers in the end. But more good than bad has
come of it, whether because he has purged some of his own
fears and hatreds, or because he has gained some of what
is good in Shago; and when he leaves the apartment, Rojack carries Shago's umbrella. It is significant that Cherry
gives it to him. He has bested Shago in the fight and also
sexually, with Cherry (although there are qualifications
to both victories), and the phallic quality of the object she
takes from her old lover and presents to the new is obvious. Her words, too, are important: "Then she saw me
looking at Shago's umbrella, and handed it to me. 'Now
you got a stick,' she said." [14] The possible ramifications of
the word *stick* in Hip argot are numerous. It can be a
marijuana cigarette; a man can be a *stick* (that is, adept)
at something; it can be a knife, and has in fact been
used a few pages earlier by Cherry to refer to Shago's
brandished switchblade. Not only do these connotations
come from Shago's Harlem domain, but each of these uses

of the word is directly related to Shago himself: he has the smell of marijuana about him, which contact leaves on Rojack's clothes (refer to quotation above, p. 141); he is a *stick* sexually, as is Rojack now; and the sense of the *stick* (umbrella) as a weapon has been suggested earlier, upon Shago's entrance:

> With his left hand he held a furled umbrella, *taut as a sword in its case* [my italics], and he kept it at an angle to his body, which returned—since his body was tall and slim—some perfect recollection of a lord of Harlem standing at his street corner.[15]

The sword simile is not idly chosen, since the umbrella is used as such by Kelly when he thrusts at Rojack on the balcony, with intent to kill. Nor is the term "lord of Harlem" (a picture suggested to Rojack partially because of the umbrella, which is as indispensable a badge of office to such a lord as sceptre or crozier) insignificant. Shago is, in fact, an aristocratic power in his world, as he makes clear before the fight:

> ". . . Listen, you," he said to me, "I should have brought my army down here. We could have put toothpicks under your nails. I'm a *prince* [Mailer's italics] in my territory, *dig?* But I came alone." [16]

There is real nobility in the choice to come unescorted, and still more in Shago's refusal to have his spirit broken. Lying badly beaten at the bottom of the stairs, Shago:

> started trying to climb the stairs on his hands and knees which released still another core of rage in me as if it were doubly intolerable that his will would not break. . . .[17]

And finally, Shago leaves on a note of noble forgiveness: "Tell you something, man. I don't hate. Never. . . . Tell Cherry, her and you, I wish you luck." [18]

Rojack carries with him, when he leaves Cherry's apartment for his meeting with Kelly, certain qualities of courage, power, and masculinity, in the umbrella which is their tangible representation. And the connection is more than metaphorical for Rojack. The handle feels "alive to my fingers" [19] and, sensitive to his moods, "felt sullen to my palm" [20] when he falters in his resolve. The simultaneous multilevel symbolism of weapon, phallus, and badge of power is maintained in the scene between Rojack and Kelly on the balcony, so obviously that it need not be belabored further.

What is of further significance here is the connection of the Shago episode to Mailer's conception of American existentialism as it is set forth in "The White Negro." In murdering Deborah, Rojack has set himself outside of the structure by which the world is governed, and as an outsider, an outlaw, he is besieged by paranoid fears which are all too well founded:

> No, men were afraid of murder, but not from a terror of justice so much as the knowledge that a killer attracted the attention of the gods; then your mind was not your own, your anxiety ceased to be neurotic, your dread was real. Omens were as tangible as bread. There was an architecture to eternity which housed us as we dreamed, and when there was murder, a cry went through the market places of sleep. Eternity had been deprived of a room. Somewhere the divine rage met a fury.[21]

Mailer has a sense of paranoia which, if one accepts his vision of the world order in *An American Dream,* must be taken as a quality necessary to survival. No matter how frightening the intuitions of dread which bombard Rojack, they must be heeded; and any false sense of security which could lead him to ignore them would result in disaster. This view is not limited to this novel. Mailer has earlier dealt with it at length in "The White Negro." One of the central contentions of the essay is that the motivations of the Hip world are based primarily upon a paranoia necessary to survival in a world of constant nuclear uncertainty, and that this paranoia is the legacy of the American Negro:

> And in this wedding of the white and the black it was the Negro who brought the cultural dowry. Any Negro who wishes to live must live with danger from his first day, and no experience can ever be casual to him, no Negro can saunter down a street with any real certainty that violence will not visit him on his walk. . . . in such a pass where paranoia is as vital to survival as blood, the Negro had stayed alive and begun to grow by following the need of his body where he could.[22]

What, then, is the hipster as Mailer sees him? Speaking of the degree of debilitating conformity in American society, Mailer states in "The White Negro":

> It is on this bleak scene that a phenomenon has appeared: the American existentialist—the hipster, the man who knows that if our collective condition is to live with instant death by atomic war, relatively quick death by the State as *L'univers concentrationaire,* or with slow death by conformity with every creative and rebellious instinct stifled (at what damage to the mind and the heart and the liver and the nerves no research foundation for cancer will discover in a hurry), if the fate of twentieth-century man is to live

with death from adolescence to premature senescence, why then the only life-giving answer is to accept the terms of death, to live with death as an immediate danger, to divorce oneself from society, to exist without roots, to set out on that uncharted journey into the rebellious imperatives of the self. In short, whether the life is criminal or not, the decision is to encourage the psychopath in oneself. . . .[23]

The concept that knuckling under to conformity poisons the body as well as the mind, resulting in a more than metaphorical cancer, had fascinated Mailer for many years before he incorporated it in *An American Dream*. The parallel corollary that indulging the psychopath in oneself (especially to the extent of committing murder) can cure or prevent cancer is also dealt with in the novel, as part of an interlocking symbolic system of real cancer (in Deborah, in Eddie Gannucci, and even momentarily in Rojack himself) which supports the metaphorical statement that American society and culture is being destroyed from within by the cancer of conformity and fear. When Rojack kills his wife, he has taken the first instinctive step toward purging his own cancerous tendencies, and toward fulfilling Mailer's prescription for the American existentialist (see quotation above): "to live with death as an immediate danger, to divorce oneself from society, to exist without roots, to set out on that uncharted journey into the rebellious imperatives of the self." This *is* what Rojack has contracted for. When his roots are cut out from under him by both of his employers, the external professions by which he is defined within society are removed, leaving him alienated. The course he takes is to face the immediate danger of death through external violence, and concurrently to make a journey into himself. But it must be remembered that this choice, though it is the only one that can lead to survival and salvation, is a voluntary and courageous one on Rojack's part. At almost any point, he can confess and have the pressure removed from him, be redefined and replaced in society's hierarchy, by going to prison.

This, then, is an existential journey which we follow in *An American Dream*. And Rojack has at the very beginning of the work the potential to define himself as an existential hero. The murder is no gratuitous accident of circumstance, but an act conditioned by the situation generated within Rojack, the primary symptom of which is the confrontation of death upon his friend's balcony in the first chapter. And this voluntary courting of destruction is repeated again and again throughout the journey to peace, not only in the dangerous confrontations with people to which Rojack is instinctively compelled, but in the last walk on Kelly's balcony at the novel's end.

But what most clearly defines Rojack as the embodiment, for Mailer, of the American existentialist, is his relationship to Shago Martin. In "The White Negro," Mailer further explains the development of the hipster:

> In such places as Greenwich Village, a ménage-à-trois was completed—the bohemian and the juvenile delinquent came face-to-face with the Negro, and the hipster was a fact in American life. If marijuana was the wedding ring, the child was the language of Hip for its argot gave expression to abstract states of feeling which all could share, at least all who were Hip.[24]

Compare to this the discussion of the conflict between Rojack and Shago Martin (see above, pp. 141–43) which is conceived, as is the above passage, in terms of sexual or marital terms, and which deals with the significance of the marijuana and Hip argot which define Shago and are transferred to Rojack. Rojack has become, in effect, the White Negro. It is no accident that this transformation takes place immediately before the confrontation with the most powerful and evil of Rojack's adversaries, Barney Kelly. For the strength derived from Shago (as he represents the best virtues and strengths of his people) is necessary to Rojack for victory.

Rojack is very much a different man at the end of the novel than he was at the beginning, and what helps to highlight the extent of the change is the tight circular structure of the plot. Certain events occur at the end of Rojack's ordeal which have obvious parallels in the early chapters. Their very external similarities serve to underline the major differences in Rojack's reactions. The most important is the brief battle with Kelly, as compared to that with Deborah in the first chapter:

> One of her hands fluttered up to my shoulder and tapped it gently. Like a gladiator admitting defeat. I released the pressure on her throat and the door I had been opening began to close. But I had had a view of what was on the other side of that door, and heaven was there . . . and I thrust against the door once more and hardly felt her hand leave my shoulder, I was driving now with force against that door: spasms began to open in me, and my mind cried out then, "Hold back! you're going too far, hold back!" I could feel a series of orders whip like tracers of light from my head to my arm, I was ready to obey. I was trying to stop, but pulse packed behind pulse in a pressure up to thunderhead; some blackbiled lust . . . came bursting with rage from out of me . . . and *crack* I choked her harder. . . .[25]

In significant contrast to the irrational but conscious decision to allow his rage to go beyond the point of control in strangling Deborah, is Rojack's ability to stop hitting Kelly:

> . . . and he lifted the tip of the umbrella to my ribs and gave a push to poke me off. But I turned as he pushed, and the tip was diverted, turned just enough to grip the umbrella as it went by, which brought me back from going off, and I jumped down to the terrace even as he let go, and struck him across the face with the handle so hard he went down in a heap. I almost struck him again, I was in a rage I could not have stopped, and in relief, some relief, wrong or right, I did not know, I turned and hurled the umbrella over the parapet—Shago's umbrella was gone. . . .[26]

Here, Rojack is again enraged, and justifiably so. Kelly has just attempted in cold blood ("His smile was pleasant," [27]) to push him over the parapet. This is more of an obvious death struggle than that with Deborah had been, and Kelly is, in both his own and Rojack's eyes, the carrier of Deborah's wrath (see quotation, p. 134 above). Despite this, Rojack throttles his rage, and after one quick retributive blow, flings the now unnecessary *stick* over the edge. This action would seem to have a dual significance: first, having internalized the qualities of masculinity and courage represented by the umbrella, he no longer needs the external symbol of them; and secondly, the umbrella's fall to the street may be seen as a final sacrifice to the drive in Rojack (now totally purged) for suicide *or* murder. (After Deborah's death, it may be remembered, he momentarily considered suicide, as though the cathartic quality of the murder could not alone purge the destructive elements within him.) It is not until this very moment that these drives are totally gone. Just as Rojack, through overcoming Shago, earned the strength to face Kelly inside the suite, he has earned by his final walk on the edge of death the right to overcome Kelly, this time in an almost merciful (and therefore Christian) manner. Of the parallels we have set out to draw, then, this is another: that the final walk is a productive and successful one, where the first was abortive and inconsequential.

Still in some control of himself, Rojack rushes from the suite, ironically retracing several parallels of his actions immediately after the murder. As he leaves, he catches a glimpse of Ruta coming toward him in a negligee, but this time he rejects the implicit invitation. Then, in a panic to be outside as great as that which prompted his headlong flight down the stairs from Deborah's apartment, he controls himself and stops midway to the street to wait for the elevator.

The most ironical of the parallels to be noted comes when Rojack arrives downtown to find Cherry dying. When a policeman attempts to hold him back as he goes to her side, he says, "She's my wife, officer," almost the same words he used when being held back from Deborah's body. Ironically, in the first instance he was telling the literal truth and in the later one a literal lie, while in moral terms the situation is reversed.

A final parallel may be cited, one which Rojack himself points out when he senses the frightful lust emanating from Kelly (see quotation above, p. 134), a desire on Kelly's part to "bury the ghost of Deborah by gorging on her corpse," an "echo of that desire to eat with Ruta on Deborah's corpse" which Rojack experienced after returning to Deborah's bedroom from Ruta's. Here is that passage:

> Let me tell you the worst. I had a little fantasy at this moment. It was beyond measure. I had a desire to take Deborah to the bathroom, put her in the tub. Then Ruta and I would sit down to eat. The two of us

would sup on Deborah's flesh, we would eat for days: the deepest poisons in us would be released from our cells. I would digest my wife's curse before it could form.[28]

We have said that Rojack, upon leaving Ruta, has given himself *almost* totally to the Devil, and this passage is indicative of the depths of mad depravity he is capable of envisioning. At the same time, it is significant that he rejects such fantasies and the madness that they represent, and does the capably satanic thing: calling the police to forge his big lie. And what he has rejected is, for a moment, more than a fantasy, as the necessary details of disposing of Deborah's bones and teeth present themselves and solutions begin to form in his mind. For Rojack, though perhaps more committed to the Devil at this point than at any other to follow, retains some small pocket of good and sanity which mitigate the blackness of his capabilities. Later, midway through the novel, drained by his latest confrontation and dreading the next, Rojack conceives, and then rejects with difficulty, a similar fantasy of escape:

> And I thought of Ruta then . . . Satan's heaven at the thought of diving into a bar, and calling her.
>
> •   •   •
>
> We would drink for hours, then disappear into some Germanic fleabag of a hotel, a bed fortified with the crazy molecules of a thousand fornications, one hundred sodomies and the Devil's tale of the tongues. We would tie one good one on, two days, three days, five empty bottles at the foot of the bed.[29]

With the exception of his decision to commit himself to love Cherry, all of Rojack's major moral decisions are won through the refusal to yield: to temptation, to cowardice, to societal pressures. This definition of oneself through negatives has been observed in several of Mailer's earlier characters, notably Red Valsen, Sergius O'Shaugnessy, and Charles Eitel.

The peculiar accoutrements and codes of the Hip world have been treated as the prescriptive requirements for the American existentialist, the White Negro. But what seems most crucial to the uniquely American existentialism Mailer posits in this novel is the commitment to a positive good represented by Rojack's decision to love Cherry bravely and unselfishly. It will be seen that such positive action is indicative of a particular quality which Mailer sees in the American character at its rare best. It takes Rojack a step further than Red Valsen, Sergius O'Shaugnessy, or even Charles Eitel could go; and it defines the note of hope in this novel which represents perhaps the most significant development in Mailer's vision of the individual. It seems necessary now to study the character of Cherry, to determine what there is in her that makes Rojack's love particularly significant in an American context.

Everything about Cherry is rife with symbolic significance. Her very name is common slang for "virginity" or "virgin," which, in a sense, she is, for Rojack. Her physical appearance is everything clichéd in mass-media sex symbols, and she is in fact defined in such terms on their first meeting: "And now I realized the detective had seen me chatting with nothing less than a blonde." [30] And she is totally American, exactly the kind of girl to turn up in an American dream:

> . . . she had one of those perfect American faces, a small-town girl's face with the sort of perfect clean features which find their way onto every advertise-

ment and every billboard in the land. . . . Her nose
was a classic. It turned up with just the tough tilt of
a speedboat planing through the water.[31]

Immediately behind these superficial characteristics
lie other less attractive ones, which give the lie to the
simplistic values generated by American mass culture.
Watching her sing at Tony's club, Rojack studies:

> the character of her bottom, that fine Southern piece.
> Occasionally she would turn, she would sing over her
> shoulder, and show that of course her butt had noth-
> ing to do with her face, no she drove it on its own
> rhythms, pleased with itself and her, practical, the
> heart of every Southern girl's pie, marvelous, just a
> little too big and round for the waist, a money-
> counter, Southern-girl ass. "This bee-hind is for sale,
> boy," said it to me, "But you ain't got the price, *you!*"
> Her face, having nothing to do with all of that, smiled
> demurely at me for the first time.[32]

And her toes are, in Rojack's vision, even more symptomatic of corruption:

> . . . five sensuous, even piggish, but most complacent
> little melons of flesh surrounding five relatively tiny
> toenails, each broader than they were long, which
> depressed me. She had the short broad foot of that
> very practical kind of woman who has time to buy
> the groceries and time to jazz the neighbor next door,
> and I looked from there up to the delicate silvery cut
> of her face, that delicate boy-girl face beneath the
> toned blonde hair. . . .[33]

There is, here, a dichotomy between the corruption represented by Cherry's body, especially her behind and her

feet, and the relative innocence apparent in her face.
Even her hair has an artificial quality about it, being
"toned." Later, in bed, Rojack is to remark upon how its
natural silkiness has been made harsh by bleaching.

In keeping with the comprehensive scope of Mailer's
concern with all of American society in this novel, Cherry
presents a remarkable tableau of experience. She comes
from a small southern town, moves northwest to Las Vegas,
and then east to New York, becoming involved with men
who are consistently corrupt, but whose power spans underworld and "legitimate" areas. Her nightclub act presents her as a series of personalities:

> And she came back with another voice, belting the
> same song now, swaying her hips, tough and agree-
> able and very American, as if she were an airline
> hostess or the television wife of a professional football
> star. There was another spot on her, an orange spot,
> Florida beaches, the red-orange tan of an athlete. . . .
> She was hard now, nightclub hard, an embodiment
> now of greed, green-eyed, brown-skinned flaming
> golden blonde—that was orange spotlight.
>
> •   •   •
>
> Well, the set went on. There was a champagne
> light which made her look like Grace Kelly, and a
> pale green which gave her a little of Monroe. She
> looked at different instants like a dozen lovely blondes,
> and now and again a little like the little boy next
> door. A clean tough decent little American boy in
> her look: that gave charm to the base of her upturned
> nose . . . yes that nose gave character to the little
> muscle in her jaw and the touch of stubbornness of
> her mouth. She was attractive, yes. She had studied
> blondes, this Cherry, she was all of them. . . . She
> could have been a nest of separate personalities if it

had not been for the character of her bottom, that fine Southern piece.[34]

Ultimately, she is most clearly defined by her origins. And the corruption in them underlines both the social criticism of Mailer's message, and the complex system of ironies which governs the human relationships in the novel. Cherry's older brother is, externally, the type of the ambitious young American boy. Orphaned, he not only supports and raises his younger sisters, but becomes Sheriff. Yet he is at the same time regularly committing incest with the oldest of his sisters. The fact of his legitimate marriage drives the latter sister to compulsive prostitution. And the self-righteously proper facade maintained by the family becomes more ludicrous in retrospect for having produced the two younger sisters, both of whom engage in miscegenation with Shago Martin.

Yet from the consummate corruption of her background there emerges a Cherry who nonetheless maintains a certain hard-core integrity. Within the brutal world she revolves in, she is effectually able to survive and to carry out the Old Testament blood vengeance which is one of its cardinal rules, as in the case of the pimp who caused her sister's death. And beneath her cynicism there is honesty. But to break through to the good in Cherry, Rojack must himself be strong and daring in a dangerous world. With a very real sense of the danger posed by Cherry he nonetheless realizes that:

> Women must murder us unless we possess them altogether . . . and I had a fear now of the singer on the stand, for her face, yes, perhaps I could possess that altogether, perhaps that face could love me. But her bee-hind! of course I could never possess that ass, no one ever had, maybe no one would, and so the diffi-

culty had gone down to her feet, yes the five painted
toes talked of how bad this girl could be.[35]

After her set, Cherry goes to the bar for a drink with
several friends of Tony, among whom is Romeo Romalozzo, the former prizefighter. One of the first of many
flashes of intuition by which his course is charted strikes
Rojack:

> . . . something now decided I must go up to Romeo
> in the next few minutes. "You'll never get past the
> police," said my mind to me, "unless you take the
> girl home from this bar. . . . I felt the anxiety of a
> man hearing he must undergo a dangerous opera-
> tion.[36]

The scene which follows is one of tense banter between
Rojack and Romalozzo, and Rojack is very much alone,
as Cherry and the others noncommitally await the outcome:

> The mulatto with the plump mandarin face and the
> goatee was staring at me from his table. He looked
> like one of those jungle crows who sit high on a tree
> and watch the lions and the lion cubs take blood, foam
> and flesh from the entrails of a wounded zebra.[37]

His fear overcome only by a rage at being used by Cherry,
Rojack stands his ground when ordered to leave by
Romeo:

> "You're going to get hurt," said his eyes. "I have
> something going for me," said my eyes back. His ex-
> pression turned dubious. The odds were not estab-
> lished for him. He had no ideas in his eyes, only
> pressure. Maybe he thought I had a gun.[38]

In any case, the duel is won, the tension broken. And Cherry, the willing spoils, leaves the group to join Rojack at his table. But more is at issue here than a barroom face-down over a woman. Rojack has overcome not only his opponent, but his own fear and weakness. Some of the slag in his soul has been burned away by an honestly courageous act, and he is one step closer to a state of grace because of it. An understanding of Romeo's attitude is important here. After backing down:

> Romeo laughed. He laughed with a big flat dead sound at the center of his amusement, a professional laugh, the professional laugh of a fighter who has won a hundred fights and lost forty, and of those forty, twelve were on bad decisions, and six were fixed, and for four he went in the tank. So it was the laugh of a man who has learned how to laugh through all sorts of losses.[39]

Compare this description to that of Detective Roberts after he informs Rojack that charges against him have been dropped:

> With each breath Roberts was becoming more genial. It was as if we'd been wrestlers and Roberts had proceeded on the assumption it was his night to win. Then the referee had whispered in his ear—his turn to lose. So he bulled around the ring. Now we were back in the dressing room exchanging anecdotes, trading apologies.

•   •   •

> He had never looked more like a cop. The dedication of his short straight nose hung above the confirmed grin of corruption at the corner of his mouth. Rectitude, cynicism, and greed threw off separate

> glints from his eyes. . . . He gave the leathery smile
> of a baseball manager who has lost a rookie he might
> have developed. . . .[40]

The men whom Rojack confronts and overcomes are
tough, but their toughness is based on total commitment
to a corrupt system. They know their places in this system,
and cannot conceive of breaking out of it. In accepting
corruption as a necessary condition of life, they support
it and become themselves corrupt. But Rojack, who has
for most of his life accepted the system and his own place
in it, has by his self-defining act of murder set himself
outside of it. His intuitions tell him that the only course
which will lead to survival is that of daring to challenge,
rather than evade, the corrupt external forces which seek
to destroy him. In doing so, he purges his own corruption
and gains increasing personal strength.

After an anticlimactic scene with Tony, in which
Cherry quits her job, the incipient lovers go to Cherry's
secret tenement apartment, and the scene which follows
represents the absolute center of Rojack's pilgrimage, the
point of no return at which he decides to make his one
positive commitment. As they enter the building and climb
the stairs, Rojack, always acutely sensitive to the significance of odors, has a sudden frightening insight into
mortality and the dangers of backsliding into his previous
self-indulgent corruption:

> The stench of slum plumbing gave a terror of old
> age. . . . "Fail here at love," said the odor, "and you
> get closer to subsisting like me." [41]

After a few moments of brutally honest self-revelation
which Rojack insists on drawing out of Cherry, they go
to bed. The sexual description is graphic, deliberate,
precise, and significant as always in Mailer's writing. At

first, the act is tentative, devoid of trust or feeling, professionally mechanical:

> But we did not meet as lovers, more like animals in a quiet mood, come across a track of the jungle to join in a clearing, we were equals.

> •   •   •

> I had never moved so well. It was impossible to make a mistake.
>
> Yet only the act was tender. Nothing was loving in her; no love in me; we paid our devotions in some church no larger than ourselves. . . .[42]

Significantly, the turning point does not come until Rojack, disturbed by the contraceptive diaphragm Cherry is wearing, removes it. And now the issue confronts him clearly, the choice to be made between the evasion or the acceptance of love with all its dangers and responsibilities. Rojack decides on love, in a passage whose style is religiously lyrical:

> I was passing through a grotto of curious lights, dark lights, like colored lanterns beneath the sea, a glimpse of that quiver of jeweled arrows, that heavenly city which had appeared as Deborah was expiring in the lock of my arm, and a voice like a child's whisper on the breeze came up so faint I could hardly hear, "Do you want her?" it asked. "Do you really want her, do you want to know something about love at last?" and I desired something I had never known before, and answered; it was as if my voice had reached to its roots; and, "Yes," I said, "of course I do, I want love," but like an urbane old gentleman, a dry tart portion of my mind added, "Indeed, and what has one to lose?" and then the voice in a small terror, "Oh, you have more to lose than you have lost already, fail at

love and you lose more than you can know." "And if
I do not fail?" I asked back. "Do not ask," said the
voice, "Choose now!" and some continent of dread
speared wide in me, rising like a dragon, as if I knew
the choice were real, and in a lift of terror I opened
my eyes and her face was beautiful beneath me in that
rainy morning, her eyes were golden with light, and
she said, "Ah, honey, sure," and I said sure to the voice
in me, and felt love fly in like some great winged
bird, some beating of wings at my back, and felt her
will dissolve into tears, and some great deep sorrow
like roses drowned in the salt of the sea came flooding
from her womb and washed into me like a sweet
honey of balm for all the bitter sores of my soul and
for the first time in my life without passing through
fire or straining the stones of my will, I came up from
my body rather than down from my mind, I could not
stop, some shield broke in me, bliss, and the honey
she had given me I could only give back, all sweets to
her womb, all come in her cunt.

"Son of a bitch," I said, "so that's what it's all
about." And my mouth like a worn-out soldier fell
on the heart of her breast.[43]

That "heavenly city" which Rojack has seen only once
before, during the act of murder, has now become attainable through love rather than hatred, positive good rather
than destruction.

The experience precipitates a clearer self-definition
in Rojack. He awakens to realize that:

. . . everything was all right inside the room. Outside, everything was wrong. Knowledge arrived from
outside—the way a Negro child might understand on
one particular morning that he is black. There was
no desire to take my pulse. I was a murderer. I was:
murderer.[44]

Leaving Cherry asleep, he fights the desire to drink, to call Ruta, to renounce his commitment, all the way to his apartment, then undergoes the telephone confrontations with his academic and television superiors,[45] and the climactic showdown with Roberts at the police station. Released from fear of legal retribution for Deborah's murder, Rojack is still fearful of the confrontation yet to come, with Barney Kelly. Drained of strength, he feels a temptation to give up his pilgrimage, retrace his steps:

> And I had a sudden hatred of mystery, a moment when I wanted to be in a cell, my life burned down to the bare lines of a legal defense. I did not want to see Barney Oswald Kelly later tonight, and yet I knew I must for that was part of the contract I had made on the morning air. I would not be permitted to flee the mystery. I was close to prayer then, I was very close, for what was prayer but a beseechment *not* to pursue the mystery. . . .[46]

And the prayer which he imagines is of enormous significance:

> "God," I wanted to pray, "Let me love that girl and become a father, and try to be a good man, and do some decent work. Yes, God," I was close to begging, "do not make me go back and back again to the charnel house of the moon." But like a soldier on six-hour leave to a canteen, I knew I would have to return.[47]

Two elements of this passage are important here. The prayer itself is the clearest articulation in the book of what Rojack discovers in himself in the course of his development: the desire for total commitment to goodness, to productivity, to fertility and love. His inability to rest upon prayer is based not upon a refusal to commit himself to God, but upon the awareness that he is not yet ready to come over to the camp of the good, for acceptance. His contract with the Devil is not yet fulfilled, there is external evil yet to be faced, and evil yet within Rojack to be purged. The Devil has kept his part of the bargain by providing the means of survival in an evil world, and "the wit to trick authority," and the Devil's gifts must be paid for before they can be renounced.

What, then, is the nature of the new contract Rojack has made, that with love? It is, to begin with, characterized by fertility. Cherry has been impregnated twice in the past, by Kelly and Shago Martin, and in both cases has aborted the pregnancy. But with Rojack she is mystically convinced that the depth of their first sexual act could not help but result in pregnancy, and both lovers are committed to bringing the hypothetical fetus to fruition. It is, in fact, Cherry's conviction that she is pregnant by Rojack which most frightens and outrages Shago when he arrives, because of the intensity of feeling which that conviction implies.

Other parallels in the system of sexual relationships presented here serve further to highlight the significance of the love between Cherry and Rojack. Certain comparisons made by Rojack himself have already been noted (see quotation above, p. 134). He is able to picture a similarity between his own sexual conflict with Ruta and that between Kelly and Cherry. And the judgment implicit in the comparison is a powerful one. Both partners in this new love have known the brutal, sterile sex of the Devil, Cherry with Kelly and Rojack with Ruta. But the qualitative worth of their sexual love together is different in kind rather than degree from these earlier contacts, just as Rojack himself has begun to become a different kind of man than the Roberts and the Romeos [48] he faces.

This love, then, which grows out of two people whose world of experience includes incest, miscegenation, anal intercourse, abortion, and murder, is nonetheless one characterized by natural fertility, tenderness and honesty. But this is bought only by courage and the desire to be good, as Rojack realizes:

> "I think we have to be good," by which I meant we would have to be brave.
> "I know," she said. Then we were silent for a while. "I know," she said again.[49]

And:

> . . . now I understood that love was not a gift but a vow. Only the brave could live with it for more than a little while. . . . love was love, one could find it with anyone, one could find it anywhere. It was just that you could never keep it. Not unless you were ready to die for it, dear friend.[50]

Love, as Mailer sees it, is a contract, not only with the beloved, but with oneself as well. It requires individual strength and courage, and the ability to stand alone, as Rojack realizes when, on his way to see Kelly, he is again tempted by fear to turn back from the right path:

> Once again I wished to rush back to her—she was my sanity, simple as that—and then I remembered the vow I had made in her bed. No, if one wished to be a lover, one could not find one's sanity in another. That was the iron law of romance: one took the vow to be brave.[51]

Just as a commitment to God cannot be made as an evasion of personal responsibility, romantic love cannot be used as a false womb in which to hide from one's frightening duties. Rojack has decided to take the path toward God and Cherry, but the mere decision to do so is not enough in itself. He knows that he must earn the right to earthly and divine love and salvation by completing the pilgrimage he has begun, and he must do it alone if it is to count.

We have stated that the sexual love for Cherry is the most crucial element by which Mailer defines the American existentialism of Rojack. It represents as well a major advance in Mailer's capacity to present in valid fictional form a consistently structured personal philosophy of sex. The extent and significance of this advance can be fully appreciated only by reference to the vague and undeveloped suggestion that sex represents hope for the individual, which closes *The Deer Park* (N). In the final paragraphs of that book, Sergius carries on the following imaginary dialogue with God:

. . . One must invariably look for a good time since a good time is what gives us the strength to try again. . . . If there is a God, and sometimes I believe there is one, I'm sure He says, "Go on, my boy. I don't know that I can help you, but we wouldn't want all *those* people to tell you what to do."

There are hours when I would have the arrogance to reply to the Lord himself, and so I ask, "Would You agree that sex is where philosophy begins?"

But God, who is the oldest of the philosophers, answers in His weary cryptic way, "Rather think of sex as Time, and Time as the connection of new circuits."

Then for a moment in that cold Irish soul of mine, a glimmer of the joy of the flesh came toward me, rare as the eye of the rarest tear of compassion, and we laughed together after all, because to have

> heard that sex was time and time the connection of
> new circuits was a part of the poor odd dialogues
> which give hope to us noble humans for more than
> one night.[52]

This closing statement may not be particularly integral
to the rest of *The Deer Park* (N) except as it is consistent,
in its vagueness, to Sergius' own confused state of non-
commitment to any clear, positive system of values. But
it does represent, in embryonic form, Mailer's intuition
that sex is somehow connected to hope and to God. The
nine years following this novel saw the development of a
clear and sophisticated view of the role of sexual love in
human hope for personal salvation, and culminated in the
statement of that view in *An American Dream*. Those
years of relative silence, however, led some critics, with
justification, to seize upon the end of *The Deer Park* as
a definitive part of Mailer's existential position. The work
of two such critics may be useful here in order further to
define the role of sex in Mailer's existentialism and the
extent of his advance on this count in *An American
Dream*.

The dissertations of James Burton Scott [53] and Samuel
Holland Hux [54] both place considerable emphasis on the
end of *The Deer Park* in treating Mailer's existentialism.
It must, in fairness, be emphasized that neither critic deals
with *An American Dream* (both dissertations apparently
being close to completion at the time of the publication
of that novel). Nonetheless, both hazard generalizations
on the present, and prognoses on the future role of sex
in Mailer's existentialism, which seem ill-founded, particularly in light of *An American Dream*, but even without
the retrospective advantage of that book.

Scott's position is the more irresponsible and simplistic
of the two. He says, in part:

> Sexual activities permitted some altogether too con-
> venient devices for enlarging upon his meanings. That
> these were too convenient, and finally specious, is in-
> dicated in *The Deer Park,* where Mailer comes to an
> acceptance of the varieties of sex on a simple ex-
> periential level. He does not try, in that novel, to make
> sex signify governmental affiliation, or political ideol-
> ogy; he does, however, still cling to the rather romantic
> notion that from sex one can come to some metaphys-
> ical conclusions about the nature of God and Time.[55]

If this statement can be considered somewhat justified by
the unformed nature of the conclusion of *The Deer Park,*
its tone of derogatory finality ("That these were too
convenient, and finally specious . . .") cannot. The super-
cilious application of the term "romantic," (with implicit
emphasis on the connotation of naiveté) to a novelist as
cynical in his view of male-female relationships as Mailer,
is singularly inappropriate. Applied in connection to *The
Deer Park,* it becomes foolish. Despite the vagueness of
the sex-time-God theory, *The Deer Park* does present a
thematically significant statement on the failures in love
of the major characters, notably Sergius and Eitel. This
failure is invested with greater significance by Mailer's
emphasis on it in his "Advertisement for *The Deer Park,*"
(see quotation and treatment above, pp. 110–111) as well
as by the fact that it represents a definite step in the
progression toward Rojack, a character who does not fail.
An American Dream may not have been available to Mr.
Scott, but *Advertisements for Myself* certainly was.

　　Mr. Hux's statements are somewhat less offensive. He
says at one point:

> The close of *The Deer Park* presents us with the hope
> of the "enormous present." Sex is time and time is
> the connection of new circuits. The most intense liv-

ing of each present as it comes, and primarily the present of sexual intercourse, provides a "hope to us noble humans for more than one night." It is at this point that Mailer's existentialism becomes clearly programmatic—search ye for the good orgasm.[56]

This is certainly a more fair and clear representation of what Mailer believed when he wrote *The Deer Park*. Yet whatever "programmatic" quality Mailer's existentialism may retain by the time of *An American Dream*, it is considerably more complex and sophisticated than "search ye for the good orgasm." Mr. Hux may not have known of the qualifications and complexities to be introduced to Mailer's conception of sex as significant human action by *An American Dream*. But his prognoses for Mailer's future fiction may be held up as inaccurate in light of that novel, particularly when he says:

> The present direction of Mailer's thought leads to certain dangers and, it seems to me, to a waste of his best talent. His increasing insistence on orgasmic ful-fillment contains a hazard quite beyond my academic concern that it could explode the bounds of his Existentialism. The hazard is that Mailer could be-come a "totalitarian" of sex, someone who offers a "quick solution for a permanent problem." Mailer does not always keep clear the distinction between the valuable and the fantastic in sex, between sex which gives hope for one more night (*Deer Park*, p. 319) and sex as the way to God.[57]

It is one of the basic contentions of this chapter that Mailer does not offer a "quick solution" through sex in *An American Dream;* and that the distinction between meaningless sex and sex as an expression of total commit-ment to love (and thereby to personal salvation) represents one of the major thematic elements of that novel. Mr. Hux is a perceptive critic, but it is dangerous to predict the future course of a writer not yet conveniently dead or unproductive.

We have said that Rojack, though consciously committed through his love of Cherry to the side of good, must still fulfill his contract with the Devil by facing Barney Oswald Kelly, before he can find his way to God. The meeting with Kelly is rendered more ominous and significant by the fact that the plot line pointedly omits any contact between him and Rojack during the course of the novel's action. Even telephone arrangements for the appointment are carried out by Rojack's answering service, rather than personally.

Rojack brings with him, to Barney Kelly's suite, all the strength he has derived from Cherry and Shago, and from his own courage in the face of the earlier confrontations. But all of this is barely enough to enable Rojack to overcome this goatlike man who himself entertains the idea that he is one of Satan's representatives. At one point, Kelly says to Rojack:

> "Well, for all we know, I am a solicitor for the Devil."
> "But you really think so."
> "On occasion, I'm vain enough." [58]

And Rojack is willing to believe that Kelly is the Devil incarnate. Arriving at the Waldorf, he:

> shivered in the open window of the cab. What was it Shago had said? "Man, I was spitting in the face [Deborah's] of the Devil." He was wrong. It was the Devil's daughter. And the memory of Barney Oswald Kelly came back. For we were approaching the Waldorf and I could feel his presence in a room near the top of the Towers. [59]

Rojack emerges from the violent scene on Kelly's balcony alive and purified, free to pursue his new life. But the bargain with the Devil is not easily settled. Both Cherry and Shago must die violently to balance the infernal books. And the systematic ironies by which they die seem to support a sense of a malevolent order which must take its due. On the way to Kelly's by cab, Rojack has experienced another intuitive flash, dictating that he go to Harlem and risk violent death in order to purge his treatment of Shago and to bless his love through gratuitous courage. Overcoming the urge by the realization that he may merely be avoiding his primary responsibility of meeting Kelly, Rojack proceeds to the Waldorf, but he is disturbed by a feeling that somewhere in Harlem a man is being bludgeoned to death in his stead. That man is Shago, killed to no apparent purpose with a length of lead pipe. And to complete the circle, Cherry is killed in revenge by a mistaken friend of Shago.

Cherry has left Rojack one further legacy, a gift of luck in gambling. Going to Las Vegas (the scene of Cherry's affair with Kelly and a city which Kelly has compared to Hell), Rojack wins enough at the tables to pay the $16,000 in debts which Deborah has left him. Significantly, Cherry has thus freed him from the financial stranglehold which Deborah had engineered. And this last formal responsibility to the earthly ills represented by commercial America is significantly dissolved through a clear victory over its most Sodom-like capital. A parallel may be seen here between the ending of this novel and the beginning of *The Deer Park,* which finds Sergius O'Shaugnessy entering the tinsel world of Desert D'Or with $14,000 won in a poker game. Sergius, too, is indirectly released from the false society in which he has lived, by his trip to Las Vegas. But it is significant that Sergius' escape is precipitated by a *defeat* at the gambling tables (which divests him of the bankroll which is his membership card in the world of Lulu Meyers). It is very much in keeping with the primary distinction hitherto drawn between Rojack and Sergius that Rojack leaves America on a note of victory over Las Vegas. For as I have earlier stated, Sergius is defined primarily in terms of negative values, while Rojack is the first of Mailer's positive characters.

These plot devices do not seem to be dictated by blind chance, for fate does seem to play a role in the works (as has been seen in the plot of *The Naked and the Dead*). In *An American Dream* it is important, particularly at the beginning, when Deborah's falling body causes a traffic pileup on the East River Drive. Not only does this effect the meeting between Cherry and Rojack, but it brings Eddie Gannucci into the hands of the police. As a result, the police are too busy to keep Rojack all night, and his temporary reprive enables him to proceed in the events later that night which lead to his relationship with Cherry. Finally, perhaps the clearest statement of the forces by which the world is governed comes from Rojack, who sees a structure, an "architecture to eternity" (see quotation above, p. 144).

There is a structure, too, to the pilgrimage which Rojack makes. The development of his character proceeds along an ascending line, each stage of which is defined by the nature of his adversary. By murdering Deborah, he takes his first faltering step into what he sees as a new life, a rebirth, and the act itself provides him the first glimpse of a heavenly city which he must try to reach. I have said that *The Deer Park* (P) is Mailer's vision of Hell. It is significant that in the world of *An American Dream,* a world viewed in as dark a cynicism as Mailer has ever held and peopled by characters perhaps

more evil than those of his previous novels, we are nonetheless presented with a vision of heaven.

The sexual episode with Ruta represents the pact
made with the Devil, and the gifts of guile which he takes
away from her bed are the last positive (though evil)
acquisitions he is to make until he is ready for Cherry.
The confrontations with Romeo Romalozzo, Roberts and
Tony are characterized by negatives: the refusal to back
down and the rejection by Rojack of the inner corruption
which he shares with these men. The relative purity of
Rojack's soul at this point enables him to take a major
positive step, that of choosing to love Cherry. The encounter with Shago (who shows not only nobility but
Christian forgiveness as well) provides Rojack with new
power, this time originating from the camp of goodness.
The ultimate test for which he has been prepared throughout his ordeal is the triumph over evil as represented by
Barney Kelly, and the consequent final release from his
pact with the Devil.

Although the structure and symbology of the course
traced by Rojack are obviously permeated by Christian
and by existential elements, there is much that is peculiarly
American here as well. Mailer is, as has been noted earlier,
very much a social critic. The degree of proximity and
accuracy with which he observes and criticizes American
society is obvious in the scope of *An American
Dream,* which encompasses the worlds of mass media,[60]
academia, politics, the stock exchange, organized crime,
local law enforcement, and the CIA. In every case, no
matter how brief the treatment, the criticism is effectively
frightening, even when ludicrous as well. The ethnic and
regional elements of the American population represented
are various, and the Rojack/Ruta passage is given greater
ironic significance by the fact that he is part Jewish and

derives brutal pleasure from "plugging a Nazi." This brief sense of the confrontation of American and European culture echoes the earlier scene in which Rojack killed the four Nazi machine-gunners. And it may be remembered that almost twenty years before Mailer chose to write about the Pacific theatre because he felt incapable of rendering the cultural impact of the European war effectively.

There are, then, two major levels upon which this novel proceeds: that of the individual and that of the society which surrounds him. Mailer's view of the American society has remained as unqualifiedly black as that set forth in *The Naked and the Dead*. But his view of the individual has changed. Although most men are corrupt, weak and evil, it is possible through great courage and luck and anguish for a man to survive the American experience and remain an individual.

Into such an individual victory enter several elements of personal ethic which are peculiar to the American character. The first is the Protestant ethic which prescribes a drive for personal success, and which states that such tangible success is symptomatic of the fact that one is among those chosen for survival. In that this doctrine has been a major rationalization for the establishment of huge capitalistic fortunes earlier in the country's history, it may be seen as not wholly admirable. And it is, in fact, the stated code of a nonadmirable capitalist in Mailer's work. The movie mogul Herman Teppis, speaking of God, says in *The Deer Park* (P): "I believe He gives His vote to the man who wins." [61] It is possible that Mailer believes this of Rojack. Certainly, the mere desire to be saved is not enough to bring Rojack to a state of grace after his involvement with the satanic elements of American society. It is necessary that he find his way to God by overcoming the establishment as it is most clearly represented by the financial, governmental, and underworld power which are brought together in the person of Barney Oswald Kelly. In that he is an underdog who succeeds against great odds, Rojack is the hero of the Protestant ethic, and that success in itself implies grace and salvation. On one level, then, the title of the novel must be taken at face value. Rojack has achieved the American dream of individual freedom. At the same time, the title is invested with great irony, for the usual connotations of the American dream (military heroism, political success, a wealthy wife, social acceptance, academic recognition, one's own television show, and numerous sexual partners) have all been achieved by Rojack by the beginning of the novel, at which time he is a weak man, an admitted failure, on the verge of despair and suicide. In showing the stereotyped American dream to be a false and shabby one, Mailer continues in this novel his consistent criticism of American society. By showing that there can be a true American dream in the achievement of personal freedom and integrity, he carries his concern with the plight of the individual in contemporary society one step further. He does this not by minimizing that plight, but by holding out a possible hope of salvation as the reward for courage.

The second major American ethic which conditions the nature and the means of Rojack's success is one of which Mailer has been acutely conscious for some time. It is the commitment of the American male to the myth of the lone hero, taken from an oversimplified history of the nation's early years and perpetuated as simplistically by the movie industry. In the Third Presidential Paper, entitled "The Existential Hero," Mailer says:

> Nowhere, as in America, however, was this fall from individual man to mass man felt so acutely, for America was at once the first and most prolific

creator of mass communications. . . . Yet America
was also the country in which the dynamic myth of
the Renaissance—that every man was potentially extraordinary—knew its most passionate persistence. Simply, America was the land where people still believed in heroes: George Washington; Billy the Kid;
. . . Hemingway; Joe Louis. . . . And when the West
was filled, the expansion turned inward, became part
of an agitated, overexcited, superheated dream life.
The film studios threw up their searchlights as the
frontier was finally sealed, and the romantic possi-
bilities of the old conquest of land turned into a
vertical myth, trapped within the skull, of a new
kind of heroic life, each choosing his own archetype
of a neo-Renaissance man, be it Barrymore, Cagney,
Flynn, Bogart, Brando or Sinatra, but it was almost
as if there were no peace unless one could fight well,
kill well (if always with honor), love well and love
many, be cool, be daring, be dashing, be wild, be wily,
be resourceful, be a brave gun. And this myth, that
each of us was born to be free, to wander, to have
adventure and to grow on the waves of the violent,
the perfumed, and the unexpected, had a force which
could not be tamed no matter how the nation's regu-
lators . . . would brick in the modern life with
hygiene upon sanity, and middle-brow homily over
platitude; the myth would not die.[62]

It is by means of this myth, within his mind, that the
common man in America attempts to maintain his sense
of individuality, while he subscribes in fact to the rules
and habits of mass media and mass society. But Stephen
Richards Rojack does in fact carry out the myth, setting
himself outside of society, wandering free, facing danger
with wily resourcefulness. To the extent that Rojack's
adventures seem to subscribe to the chichéd Hollywood
myth, the novel's success is mitigated for many readers.

But what makes Rojack's adventures credible, for the most part, is the fact that they proceed naturally out of his character; and that character is a substantial creation. Rojack is no stereotyped, square-jawed, unfaltering Hollywood hero, but a man who is weak, frightened and unsure in the face of challenge. That he forces himself to overcome his own weakness and to face his antagonists successfully is rendered credible by Mailer's sophisticated establishment of the rational and emotional forces operating within the narrator's mind at each confrontation (for example, the compulsion to face Romeo). Once again, then, Rojack's story represents the achievement of a real American dream, the desire to be free and brave. And once again, the simplistic aspects of that dream as seen by the popular eye are implicitly rejected.

A final statement on the source of Rojack's strength is in order. It is significant that among the various interlocking layers of aristocracy and royalty existing in this ostensible democracy (princes of Harlem, of the Mafia, of finance, and of the social elite abound and are described as such) it is from the supposedly lower strata that Rojack derives his strength. He is himself a sort of sophisticated Horatio Alger figure, and those two people who give of themselves (and ultimately their lives) for his victory are a Negro and a Poor White Southerner. It is not that Mailer has changed his opinion of the common man in general since the writing of *The Naked and the Dead,* but rather that he seems to believe that whatever will enable the common man to achieve personal salvation must come from the strength of today's particular downtrodden groups, especially the Negro. Whether or not this potential strength can save America itself in Mailer's view is questionable. For Rojack, after his own purgation, does not commit himself to helping cut out America's considerable cancers, but instead leaves the country. The message, then, is one of very limited hope, but hope nonetheless, and from the author of *The Naked and the Dead,* this is something remarkable.

Notes

1 *An American Dream,* p. 24.
2 *Ibid.,* p. 20.
3 *Cannibals and Christians,* p. 114.
4 *An American Dream,* p. 237.
5 *Ibid.*
6 *The Deer Park: A Play,* pp. 101–102.
7 *Advertisements for Myself,* pp. 501–502.
8 *An American Dream,* pp. 47–49.
9 *Ibid.,* p. 44.
10 *Ibid.,* p. 52.
11 *Ibid.,* p. 181.
12 *Ibid.,* p. 182.
13 *Advertisements for Myself,* p. 332.
14 *An American Dream,* p. 189.
15 *Ibid.,* p. 173.
16 *Ibid.,* p. 181.
17 *Ibid.,* p. 182.
18 *Ibid.,* p. 183.
19 *Ibid.,* p. 190.
20 *Ibid.,* p. 191.
21 *Ibid.,* p. 192.
22 *Advertisements for Myself,* pp. 340–41.
23 *Ibid.,* p. 339.
24 *Ibid.,* p. 340.
25 *An American Dream,* pp. 35–36.
26 *Ibid.,* p. 243.
27 *Ibid.*
28 *Ibid.,* p. 52.
29 *Ibid.,* p. 126.
30 *Ibid.,* p. 63.
31 *Ibid.,* p. 62.
32 *Ibid.,* p. 95.
33 *Ibid.,* p. 97.
34 *Ibid.,* pp. 94–95.
35 *Ibid.,* p. 97.

[36] *Ibid.,* pp. 100–101.

[37] *Ibid.,* p. 103.

[38] *Ibid.*

[39] *Ibid.,* p. 104.

[40] *Ibid.,* pp. 151–52.

[41] *Ibid.,* p. 116.

[42] *Ibid.,* pp. 120–21.

[43] *Ibid.,* pp. 122–23.

[44] *Ibid.,* p. 123.

[45] Ironically, through a passing reference made by the latter, Rojack learns Cherry's last name for the first time.

[46] *An American Dream,* p. 153.

[47] *Ibid.*

[48] Could there possibly be some significance in the vague similarity these names have to Rojack's own? It is, after all, one of Mailer's points that he renounces his similarities in character to these men.

[49] *An American Dream,* p. 155.

[50] *Ibid.,* p. 156.

[51] *Ibid.,* p. 191.

[52] *The Deer Park,* pp. 318–19.

[53] James Burton Scott, "The Individual and Society: Norman Mailer versus William Styron" (unpublished Doctoral dissertation, Syracuse University, 1964).

[54] Samuel Holland Hux, "American Myth and Existential Vision: The Indigenous Existentialism of Mailer, Bellow, Styron and Ellison" (unpublished Doctoral dissertation, University of Connecticut, 1965).

[55] Scott, *op. cit.,* p. 154.

[56] Hux, *op. cit.,* p. 201.

[57] *Ibid.,* p. 209.

[58] *An American Dream,* p. 221.

[59] *Ibid.,* p. 192.

[60] The telephone conversation with the humorously despicable TV producer has already been mentioned. Another brief but telling jibe is implicit in the irresponsible newspaper treatment of Deborah's death, to which a parallel may be found in the gossip column reference to Sergius in *The Deer Park.*

[61] *The Deer Park: A Play,* p. 167.

[62] Norman Mailer, *The Presidential Papers* (New York: G. P. Putnam's Sons, 1963), pp. 39–40.

5

Why Are We in Vietnam?

Why Are We in Vietnam? is Mailer's latest novel. It comprises most of the thematic concerns found in the first four novels and employs a system of metaphor similar to that of *An American Dream*. Thus, the novel is very much a part of the continuum established thus far by the Mailer canon. But structurally and stylistically, *Vietnam* represents a retrogression rather than an advance in the development of Mailer's art.

The novel does not deal directly with Vietnam, but the significance of the title is fairly obvious, as the book jacket hastens to point out:

> . . . Vietnam is mentioned only once in the book, and then on the final page. Nor does the author once refer to international affairs or American involvement overseas. Why then the title? Could it be that in this scandalous, ribald, hilarious, frightening account of a hunting expedition in Alaska's Brooks Mountain Range, Mr. Mailer is drawing a dread parallel? Or

that in the behavior of a few hunters from Texas a reader may sense why America goes to war? . . .[1]

It could be, and is. The "dread parallel" is a well chosen one, but the execution is weak. Eliot Fremont-Smith, who holds a high opinion of the book's political message, points out at the outset of his review that the novel:

> was, by the author's admission, written "in a great hurry"; it is difficult to get into, messy, insulting . . . and deliberately relentless in its use of revolting imagery. It will be mistakenly reviled . . . and mistakenly thought a "swinging" book.[2]

But Fremont-Smith goes on to say that:

> It is also the most original, courageous and provocative novel so far this year. . . . Norman Mailer, who is, among other things, this country's most intrepid polemical metaphorist, not its Hemingway but its Swift, has said that his novel is an attempt to place "the shortest possible equals sign" on the Vietnam war. He sees the war as a wholly destructive, wholly brutalizing exercise of American violence whose only rationale now is the verification of a vulgarized self-image of potency, toughness, masculinity. Why are we in Vietnam? Because it's there, man. And violence is as American as cherry pie.[3]

What is indisputable here is the reviewer's understanding of Mailer's political position and artistic intention in the novel. Less acceptable are Fremont-Smith's generous superlatives. But in order to dispute these, we must first outline the plot structure of the novel.

The major characters are D.J., the narrator; Rusty, his father; Tex Hyde, his best friend; and Big Luke Fellinka, their hunting guide. The narrative is carried out

in stream-of-consciousness form within D.J.'s mind as he
sits at a formal dinner in his parents' Dallas mansion on
the night before he and Tex leave to fight in Vietnam.
The Alaskan hunting trip with which the novel deals has
taken place two years before, when D.J. was sixteen. The
narrator suggests that his initials stand for "disc jockey"
and for Dr. Jekyll. The tone of the text often resembles
the patter of a disc jockey, and D.J. tells us that he is
"Disc Jockey to America"[4] speaking into a tape recorder
for the ear of God. The Dr. Jekyll motif has several
reverberations which become clearer later in the book.
First, D.J. and Tex *Hyde* are to undergo a communion
which will fuse them into "killer brothers." Secondly, the
narrator himself is a split, Jekyll-Hyde personality. D.J.
tells us repeatedly that he is not merely a white Texan,
but also a crippled Negro writing or transmitting from
Harlem. The story is told in chapters (called "Chaps"),
with an "intro beep" introducing each. Both chapters and
intro beeps are related by D.J., although he usually refers
to himself in the third person in the chapters. The
chapters are more directly relevant to the plot line, and
sometimes more coherent than the intro beeps.

The story of the hunting trip embodies certain mythic
elements (notably the initiation into manhood of D.J. and
Tex) and proceeds along a line of progressively more
crucial conflicts between man and nature. In this respect
the structure is similar to that of *An American Dream,*
but the narrative stance makes the execution of the later
novel far less effective. The initial conflict takes place
between Rusty and Big Luke, in the very American and
artificial bar of a deluxe motel in Fairbanks, the description of which makes it clear that the urban portions of
Alaska have become very much a part of commercial
America. Rusty is the archetypal Ugly American: a top-
level corporation executive (who brings two corporate

sycophants along on the hunt) and ex-All-American tackle. He is in search of a reassuring moment of truth of the sort that has become permanently associated with Hemingway,[5] and only killing a grizzly bear will satisfy him. The tension generated by his first failures to realize this aim while other members of the party do kill bear is strikingly similar to that which helped spur the narrative of *Green Hills of Africa,* in which Hemingway is repeatedly frustrated in his desire to shoot a Greater Kudu. But the similarity highlights the significant differences. This is not Africa, but Alaska, a place very much a part of the United States. For this is a totally American novel, very much in the stream of social consciousness which has been observed in all of Mailer's earlier work. The fact that the hunting party comes from Texas is significant, for Mailer portrays that state as the repository of the most undiluted and unabashed American qualities of vulgarity and commercialism. Rusty wants his moment of truth as a commodity, one he can hold up for public inspection back home (which is, as D.J. suggests, why his two corporation inferiors are along, so that they can later substantiate and embellish the story); and one with a lifetime guarantee: ". . . so I'll never have to be so scared again, not until I got to face The Big Man." [6]

Big Luke's position is that he cannot guarantee Rusty a shot at a bear. His reasons are several. The Brooks Range has been invaded by too many clumsy hunters, who wounded bear and left them to suffer and survive, growing in cunning and hatred of man. Big Ollie, Luke's Indian assistant, elaborates on the upsetting of nature by man:

> He talks like a cannibal in a jungle bunny movie. "Brooks Range no wilderness now. Airplane go over the head, animal no wild no more, now crazy." [7]

Big Luke is influenced by another consideration as well, as D.J. points out:

> Big Luke used to be a big hunter, but those grizzly scratches have weakened his Arnold Toynbee co-efficient—he interested less in challenge than response —if he caught his share of the three grand a head without having to lead various grades of assholes and tough but untrained adolescents into the brush to look for Mr. Wounded Honey Grizzly holding the head of a magnum in his bear gut and a last dream of murder in his bear eye, well, Big Luke, despite the big man death-guts charisma, may have had his day. Who's to say there is no actors in Alaska? [8]

Thus, though D.J. has described Big Luke as very much a man,[9] he is not to be seen as an unqualified representative of nature. American civilization has tainted him as well as it has Alaska. He wins the confrontation with Rusty in the motel bar partly because he is a better man, but partly because his skill as a guide has become known as the best of that commodity available on the market. Luke guides only the social and political elite, and so when he hints that Rusty can have his deposit back and forget the hunt, Rusty must back down. It is far worse to go home a rejected client of Big Luke than to accept the safari on Luke's terms and risk getting no bear.

Big Luke is midway between the totally corrupt Rusty and nature. When, on the first morning in camp, Tex cleanly kills a wolf, Luke performs the ritual of giving each of the boys a cup of blood to drink. But when the degree of inept impatience which characterizes this group of clients becomes clear to Luke, he commits himself to compromise. Barely conforming to hunting regulations, and renouncing any pretense of sportsmanship, Luke brings in a helicopter and thus enables each member of the party to bag mountain goat and caribou effortlessly.

Bear are another matter entirely. Even from the air, they are difficult to find. When one is finally encountered, Rusty experiences a failure of nerve and is ignominiously saved from the bear's charge by the patently artificial aid of the helicopter. The failure brings the situation to a sharp focus, in Rusty's mind and that of the reader. What is at stake is Rusty's manhood, and the sleepless conclusion he reaches that night is conceived in sexual terms and related directly to Rusty's relationship with Hallie, D.J.'s mother:

> Rusty was sick. *He had to get it up.* [My italics] They had to go for grizzer now. Well, he was man enough to steel his guts before necessity, he not D.J.'s father for naught. . . .
>
> •   •   •
>
> Blasts of rage and gouts of fear burn like jets and flush like bile waters and he is *humped* [my italics] in his mind on Hallie. D.J.'s own father, Rusty, married twenty years to a blonde beauty he can never own for certain in the flesh of his brain.[10]

The passage is significant in terms of point of view as well as symbolism. The sexual nature of Rusty's drive to kill is made patently obvious. But D.J.'s view into Rusty's mind seems not so much a tendency to omniscience as a capacity to identify with his father's plight. The differences between father and son may be conditioned primarily by the discrepancy in age and experience, rather than innate personality traits. In this sense, Rusty's name is of some significance. He is rusty in the ways of courage because he has been corroded for twenty years by corporate falsity as well as emasculation at the hands of a representative of tough American womanhood.

The next bear episode is a failure as well. Two are sighted, and Tex kills the male immediately. Although Rusty hits the female, the kill is awarded to one of his subordinates. Everyone involved is immediately sorry for the decision when it becomes clear how crucial a bear kill now is to Rusty. D.J., too, is anxious to get a bear. His own performance up to this point is disappointing to him for several reasons. First, Tex, with whom he has a competition in every endeavor, has both a bear and a wolf, while D.J. "had blown up in bull buck bear fever," [11] and failed even to shoot at the female bear. Father and son are closer in character and motivation at this point than they have ever been:

> Rusty scurries about in his gut and reamasses his cool. He is getting to feel taut and not without his ready—D.J. is more so than a young assassin with a knife. He too has got to get grizzer. The wolf is burning fever in him now, best future of his blood is going to boil off if he can't get on a bear. . . . [12]

Rusty has a certain potential for courage, and he is ready to rise to the occasion. But D.J., I have said, has one additional motivation. He has begun to sense the force of natural Alaska. In shooting his mountain goat earlier, D.J. has begun to recognize the falsity represented by helicopter hunting:

> . . . and when he [the goat] died, *Wham!* the pain of his exploding heart shot like an arrow into D.J.'s heart, and the animals had gotten him, they were talking all around him now, communicating the unspoken unseen unmeasurable electromagnetism and wave of all the psychic circuits of all the wild of

Alaska, and he was only part of them, and part he was of gasoline of Texas, the asshole sulfur smell of money-oil clinging to the helicopter, cause he had not gotten that goat by getting up in the three A.M. of morning and climbing the mountain.[13]

And so it is that father and son elude the rest of the hunters and set off together after bear.

The mixed feelings between father and son have been established earlier by two flashbacks to D.J.'s childhood, both of which are involved with sexuality and conflict. One establishes a classically Oedipal situation, while the other involves an incident of open physical conflict between father and son. But now, for a few hours alone in the woods, D.J. and Rusty are on the same frequency. Their paths coincide briefly before they diverge forever. The two find a bear, both shoot, and the wounded grizzly escapes into dense undergrowth. Frightened but determined, the two follow. They find the bear dying quietly. The difference between their two reactions defines the direction that each has chosen for life:

> . . . Rusty was for pouring in some lead just to make shit-and-sure, but peace was coming off that bear . . . and so Rusty contented himself—being a camera-conscious flash-bulb poking American—to heist a little stone and bap that bear on the hide.
>
> • • •
>
> Rusty raised his gun, but D.J. touched the rifle slightly with a little salute, and started walking down toward the bear.
>
> • • •
>
> . . . and D.J. looked in from his twenty feet away and took a step and took another step and another step and something in that grizzer's eyes locked into

his, a message . . . those eyes were telling him something, singeing him, branding some part of D.J.'s
future. . . .

•   •   •

. . . and when D.J. smiled, the eyes reacted, they
shifted . . . they looked to be drawing in the peace
of the forest preserved for all animals as they die . . .
and Rusty—wetting his pants, doubtless, from the excessive tension—chose that moment to shoot, and griz
went up to death in one last paroxysm . . . all forgiveness gone.

•   •   •

D.J. didn't speak to Rusty on the way back. And when
they hit camp at dark, Big Luke so relieved he
couldn't even read various prescribed riot acts, they
asked at last who had got the bear, and D.J., in the
silence which followed, said, "Well, we both sent
shots home, but I reckon Rusty got it," and Rusty
didn't contradict him—one more long silence—and
Rusty said, "Yeah, I guess it's mine, but one of its
sweet legs belongs to D.J." Whew. Final end of love
of one son for one father.[14]

Rusty has come closer than ever before to true manhood,
and then retreated. He has been for too long committed
to the American ethic, and so he chooses to claim the
trophy and the public manhood implicit in it, over the
true courage and commitment to nature toward which
D.J. is progressing.

One final confrontation remains, and it is the most
crucial and revealing. Tex and D.J., disgusted by the
artificiality of the hunt, awake long before dawn the next
day and spend a day and a night in the woods alone. With
an intuition closely parallel to that of Ike McCaslin in
Faulkner's *The Bear*, the boys divest themselves of guns,

knives and compasses, purifying themselves by giving up
the protection of manmade instruments. Tough in the
face of their fear, they encounter a wolf (whom they
frighten off by sheer concentrated waves of psychic murder)
and a bear (whom they watch, unobserved, from a tree).
They spend the night in bedrolls, closely skirting the
edge of a murderous love/hate homosexual union similar
to those approached by Rojack with both Shago Martin
and Barney Oswald Kelly. Then, through communion
with nature they become united in a new telepathic sense:

> . . . something in the radiance of the North went
> into them, and owned their fear, some communion
> of telepathics and new powers, and they were twins,
> never to be near as lovers again, but killer brothers,
> owned by something, prince of darkness, lord of light,
> they did not know; they just knew telepathy was on
> them, they had been touched forever by the North
> and each bit a drop of blood from his own finger
> and touched them across and met, blood to blood . . .
> and they left an hour later in the dark to go back to
> camp and knew on the way each mood of emotion
> building in Rusty and Big Luke and Ollie and M.A.
> Bill and Pete and their faces were etched just as they
> had foreseen them and the older men's voices were
> filled with the same specific mix of mixed old shit
> which they had heard before in the telepathic vaults
> of their new Brooks Range electrified mind.[15]

It is significant that D.J. and Tex are shown, at the end
of this last chapter, in clear contrast to the older men,
not excepting Big Luke. D.J. has told the reader early in
the book that he "sees right through shit," [16] and it now
becomes clear where both he and Tex gained this faculty.
Eliot Fremont-Smith calls the book "profoundly pessimistic," [17] and it is indisputably that. But there seems to

be a glimmer of hope held out in D.J. and Tex: in their capacity to "see through shit," to recognize and reject the false ideals and national motives disseminated by the older men who govern America; and in their peculiarly American initiative and, if you will, pioneer spirit.

The "Terminal Intro Beep and Out" following the last chapter qualifies this hope drastically, perhaps destroys it. For on the last page of the novel, D.J. reveals that:

> . . . tomorrow Tex and me, we're off to see the wizard in Vietnam. . . . This is D.J., Disc Jockey to America turning off. Vietnam, hot damn.[18]

The question, then, is whether the energy and insight attributed to the new generation of American males as they are represented by Tex and D.J. is meant by Mailer to imply some hope for the future of the country. Certainly, the boys have rejected the American faults and blindnesses represented by the older men. But the arena in which they choose to define their future, and the eagerness in which they choose it ("Vietnam, hot damn."), raise the question of whether the aims of the new generation are not as wrong as those of the old, however different their methods and motives. In this light, the indictment of American society intended by Mailer may appear all the more bitter for the degree of youthful potential which is wastefully misdirected. The issue is somewhat ambiguous, but what resolution there is must be understood in terms of the nature of the purification which the boys undergo.

This purification is tied to the use of obscenity in the book. It is significant that the amount of obscenity drops as the narrative proceeds. D.J. suggests a reason for this early in the lone expedition with Tex:

> Listen, fellow Americans, and D.J. here to tell you,
> don't get upset by the boys' last dialogue, they so full
> of love and adventure and in such a haste to get all
> the mixed glut and sludge out of their systems that
> they're heating up all the foul talk to get rid of it in a
> hurry like bad air going up the flue and so be ready to
> enjoy good air and nature. . . .[19]

The purifying effect of giving free rein to obscenity in
one's speech or writing is a theory in which Mailer truly
believes. He elaborates further on it in *The Armies of the
Night:*

> He [Mailer] was off into obscenity. It gave a hearti-
> ness like the blood of beef tea to his associations.
> There was no villainy in obscenity for him, just—
> paradoxically, characteristically—his love for America.
> . . . what none of the editorial writers ever men-
> tioned was that [the] noble common man was obscene
> as an old goat, and his obscenity was what saved him.
> The sanity of said common democratic man was in
> his humor, his humor was in his obscenity.[20]

But "The war in Vietnam was an obscene war," [21] and
Mailer explains why America's leaders are opposed to
verbal obscenity:

> Yes, the use of obscenity was indeed to be condemned,
> for the free use of it would wash away the nation—
> was America the first great power to be built on bull-
> shit? [22]

Those who ban obscenity are, like the Rustys of America,
bottling up their own rages and fears, which are then
channeled into an obscene war:

> . . . the American corporation executive, who was
> after all the foremost representative of Man in the

world today, was perfectly capable of burning unseen women and children in the Vietnamese jungles, yet felt a large displeasure and fairly final disapproval at the generous use of obscenity in literature and in public.[23]

And, speaking particularly about obscenity in *Why Are We in Vietnam?*, Mailer made a statement last year on the Merv Griffin television show to the effect that "one day in the life of General Westmoreland is more obscene" than all the obscene books ever published in this country. The audience booed him.

The result of the purging of obscenity does effect a purification in D.J. and Tex, one which culminates in the mystical communion with nature (see quotation above, p. 188). But why do the boys take their new sensitivity and awareness to Vietnam? John W. Aldridge, in an excellent article on this novel, takes the following position:

> It may be an irony that on the last page of the novel D.J. reveals that he and Tex are on their way to the Army and Vietnam. But the point, one suspects, is that by now they have conquered the impulse to Vietnam in themselves. They do not *need* Vietnam as an outlet for their hostilities, and so it is certain that they will be as derisively antagonistic to the war as they have been to the sick pretensions of Rusty's world.[24]

This seems to me a somewhat suspect interpretation of the novel's end. Not only are D.J. and Tex anxious to get to Vietnam, but their communion with nature and with one another has turned them into "killer brothers" [25] told by God to "Go out and kill—fulfill my will, go and kill." [26] All of their heightened awareness and purified energy is defined in terms of violence, and the implication is that such powers can be effectively channeled only into killing. In this sense, America's presence in Vietnam may be seen as the natural outgrowth of the character of the new generation of Americans, represented by the "killer brothers," D.J. and Tex. Mailer expresses a sympathetic understanding of the situation of the young Americans fighting in Vietnam, in *The Armies of the Night* when he speaks of the

> very air of the century (this evil twentieth century with its curse on the species, its oppressive Faustian lusts . . . its entrapment of the innocence of the best —for which young American soldiers hot out of high school and in love with a hot rod and his Marine buddies in his platoon in Vietnam could begin to know the devil of the oppression which would steal his soul before he knew he had one. . . .[27]

These young men are not of Rusty's ilk, but their courage and idealism are misdirected. And D.J. and Tex, though not as innocent and unaware as the hypothetical soldiers Mailer describes, are nonetheless governed by the same "air of the century." The God who speaks to D.J. and Tex in the Brooks Range and sends them off to kill is "a beast, not a man," [28] the representative of those "Faustian lusts" of which Mailer speaks.

Thus, although Mailer's criticism of the American character in *Why Are We in Vietnam?* is mitigated somewhat by the fact that D.J. and his generation are more honest and courageous than their fathers, they are still governed by the violent tone of our time, and we are still in Vietnam. A very crucial further step will be taken in Mailer's position less than a year later, in *The Armies of the Night.* In that book, the best of the younger generation is shown as capable, not merely of rejecting outmoded values in American society, but of courageously combatting the national violence which informs support of the war. Their courage is tested, as Mailer sees it, in a war here at home.

Samuel Holland Hux, toward the close of his discussion of Mailer, states; "I would like to see Mailer become the American political novelist. . . ." [29] This was certainly a reasonable hope to have held for the future direction of Mailer's fiction, considering the novelist's consistent interest in the political climate of America; and Mailer's work in 1968, *The Armies of the Night* and *Miami and the Siege of Chicago*, certainly fulfill that hope. But *Why Are We in Vietnam?* seems a rather unfortunate confirmation of Hux's projection. It should be evident from what has been said up to this point that this novel is as much a vehicle of Mailer's concern with social ills as any of his previous work, perhaps more explicitly so than any. But how effectively is this polemical message presented by the work of art of which it is ostensibly an integral part? Is Mailer's artistic development, the progressively greater maturity and control that I have been at pains to document, carried further in this novel?

Certainly, Mailer has dealt once again with his recurring theme of the individual in American society. And D.J., like Rojack, is able to reject much of the falsity of that society. But I do not believe that Mailer has continued, in this book, his progress toward a fresh, essentially nonimitative art. His failure here lies, I believe, in the problems of point of view and the novelistic form dictated by it. And central to these problems are the metaphorical patterns established by D.J.

The metaphorical patterns which lace this novel are complex, but a few examples should suffice to show that these are essentially the same as those employed in *An American Dream*, with minor shifts of emphasis. The concept of cancer as a communicable byproduct of inner

frustration is transmitted almost intact by Mailer from
the mind of Stephen Richards Rojack to that of D.J.:

> This ain't young cunt from which you cop the goods—
> this is used cunt, burnt meat, cliff-hanging menopause
> types which can't get rid of the poisons by any hole
> but the pussy hole. . . . they get more out of you in
> three hours than a new chick emanating happy fucks
> would elicit in a day and a night. And the tooth and
> cunters are converting their schizophrenia into cancer
> juice for you.[30]

And there is a parallel theory involving urination:

> Well, this is deep stuff. Excrement is defeat. Liquid
> excrement otherwise known as You're-In Spa-ce-man
> is the defeat which comes from stand-up ventures
> where you had to wait. Someone talking, and you
> want to interrupt but you hold your tongue—that
> makes for piss. Gather near, D.J. tell you why. An
> impulse once it is frustrated crystallizes the chemicals
> which had been interacting in order to fuel the move.
>
> •   •   •
>
> Urine is a pipe running the dissolution of all unheard
> messages. That's why people piss like horses at good
> parties and bad—they are getting uncouth oceanic
> messages from all over the room: come here, I want
> to fuck you; go there, I want to kill you. Whoo-ee!
> That bladder gets full of piss.[31]

The metaphorical emphasis has shifted slightly, so that
excretory images are slightly more numerous than sexual
ones, whereas in *An American Dream* the reverse was true.
Eliot Fremont-Smith makes some perceptive points about
the significance of the fact that "the rhetoric is not genital
but anal." [32] But my point is that this is nothing new in

Mailer's work, and that as old thought in a new book it is highly suspect. The issue is whether this is "courageous" writing, as Fremont-Smith suggests, or merely lazy writing. Concern with anal function in Mailer's work takes two forms: excretory and sexual. The first has been dealt with in *The Presidential Papers,* in both a short fictional fragment [33] and an interview.[34] Even earlier, in the "Prologue to a Long Novel," the scatological element was present as a complex and apparently significant metaphor. D.J. says "excrement is defeat." The very complex theory of defecation presented in the three pieces mentioned above states, to oversimplify somewhat, (1) that defecation represents the ultimate in rejection, and (2) that one's feces reflect, in their contents, our personal failures. It seems, then, that D.J.'s theories on the subject represent no major new thought on Mailer's part.

Anal intercourse, both heterosexual and homosexual, figures significantly in *An American Dream.* The latter looms particularly large in the scene between D.J. and Tex alone in the wilderness, toward the end of *Why Are We in Vietnam?* Consider the following passage, which includes the themes of simultaneous hate and love (for which Mailer is indebted to Freud); the struggle between God and the Devil and one's commitment (often unclear) to one or the other; and the capacity of the aggressive partner to assimilate the strengths of the passive one through anal intercourse. All of these elements, it should be remembered, are significantly present in parallel scenes in *An American Dream:*

> . . . and D.J. breathing that in by the wide-awake of the dark with Aurora Borealis jumping to the beat of his heart knew he could make a try to prong Tex tonight, there was a chance to get in and steal the iron from Texas' ass [35] and put it in his own and he

was hard as a hammer at the thought and ready to give off sparks and Tex was ready to fight him to death, yeah, now it was there, murder between them under all friendship, for God was a beast, not a man, and God said, "Go out and kill—fulfill my will, go and kill," and they hung there each of them on the knife of the divide in all conflict of lust to own the other yet in fear of being killed by the other and as the hour went by and lights shifted, something in the radiance of the North went into them, and owned their fear, some communion of telepathies and new powers, and they were twins, never to be near as lovers again, but killer brothers, owned by something, prince of darkness, lord of light, they did not know. . . .[36]

The question of the validity of these theories and of their effectiveness as metaphor is not at issue here. The issue is whether they are integral to the narrative voice which presents them, or merely scattered irresponsibly and self-indulgently through the book by the author. It seems reasonable that a system of perceptions originating from and characterizing a forty-three-year-old Professor of Existential Psychology who has just killed his wife cannot be accepted with equal credibility as the original thought of an eighteen-year-old Texan, no matter what degree of peculiarly American identity they may share.[37]

What sort of narrative voice is D.J.? The book jacket and some of the reviews call him a genius, and compare him to Huck Finn and Holden Caulfield. As for D.J.'s being a genius, it must be so, for he tells us himself early and often. The genius label, meant to be taken quite seriously, seems to be no more than an attempt on Mailer's part to make the many long digressions (on such topics as existentialism and mass media, as well as urine and cancer) acceptable as part of D.J.'s consciousness. It is also meant to make more credible the fantastic rate and scope of D.J.'s name dropping. This habit is, in fact, the direct source of the currently popular parallels drawn by book reviewers to Holden and Huck. For D.J. has, early in the book, suggested these earlier narrators as possibly comparable to himself, then immediately dismissed them as inferior. The tone is offensively sneering, intentionally so. For D.J., as a genius, but still a tough outdoorsman and stud who "sees through shit," can knowledgably drop a name (such as, Marshall McLuhan, Soren Kierkegaard) and dismiss it immediately with a knowing sneer at both the reader and the name.

Perhaps D.J. can afford such sneers. Mailer, as the consciousness behind the narrator (which he all too evidently is) certainly cannot. This becomes an important issue in terms of the aesthetic form of the novel. D.J. makes references to James Joyce and William Burroughs, upon the latter of which he bestows a rare approval. Mailer seems unwilling to allow either his narrator or his novel's form to stand on their own merits and themselves to elicit comparisons from critics. Instead, using a clumsy device, he suggests parallels to other novels, implying first the acceptability of this work because of its literary forbears, and then its superiority to them. The repeated mention of Burroughs serves another purpose as well. D.J. admits to being on pot, and later hints at the fact that it may be acid or horse instead. The admission that the narrative line is conditioned by marijuana, LSD or heroin would make more credible the rambling irrelevance of much of the text, but it is also suspect as an easy rationalization for a sloppy book "written in a great hurry." [38] The parallel to Burroughs has a great deal of validity, that to Joyce almost none. Mailer has taken the license granted by the stream-of-consciousness form but abandoned any pretense of economy. Because D.J.'s ideas themselves seem lifted from

An American Dream rather than proceeding as the natural outgrowth of a new narrative voice, it does not seem reasonable to assume that the unchecked narrative style is a carefully purposeful one. No matter what he would have us believe, Mailer has not retained even a semblance of the *control* which distinguishes the work of Joyce.

Besides the references to *Huckleberry Finn* and *Catcher in the Rye* and to the work of Joyce and Burroughs, I have cited certain parallels in plot and theme to particular works of Hemingway and Faulkner. Considerable stress has been laid throughout this study on the derivative quality of Mailer's early work, and the importance of his attempts to divorce himself from such influence. It is all too easy to conclude, from the sloppiness of style and form, and the use of secondhand themes and metaphors, that these literary analogues represent a return by Mailer to the easy, secure method of imitation, but without the admirable qualities of originality and careful limitation of form to be found in *The Naked and the Dead. Why Are We in Vietnam?* is lazy rather than courageous writing. Although at the time of this writing at least one reviewer [39] sees the book as praiseworthy primarily because its form is an effective vehicle for its message, precisely the opposite is true.

The most intelligent reading of *Why Are We in Vietnam?* of which I am aware at present is the article (mentioned earlier) by John W. Aldridge. Nonetheless, his is a position with which I am in substantial disagreement. Mr. Aldridge explains at the outset that Mailer draws the basis of his story line from earlier American novels, but goes on to state that the book is made fresh and effective by the use of D.J. as narrative voice. This judgment is precisely antithetical to my own, although I am in accord with many of Aldridge's perceptions about the *intended* function of D.J. in the novel. The distinction I would like to draw is this: while I agree with Aldridge that the novel succeeds or fails in proportion to the effectiveness of D.J. as its narrative voice, I feel that that voice is a failure, a cop-out rather than a breakthrough. Mr. Aldridge has succinctly and incisively struck to the heart of what Mailer intended to do in this novel; but I think he has confused intention with execution. Mailer gets credit for yardage, but no touchdown.

One aspect of the narrative voice in this novel must be discussed further: the Negro alter-ego through which D.J. periodically addresses the reader. Two passages may be necessary to make clear the nature of this other identity. These passages, although cut away from the far less relevant material which surrounds them, also provide an honest representation of the style and tone of the intro beeps. The last passage is the very end of the novel.

> Or maybe I'm a Spade and writing like a Shade. For every Spade is the Shade of the White Man, and when we die we enter their mind, we are part of the Shade. And when Spades die?—well, that depends on how you dig Niggers you white ass chiggers says D.J. Come on now, says D.J., what if I'm not the white George Hamilton rich dear son of Dallas, Texas, and Hallelujah ass but am instead black as your hole after you eat licorice and chew black cherries, what then, what if I'm some genius brain up in Harlem pretending to write a white man's fink fuck book in revenge. . . . So you can't know if I'm true-blue Wasp-ass Texas even if I know. . . .[40]

> . . . tomorrow Tex and me, we're off to see the wizard in Vietnam. Unless, that is, I'm a black-ass cripple Spade and sending from Harlem. You never know. You never know what vision has been humping you through the night. So, ass-head America con-

template your butt. Which D.J. white or black could possibly be worse of a genius if Harlem or Dallas is guiding the other, and who knows which? This is D.J., Disc Jockey to America turning off. Vietnam, hot damn.[41]

Several possible purposes are suggested by this device. The schizophrenic narrator may be seen as another reverberation of the Jekyll-Hyde motif established by the D.J.-Tex Hyde fusion. On another level, the split in D.J.'s personality may reflect the fact that the parallel issues of the war in Vietnam and the civil rights movement have polarized the country. This polarity may be even more explicitly emphasized by the antithetical political climates of D.J.'s Texas (home of the Rustys and scene of President Kennedy's assassination) and the nameless Negro's New York (with its vocal liberal establishment).

In *An American Dream*, Rojack derived much of his strength from the Negro race as represented by Shago Martin, Prince of Harlem. Insofar as D.J. is to be seen as representative of the new American generation, Mailer may be making a similar statement here. His implication may be that much of the strength and motivation of D.J.'s generation to reject the old values is to be drawn from the anger of the Negro youth. Such a parallel is reinforced by Mailer's portrait of Rusty, in which he implies (as he often has in previous works) that white bigotry has a basis in fear of the sexual supremacy of the Negro. Since D.J., too, presents a sexual threat to Rusty (particularly in the Oedipal scene mentioned above, p. 186), this may be seen as a function of his Negro (and, by implication, potent) half.

If these are Mailer's intentions, the presence of the Negro alter-ego is more than a puckish whim. But I don't think the author succeeds here in establishing reader credibility in the world of his novel. The presence of Mailer himself in the novel is, unfortunately, more palpable than that of the nameless Negro. Perhaps the most reasonable view is to see the Negro narrator as a metaphor for Mailer himself, a hip consciousness standing behind D.J., critical of Texas values and writing from New York.

In his earlier novels (particularly *The Deer Park* and *An American Dream*), Mailer compromised the ambition to write a massive, loosely controlled work by limiting himself to a more modest form in which his considerable talent could be brought effectively and powerfully to bear. In his latest novel, he seems to have forsaken both high ambition and control. Yet when one reads of the ambitious goal he set himself in *Advertisements for Myself* it is tempting to slough *Why Are We in Vietnam?* off as a temporary pause in the development of his fiction. Speaking in *Advertisements* of a projected major novel, Mailer predicts:

> . . . The book will be fired to its fuse by the rumor that once I pointed to the farthest fence and said that within ten years I would try to hit the longest ball ever to go up into the accelerated hurricane air of our American letters. For if I have one ambition above all others, it is to write a novel which Dostoyevsky and Marx; Joyce and Freud; Stendhal, Tolstoy, Proust and Spengler; Faulkner, and even old moldering Hemingway might come to read, for it would carry what they had to tell another part of the way.[42]

The ten years are almost up, and that ambitious project has not materialized. Although at the time of this writing Mailer has recouped substantial critical recognition as a result of *The Armies of the Night*, the period immediately following the publication of *Why Are We in Vietnam?*

saw critics divided in their estimates of his current worth. Perhaps the most perceptive and sane position of those set forth in the early reviews of *Why Are We in Vietnam?* is that of Granville Hicks. Hicks, too, looks back to *Advertisements for Myself* and remarks caustically and sadly upon the fact that the latest novel falls so far below the potential of Mailer's talent. He goes on to say:

> Why do we—why do I—go on bothering with Norman Mailer? Not merely because he once had talent but because he still has it. There are passages in this book that nobody else could have written—as well as passages that, I hope, nobody else would have written. . . . Mailer has grown a great deal in power of language since he wrote *The Naked and the Dead.*

•   •   •

> After the success, critical and financial, of *The Naked and the Dead,* he felt that he had been, so to speak, nominated for the presidency. He wanted to be and believed that he could be not only the best novelist of his generation but a decisive influence on generations to come. . . . If he had been able and willing to do the best he could, without worrying about being President, he might have made a contribution to American letters commensurate with his abilities.[43]

Such constructive concern with Mailer's tendency to waste his talent shows a sympathy on Hicks' part which is not paralleled by any of the other critics who recognize the novel's failure. Those publications whose political leanings favored administrative policy in Vietnam treated *Why Are We in Vietnam?* as an obscene and offensive book of no serious merit. And one New York critic evinced the most cavalier attitude of all to Mailer's work, in a review which (by several glaring factual errors bearing upon crucial elements of the plot) betrayed a blatantly careless reading of the text.

This same critic concluded his review with a statement which implied that *An American Dream* and *Why Are We in Vietnam?* were of a kind, and were both failures. Perhaps it is time that Mailer's novels were read more closely, and that a qualitative distinction were drawn between those which fail, like *Why Are We in Vietnam?* and those which succeed but pose more critical problems than most readers feel they are worth. It is my contention that *An American Dream* is a more commendable and significant novel than any other Mailer has yet written, including *The Naked and the Dead*. In it, narrative stance, metaphorical patterns and a highly personal existential vision are integrally combined to effect an artistic statement which is exceedingly relevant to the life of every thinking American.[44] It is the lack of such integration upon which the failure of *Why Are We in Vietnam?* ultimately rests. Although the latter novel's political message is a valid and justly well-received one, its artistic value is small. Its system of metaphor is too little changed from that in *An American Dream* to be rendered integral to its entirely different fictional situation and narrator.

Mailer has admitted the considerable difficulty which point of view caused him in the early novels. The achievement of considerable control over a first person narrator (and concomitantly over a formal structure integral to him) in *An American Dream* seemed to imply that he had overcome this problem. But narrative voice and structural form in *Why Are We in Vietnam?* are clumsy and not credibly linked. Nevertheless, this novel represents no more than a momentary lapse in Mailer's progress. The two works of nonfiction which immediately follow it, *The Armies of the Night* and *Miami and the Siege of Chicago,* are highly controlled narratives, structured much like novels. These books are very much an outgrowth of Mailer's fiction, but they are also largely influenced by his earlier nonfiction works; and it is these to which we must first turn if we are fully to appreciate the significance of Mailer's most recent work.

Notes

1 Norman Mailer, *Why Are We in Vietnam?* (New York: G. P Putnam's Sons, 1967), jacket flap.
2 Eliot Fremont-Smith, "Norman Mailer's Cherry Pie," *The New York Times,* CXVI (September 8, 1967), p. 37.
3 *Ibid.*
4 *Why Are We in Vietnam?*, p. 208.
5 This book is significantly rife with parallels and references to the works of other authors.
6 *Why Are We in Vietnam?*, p. 62.
7 *Ibid.,* p. 65.
8 *Ibid.,* p. 60.
9 *Ibid.,* p. 46.
10 *Ibid.,* pp. 106–107.
11 *Ibid.,* p. 121.
12 *Ibid.*
13 *Ibid.,* p. 99.
14 *Ibid.,* pp. 145–147.
15 *Ibid.,* p. 204.
16 *Ibid.,* p. 49.
17 Fremont-Smith, work cited above.
18 *Why Are We in Vietnam?*, p. 208.
19 *Ibid.,* pp. 179–180.
20 Norman Mailer, *The Armies of the Night* (New York: The New American Library, 1968), p. 47.
21 *Ibid.,* p. 79.
22 *Ibid.,* p. 201.
23 *Ibid.,* p. 49.
24 John W. Aldridge, "From Vietnam to Obscenity," *Harper's Magazine,* 236 (February, 1968), 97.
25 *Why Are We in Vietnam?*, p. 204.
26 *Ibid.,* p. 203.
27 *The Armies of the Night,* p. 114.
28 *Why Are We in Vietnam?*, p. 203.

29 Samuel Holland Hux, "American Myth and Existential Vision: The Indigenous Existentialism of Mailer, Bellow, Styron and Ellison" p. 210.

30 *Why Are We in Vietnam?*, p. 156.

31 *Ibid.*, p. 151.

32 Fremont-Smith, work cited above.

33 Norman Mailer, *The Presidential Papers* (New York: G. P. Putnam's Sons, 1963), p. 271.

34 *Ibid.*, p. 277.

35 Not only does Tex's last name, Hyde, complement D.J.'s Dr. Jekyll, but his first name, in the context quoted here, seems to imply that he is the incarnation of the state of Texas, from which D.J. hopes to draw strength ("steal the iron").

36 *Why Are We in Vietnam?*, pp. 203–204.

37 In fairness, I must quote a remark from *Armies of the Night* which may bear upon this (p. 9):

> Mailer had never had a particular age—he carried different ages with him like different models of his experience: parts of him were eighty-one years old, fifty-seven, forty-eight, thirty-six, *nineteen*, etcetera [My italics].

D.J. may very well be a valid representative, to Mailer, of the teen-aged part of his mind. This may help us understand why Mailer chose this narrator, but I don't think it makes D.J. any more credible or integral to the metaphorical patterns of the novel.

38 Quoted by Eliot Fremont-Smith (see quotation above, p. 180). Mailer makes a further point of the fact that the book was written in four months in his interview with himself which accompanies the review of the novel in *The New York Times Book Review*, September 17, 1967. Although this seems offered as an apology for the novel, the author states in the same interview that it is "certainly the 200 pages least alienated from genius" of all his work; and later, "I do not know if I love the new novel or am indifferent to it." Ultimately, of course, the book's worth must be determined by a study of the text itself, but the author's own apparent vascillation in his feeling for it may be symptomatic of the uneven quality of the work: the discrepancy between the valid political statement it makes and the less valid formal structure which carries it.

39 Jack Kroll, "The Scrambler," *Newsweek*, LXX (September 18, 1967), 100–101.

40 *Why Are We in Vietnam?*, p. 26.

41 *Ibid.*, p. 208.

42 *Advertisements for Myself* (New York: G. P. Putnam's Sons, 1959), p. 477.

[43] Granville Hicks, "Lark in Race for Presidency," *Saturday Review*, L (September 16, 1967), 40.

[44] It must be admitted that even Granville Hicks, in the excellent review quoted above, refers to *An American Dream* as "an absurd and badly written book," and states that Mailer prefers "to describe the novel as a potboiler." Nonetheless, in his interview with himself (dealt with above) Mailer says:

> I did *An American Dream* in installments because I was in debt and had to make a small fortune in a hurry. That didn't make it a bad book. I think it's my best book. I confess I still believe sentence for sentence *An American Dream* is one of the better written books in the language.

6

Deaths for the Ladies and Other Disasters

When Mailer is good he can be very good, and when he is bad there is no one worse. But it must be said that the most dismal failures of his art proceed from the same persistent motivation: the desire to go beyond what he has already achieved, into unexplored regions of his talent. Thus, in his refusal to remain static, he may desert a successful formula only to fail, as in *Barbary Shore* or *Why Are We in Vietnam?;* or he may succeed in his experiment, as in *An American Dream.*

Similarly, Mailer has made periodic excursions into other genres, and here, too, his failures glare garishly enough to obscure his successes. Within the province of fiction, he has accomplished little with the short story, that traditional laboratory and financial supplement of the novelist.[1] In the drama, on the other hand, he has been relatively successful. The play version of *The Deer Park* (which I saw on March 3, 1967) is not great literature, but it is substantial, entertaining theater; and it earned a reasonably sympathetic critical reception. Lately, Mailer has turned his hand to making movies. His first film, "Wild 90," is embarrassingly bad. It is a tedious story of three criminals in a hideout, which I found difficult to sit through. The second movie, "Beyond the Law," which I have not yet seen, has been better received by some critics, and cannot help but be an improvement over "Wild 90." Mailer's third movie, "Maidstone," which has not yet been released at the time of this writing, has already attracted considerable attention because of the bizarre, party-like circumstances under which it was shot.[2] Since each of these movies features Mailer as star, as well as producer and director, his cinematic efforts increase still further the considerable influence which his flamboyant personality exerts upon the public's conception of him. (The relation between this public image and the critical reception of his books will be discussed in my next chapter.) Whether or not Mailer's later movies achieve any real artistic stature, they do represent some sense of serious experimentation on his part, one which is underlined by the substantial investment (both in finances and reputation) which he has made in them.

The most painful disappointment to someone interested in Mailer's work (but who does not wish to assume the role of Mailer apologist) is his poetry. Almost every poem Mailer has ever written appears in a volume entitled *Deaths for the Ladies and Other Disasters*,[3] although many of these poems and a few new ones are sprinkled through the nonfiction collections, and one or two are worked into *The Deer Park* (N) and *An American Dream*.

Deaths for the Ladies is one book which it appears Mailer was more foolhardy than brave to publish, for there is no significant literary merit anywhere in it. The few worthwhile poems which are included are not worthy of an entire volume, and most of the pieces are not worthy of the entire page which each occupies. It is certain that

no major American publishing house would have considered the book without the benefit of Mailer's name to
help sell it. Nonetheless, it is unfortunate that the book
is pejoratively associated with Mailer's reputation but not
usually associated with his other work; for it is only in
the context of the entire body of his writing that the
poetry assumes any interest. Just as *An American Dream*
(which may seem at first to some readers a sloppy, self-
indulgent fantasy) appears clearer in purpose and execution when read in light of what precedes it, *Deaths for
the Ladies* is largely incomprehensible without extensive
reading in Mailer's prose. But unlike *An American Dream*,
it cannot be justified as a significant book even after
careful study has unearthed some coherence in the patterns
it presents.

For what it is or isn't worth, the book is conceived
as a whole, an intention which is partially implemented
by the device of omitting any pagination.[4] Refrains and
echoes of early pages reappear later in the book, suggesting
that Mailer is attempting to erect and reinforce a structure
from his grab-bag of minor perceptions, epigrams, and
personal horrors. In order not to overemphasize the very
limited extent to which this attempt is successful, I would
first like to establish some perspective by quoting a few of
the more precious poems. (Mailer calls them "short hairs.")

A few attempt to explain the nature of the book itself,
as:

> The art of
>   the
>   short hair
>   is that
>   it
>   don't
>   go on
>   for
>   too long.

And:

> This is
> genteel
> poetry.
> One thought
> at a time.

But the clearest insight into the form of this poetry and into Mailer's own attitude toward its publication comes from this poem:

A writer who
has power
should use it
to extract
such benefits
from his
publisher

     as
   give
        his
   words

    room

to

    breathe

   I
     w
      a
       n
        t
         m
          y
           l
           i
           n
           e
           t
           o
             s
              t
              r
             i
              k
               e
                l   e
                i   k
                k   a
                e   n
                  a   s

              A s n a k e
              can't strike
              in a box

The poem suggests that Mailer is waggishly aware of the
fact that it is the power of his name rather than the
merit of his poetry which has persuaded the publisher to
allow him *carte blanche* in presenting this material. This
poem is also a good example of Mailer's derivative use of
the devices of other poets. On the next page, he acknowl-
edges the influence of E.E. Cummings evident here:

```
         you  break
         up your
          line
          like
             ee
             cum
               mings
       I  notice


             n
   o  heb      re   a
   ksitu       pd
         iffe
         r
         e
         nt

     •        •        •

                       r)


                     ette
```

            besi desh e'sb

And on the following page, within his own poem, he
italicizes this echo of Wallace Stevens:

> *the emperor is the*
> *emperor of ice cream*

Other literary influences are advertised as well. For example, Mailer uses a quotation from T.S. Eliot as an epigraph to a poem and dedicates two "wanderings in prose" to Hemingway. The latter are highly personal and rather poignant pieces about Mailer's own life. And in "Farewell to Arms Revisited," Mailer deals wittily with how Catherine and Frederick Henry would feel had they been married for twelve years.

Some of the individual poems are interesting in themselves, worth a chuckle or a wince:

Cheerleader

She
went to
Southern
Baptist
U
but
somehow
she nev-
er did
find out
who
John
the Bap-
tist was.

•   •   •

Definition of a Hero:

He
thrives
in
dikes.

•   •   •

Exodus

goodbye America,
    Jesus said.
Come back, *boy!* [5]
    we cried
    too late.

•   •   •

        If
Harry Golden
is the gentile's
Jew
    can I be-
come the Golden
Goy?

•   •   •

Men
who are not
    married
    and grow beards
    are insecure,
    said the CIA
    before
    it went
    to Cuba.

The most serious artistic attempt which Mailer seems to be making in this uneven book is to present the entire volume as one continuing experience. The device upon which this attempt at structure and continuity rests is the use of fugue-like repetitions from one part of the book to another. One of these provides a particularly good example of the way in which repetition establishes and reinforces a thematic statement:

> doing the limbo bit
> doing the limbo bit
>   it's good enough
>   for me

This bit of doggerel, taken from a popular song, appears several times, at intervals. Two primary associations occur immediately, and are reinforced by the monotony of repetition. First, the obvious derivation of the poem from a particularly mindless example of popular entertainment implies that our popular culture is tasteless and without meaning. Secondly, the speaker, in "doing the limbo bit," is saying in popular parlance that he is in a limbo (although the song itself means literally that he is doing the dance called the limbo). Both of these associations are encompassed by the intentional irony of the last line, "it's good enough for me," in which the speaker makes it clear that he is quite willing to accept the status quo of a personal limbo within a vacuous society.

Within the structure established by such repetitions, Mailer introduces a number of themes to which he returns throughout the book. One of these is the metaphor of cancer (already dealt with above in terms of the novels), which is viewed in a number of contexts, as:

> Cancer Gulch
>
> What's
>   he got?
>
> (Made
>   a little
>   money
> Lost
>   a little
>   love)
>
> Miami.

Cancer has been shown previously to be a metaphor of particular importance to Mailer, one which recurs throughout his work. And the title, "Cancer Gulch," is a favorite Mailer term for the geographical or mental situations in America which are most artificial, most antipathetic to true emotion. Thus, the playland of Miami comes to represent the false, materialistic values of those who visit it, and by implication, those of most Americans. Other poems about cancer include:

Circumcision

They say
  that
  women
  don't get
  cancer
  of the
  cervix
  as much
  from Jewish
    men.

They don't.

They give
    it
    to
    Jewish
      men.

and:

Cancer
is growing
ivy
professor
which   spreads
like college

and:

> You have
> so many
> poems
> about
> cancer.
>
> It's me.
> or
> my readers.

The first of these poems ties into several other thematic patterns in the book. It reinforces Mailer's usual theory that cancer comes from stifled emotion; it provides another in a series of perceptions about the sexual identity problems of Jewish males (an issue dealt with more here than in any other of Mailer's books, despite the fact that he is himself Jewish); and it is related to the theme of disappointment in marriage which informs many of the poems. The other cancer poems quoted above further emphasize Mailer's contention that every aspect of American culture (even the academy) and most of the populace are touched by the cancer of stagnance and falsity.

If the numerous themes treated briefly (and sometimes rather superficially) by Mailer in this book are obviously representative of his cerebral preoccupations in the early nineteen-sixties, it should be no surprise that many of them correspond to those which govern *An American Dream*, which Mailer was to write two years later. Actually, this book might serve as a companion volume to *An American Dream* (although the juxtaposition certainly would not do Mailer's reputation any good in those quarters where the novel was badly received). Not only does the poetry reveal Mailer's earlier concern with themes and metaphors which appear in *An American Dream*, but sometimes actual plot situations are previewed, such as:

                              One
                               nerve
                              screams
                              before
                               you
                                fall
                               said
                                the
                               ledge
                                 on
                                the
                              window
                                 in
                                the
                             nineteenth
                               floor
and:

                           something
                           about
                           the
                           smell
                           of a cop
                           when he's
                           groping
                           you

And even Rojack's note to Cherry upon leaving her asleep
appears first here:

                           Hey—
                              you
                               sleep
                               deep—
                             but what a sight
                               see
                               you
                                 soon
                               beautiful
                               I hope

Other themes and metaphors in the poetry which figure in Mailer's prose works include witches, cannibals, urine, and the smell of corporation. But the most effective development of a theme within a single poem occurs at the end of *Deaths for the Ladies,* in the long poem entitled "The Inaugural Ball."

1.

There was a time
    when fornication
    was titanic
and the Devil
    had to work
    to cheat a womb.

    (pride of his teeth
      on a root
      long enough
        to
      pluck it out
      the green wet sea
      of the pussy slue
      and down a falling
        flight
      of cellar stairs
      hard, dark, deep
      into the maiden brown
      rooting out the bowels
      which fell
      like assassins
        upon the white foam
        of God's arrow)

•   •   •

3.

But now the devil
        smokes a cigar
        and has his nose
        up U.S. Phar-
        maceutical
The assassins
        who fall on God's
        white arrow
        give off the fumes
        of chemical
        killer bedded
        in vaseline
        as heroic
        in its odor
        as the exhaust
        which comes off a
        New York City
        Transportation
        System Bus.

There is more to the poem, but this will suffice. The first
section quoted above presents in abstract form the bedroom scene between Rojack and Ruta in *An American
Dream,* and the central metaphor established by that scene:
the conflict between God and the Devil as represented in
the choice between Ruta's two orifices. The second excerpt
carries the idea further, by implying that the American
experience, conditioned by the influence of mass tech-
nology has further stacked the odds against the victory of
the fertile forces of God. In the fourth and final section
of this poem, Mailer looks to the future, hoping that the
contest will once again become an equal one. The central
metaphor is effectively developed here, perhaps better than
in any other of his poems. Yet the idea is much more

precisely and effectively given literary form in the Ruta passage of *An American Dream*. And this is a judgment which I feel extends to all Mailer's poetry. *Deaths for the Ladies and Other Disasters* is a strange and uneven book, sometimes witty, often merely cute. But even in its better aspects, the few good individual poems and Mailer's intention to make the book one cumulative experience, the experiment falls far short of the achievement of Mailer's prose. It is certainly less than one would like to expect from him.

Notes

1 All of Mailer's short fiction to date has been issued in a recent paperback collection: *The Short Fiction of Norman Mailer* (New York: Dell Publishing Company, 1967). This edition offers almost nothing that has not already been published in the three non-fiction collections, but the short introduction by Mailer is of some interest. In it, among other things, he reiterates his feeling that the short story is a form inferior to the novel (p. 9):

> The short story bores him [Mailer] a little. . . . he rarely reads them. He is, in secret, not fond of writers who work at short stories . . . he thinks the short story is relatively easy to write. You only have to be good for a day or a week. . . .

2 For a sense of those circumstances, see James Toback, "At Play in the Fields of the Bored," *Esquire,* December 1968, pp. 150–155.

3 New York: G. P. Putnam's Sons, 1962.

4 Where it seems relevant, it will be made clear whether a poem precedes or follows another, or whether it appears early or late in the book.

5 The emphasis on the italicized word *boy,* the traditional Southern term of address for a Negro, makes plain Mailer's condemnation of American arrogance and moral blindness.

7

Advertisements for Myself, The Presidential Papers, and *Cannibals and Christians*

Advertisements for Myself (1959), *The Presidential Papers* (1963), and *Cannibals and Christians* (1966) have been referred to in earlier chapters when they provided material directly relevant to Mailer's novels. They are also significant as stages in the development of Mailer's non-fiction voice, which is to reach its finest expression to date in *The Armies of the Night* (1968).

Advertisements for Myself, the richest and most varied in content of the three, is also the most interesting in that it provides direct insights into the state of Mailer's mind in the late 1950's. The "advertisements" themselves treat personal experience with candor and perception reminiscent of Fitzgerald's "The Crack-Up." And the situation in which Mailer found himself at the time is parallel to that of Fitzgerald in his slump. Early in the book, he tells us:

I've burned away too much of my creative energy. . . . I may have fatigued the earth of rich language beyond repair. . . . There may have been too many

fights for me, too much sex, liquor, marijuana, benze-
drine and seconal. . . .[1]

This is a painfully candid admission for a thirty-five-year-
old writer who has, a few pages earlier, confided the
enormous extent of his ambition:

> The sour truth is that I am imprisoned with a percep-
> tion which will settle for nothing less than making a
> revolution in the consciousness of our time.[2]

This is a book, then, not of ambitions unfulfilled, but of
ambitions yet to be attained. Just as Fitzgerald was to go
on to a new affirmation of his talent in *The Last Tycoon,*
Mailer was eventually to go beyond the fragmentary state
of his work in 1959 to new and valid artistic forms.
Advertisements for Myself serves an important function
in the drive toward those later works. Mailer remarks, in
"A Note to the Reader," that "one of the purposes of this
collection is the intention to clear the ground for [his
next] novel." [3] The process of establishing an ordered
form within which to present the various pieces which
make up *Advertisements* was a project intended to provide
Mailer with a clearer view of what he had done and what
he wished yet to do in his writing. It provides the reader
with an insight into Mailer's artistic intentions. But something else is given concrete form here: the flamboyant
public image which, since the publication of *The Naked
and the Dead,* had served to spotlight Mailer's career, and
which tended (and still does) to obscure rather than eluci-
date the literary value and intentions of his work. Perhaps
no writer since Hemingway has had a public image so
attractive or repulsive to so many people, and so unfortunately influential in the critical reception of his fiction.
To an extent, this notoriety was forced upon Mailer after

the publication of *The Naked and the Dead,* as he laments
in *Advertisements:*

> . . . from now on, people who knew me would never
> be able to react to me as a person whom they liked
> or disliked in small ways, *for myself alone* (the inevi-
> table phrase of all tear-filled confessions); no, I was
> a node in a new electronic landscape of celebrity,
> personality and status. . . . I had been moved from
> the audience to the stage. . . .[4]

But to a greater extent, it is clear, Mailer lived and wrote
in such a manner as to create a public personality characterized by excesses. Within *Advertisements for Myself,*
we get a view of these excesses telescoped together like a
two-hour movie of a man's life. Thus, within a few pages,
Mailer can both affirm the enormity of his ambition and
confess his fears that he may already have burned out his
talent. Later in the book, he makes clear why he feels it
worthwhile to risk the death of his talent in the gamble to
increase it through deeper self-knowledge:

> . . . in admiration for Hemingway's strength and
> with distaste for his weaknesses, I was one of the few
> writers of my generation who was concerned with
> living in Hemingway's discipline, by which I do not
> mean I was interested in trying for some second-rate
> imitation of the style, but rather that I shared with
> Papa the notion, arrived at slowly in my case, that
> even if one dulled one's talent in the punishment of
> becoming a man, it was more important to be a man
> than a very good writer, that probably I could not
> become a very good writer unless I learned first how
> to keep my nerve. . . .[5]

After *The Deer Park,* Mailer was at an impasse in
his struggle to become a man and a writer. Ridden with

doubts at his failure in the decade following *The Naked and the Dead* to write the great novel he still aspired to, befuddled by his own confused mind and the drugs he had used to explore it, he found himself unable to write at all:

> . . . I could not write; my mind would have fine moments, but its powers of connection were dim; my brain seemed stuffed in cotton.
> It was the first pause I had had in years, and it seemed to me that I was punch-drunk. In company I felt stupid. . . . I began to live with the conviction that I had burned out my talent.[6]

It was under these circumstances that the events which prompted Mailer to write "The White Negro" occurred. Encouraged by Lyle Stuart, Mailer wrote a few paragraphs about his theory that the integration problem in the South had as its basis the white man's fear of the sexual potency of the Negro. The piece was printed in Stuart's monthly newspaper, and copies sent to a number of people, including William Faulkner, who dismissed it with a short note which ridiculed Mailer. Despite the fact that he answered with arrogance, Mailer was disturbed, and this led to the writing of "The White Negro."

> . . . I had been dismissed by a novelist who was to me a great writer, and in reflection from the ice of his few lines had been cast the light of how I would properly be seen if I could not flesh the bold loud air of my pronouncements with writing better than I had so far done. Like a latent image in the mirror of my ego was the other character Faulkner must have seen: a noisy pushy middling ape who had been tolerated too long by his literary betters. So I owe Faulkner the Biblical act of banishing me. Fearful of consequence,

I had at last no choice but to begin the trip into the psychic wild of "The White Negro." [7]

If *Advertisements for Myself* lies at the heart of the development of Mailer's ideas between the 1950's and the 1960's, "The White Negro" is indisputably the heart of *Advertisements*. As has been stated at the outset of this book, "The White Negro" begins with a more sophisticated and more clearly articulated statement of a theme which Mailer rendered well in *The Naked and the Dead:* that after the Second World War man was forced to look at his society and to recognize not only that it was a sick and perverted one, but that something in each of us was responsible for its creation, and thus that we were sick as well. In a world which reeked of totalitarianism (which, Mailer maintains, was by no means totally destroyed in the war), each man must choose whether to die a slow and anonymous death at the altar of conformity or to strike out into a bold search for individual selfhood:

> A totalitarian society makes enormous demands on the courage of men, and a partially totalitarian society makes even greater demands, for the general anxiety is greater. Indeed if one is to be a man, almost any kind of unconventional action often takes disproportionate courage.[8]

He goes on to state that the reason the Negro is the source of Hip is that he "has been living on the margin between totalitarianism and democracy for two centuries." [9] The resultant life style of the Negro, the functional paranoia which enables him to survive and commits him to the present more than the future, have been adopted by the American existentialist, the hipster or White Negro.

Certainly Mailer cerebrates so intensely that he goes

far beyond the intuitive values of the hipster. In "The White Negro," he articulates a series of nice distinctions which clarify precisely the nature and limits of his own existential philosophy, one which shares certain basic assumptions with other thinkers but which, in its entirety is unique to Mailer. His basic premise is that one must combat totalitarianism by a commitment to constant growth through experience. The threat of totalitarianism is not merely an external one, but internal as well. At the same time that he must guard against the deadening of his individuality by the pressure exerted by a conformist society, the existentialist must beware of becoming static himself, of commiting himself *permanently* to any idea or habit which is momentarily valid, and thus becoming, himself, totalitarian. The key idea is that the existentialist must be always dynamic, and that he must *act* in order to develop, rather than accept experience passively.

Mailer draws a clear distinction between the atheistic existentialist and the mystic, and himself embraces the values of the latter. The central difference lies in the attitude towards death. Where the atheist rejects any appreciation of the proximity of death because he refuses to romanticize it, the mystic sees the awareness of the presence of death as a meaningful experience.

> . . . the mystic is the one finally who has chosen to live with death. . . . His inner experience of the possibilities within death is his logic. So, too, for the existentialist. And the psychopath. And the saint and the bullfighter and the lover. The common denominator for all of them is their burning consciousness which the possibilities within death has opened for them. There is a depth of desperation to the condition which enables one to remain in life only by engaging death, but the reward is their knowledge that what is happening at each instant of the electric present is

good or bad for them, good or bad for their cause, their love, their action, their need.[10]

Certainly this concept is recognizable as one of the primary motivations which inform the character of Rojack in *An American Dream,* as he makes repeated excursions to the edge of death in the attempt to define himself and to grow as a man.

Another distinction which Mailer goes to great lengths to draw is that between the psychotic and the psychopath. The latter term is very definitely not a pejorative one to Mailer, since he feels that the American existentialist is, by the very nature of his commitment to his own needs and his rejection of societal restrictions a "philosophical psychopath." Further, this is a condition which must be maintained by the White Negro if he is to survive as an individual. The concept of the psychopathic state as a positive good ties in with Mailer's idea of himself as a "psychic outlaw," [11] and certainly Rojack assumes this role.

Because Mailer considers the term *psychopath* so central to his definition of the White Negro, and because his understanding of it can be so easily misapprehended when removed from the sophisticated context within which he uses it, the salient points of his definition should be presented:

It may be fruitful to consider the hipster a philosophical psychopath, a man interested not only in the dangerous imperatives of his psychopathy but in codifying, at least for himself, the suppositions on which his inner universe is constructed. By this premise the hipster is a psychopath, and yet not a psychopath but the negation of the psychopath, for he possesses the narcissistic detachment of the philosopher, . . . extrapolates from his own condition, from the inner certainty that his rebellion is just, a

radical vision of the universe which thus separates
him from the general ignorance, reactionary prejudice, and self-doubt of the more conventional psychopath.

•   •   •

Before one can say more about the hipster, there
is obviously much to be said about the psychic state
of the psychopath—or, clinically, the psychopathic
personality. Now, for reasons which may be more
curious than the similarity of the words, even many
people with psychoanalytical orientation often confuse
the psychopath with the psychotic. Yet the terms are
polar. The psychotic is legally insane, the psychopath
is not; the psychotic is almost always incapable of
discharging in physical acts the rage of his frustration,
while the psychopath at his extreme is virtually as
incapable of restraining his violence.[12]

Mailer goes on to show that while the psychotic may move
in and out of his insane state, the psychopath maintains
a constant, long-term, antisocial attitude and is not characterized by the hallucinations and other dramatic symptoms
displayed by the psychotic. The distinction, then, is one
of rationality and of voluntary choice. That is, the psychopath is a sane man, living rationally in the real world,
but motivated by an antisocial attitude. The "philosophical psychopath," Mailer's White Negro, goes a step beyond
the more conventional psychopath, whose selfish needs are
pursued in an antisocial but socially conditioned (hence
rather trite—almost conventional) manner (such as rape).
Rather, the hipster's actions are motivated by a conscious
desire to "codify . . . the suppositions on which his inner
universe is constructed." While his actions are not always
rational (he is "incapable of restraining his violence"), the
underlying philosophy which informs and encourages them

very definitely is. He may not be able or willing to control his psychopathic state, but he does wish to understand it. Although it is not socially acceptable, it forms for him a personal "inner universe"; a dynamic system of values to which he subscribes in place of externally imposed societal values. Thus, Mailer himself and his more recent fictional protagonists, Rojack and D.J., attempt to establish their own inner worlds, by means of which they can survive on the outskirts of society.

The idea that "the psychopath at his extreme is virtually . . . incapable of restraining his violence" makes it clear that Rojack's murder of his wife is intended by Mailer as more than a mere expression of desperate rage. It is the index of his psychopathic state, one which Rojack must struggle to understand through seeking further dynamic experiences, no matter how fearful. Rather than take the easier path of allowing society to define him within its terms by confessing his guilt and accepting society's evaluation of him, its prescribed punishment, and, implicitly, its forgiveness, Rojack elects to take the frightening trip into his own soul and to come to terms with his psychopathic state by defining it in his own terms.

At the beginning of *An American Dream*, Rojack is not particularly courageous, nor does he have a clear idea of the state of his own psyche. What is it that prompts him, after some vacillation, to avoid societal judgment after the murder? Perhaps the answer lies here:

> The strength of the psychopath is that he knows (where most of us can only guess) what is good for him and what is bad for him at exactly those instants when an old crippling habit has become so attacked by experience that the potentiality exists to change it, to replace a negative and empty fear with an outward action, even if . . . the action is to murder.

> The psychopath murders—if he has the courage—out
> of the necessity to purge his violence, for if he cannot
> empty his hatred then he cannot love, his being is
> frozen with implacable self-hatred for his cowardice.[13]

As a psychopath, then, Rojack murders Deborah because
he has reached one of those crucial points to which Mailer
refers. Afraid and empty, tied to the habit of Deborah
and reduced by her power over him to a passive and
negative life which he is on the verge of ending, he
instinctively *acts,* and thus begins to change his life. And
it is this act of murder which, as Mailer has prescribed,
purges his violence and hatred and unfreezes his being
so that he can love Cherry. The very act of murder gives
him the added courage he needs to lie to the police, and
thus to commit himself to the series of further actions
which will lead him to self-knowledge and salvation.

The series of confrontations with hostile people which
is the means by which Rojack grows in strength and
understanding has been dealt with at length earlier. But
some further understanding of how central such a path
of development is to Mailer's view of life (and of how
long he has felt thus) may be gained by his statement in
"The White Negro" that:

> . . . life is a contest between people in which the
> victor generally recuperates quickly and the loser takes
> long to mend, a perpetual competition of colliding
> explorers in which one must grow or else pay more
> for remaining the same (pay in sickness, or depres-
> sion, or anguish for the lost opportunity) but pay or
> grow.[14]

Rojack is the victor in a series of crucial collisions with
other people, and this is why he grows throughout *An
American Dream* and emerges as a whole man. But the

most recent of Mailer's books will show that he has not developed this view of human conflict only in his fiction; it is applicable to his own life as well. In *The Armies of the Night,* Mailer, as narrator and protagonist, will be shown to undergo a series of confrontations with other people and with his own fears which parallels that of Rojack.

I have emphasized earlier that Rojack's greatest strength grows out of his love for Cherry, a love characterized by a fertile sexuality which is described in heavenly terms. The idea of "good" sex as an ideal to be sought by the existentialist figures in "The White Negro"; and since Mailer's emphasis on this ideal has been attacked by some critics,[15] it may be fair to quote his statement:

> At bottom, the drama of the psychopath is that he seeks love. Not love as the search for a mate, but love as the search for an orgasm more apocalyptic than the one which preceded it. Orgasm is his therapy—he knows at the seed of his being that good orgasm opens his possibilities and bad orgasm imprisons him.[16]

Mailer goes on to stipulate further that the hipster must "find his courage at the moment of violence or equally make it in the act of love." [17] This is the "good time" of which Sergius speaks at the conclusion of *The Deer Park* (N) as the source for new hope in human life. The concept is more clearly defined in "The White Negro" than it was in *The Deer Park,* but even here it is only the embryo of the far more hopeful idea which takes form in *An American Dream:* that the good time and the good orgasm are only momentary goals which are transcended by the passion and fertility of a courageously selfless love. Thus it is clear that while many of the themes Mailer develops in *An American Dream* are the direct products of his defini-

tion of the American existentialist in "The White Negro,"
he has continued to develop and refine his personal philosophy. The mature statement of *An American Dream*
that love for one mate can represent the greatest single
positive hope for the individual brave enough to earn it,
is a significant departure from the more cynical theory of
the apocalyptic orgasm expressed in "The White Negro."

It has repeatedly been emphasized here that Mailer's
psychopath/existentialist/hipster is antisocial and selfish
in his actions and aims. Stephen Richards Rojack, a somewhat more mature version of the White Negro, has been
held up as an example of Mailer's hope that the individual
can survive in a corrupt and hostile society; but *An
American Dream* criticizes that society without holding
out any hope for its improvement. Perhaps a muted note
of optimism may be seen towards the end of "The White
Negro," when Mailer states candidly that although the
hipster, bent on releasing his hatred and violence, could
easily be an elite storm trooper, it is as probable that he
might recognize the necessity to work for all men's freedom
in order to gain his own:

> . . . given the desperation of his condition as a
> psychic outlaw, the hipster is equally a candidate for
> the most reactionary and most radical of movements,
> and so it is just as possible that many hipsters will
> come—if the crisis deepens—to a radical comprehen-
> sion of the horror of society . . . may yet come to
> an equally bitter comprehension of the slow relentless
> inhumanity of the conservative power which controls
> him from without and from within. And in being so
> controlled, denied and starved into the attrition of
> conformity, indeed the hipster may come to see that
> his condition is no more than an exaggeration of the
> human condition, and if he would be free, then every-
> one must be free.[18]

The crisis in individual freedom of which Mailer wrote in 1957 is primarily represented by the plight of the Negro. That crisis has deepened, and Mailer has continued to speak out for individual human rights. But an additional crisis besets us today, in the division of America over the war in Vietnam. In the context of his statements about personal growth through the expression of violence, Mailer states in "The White Negro" that ". . . individual acts of violence are always to be preferred to the collective violence of the state. . . ." [19] Mailer's theories of violence are applied fictionally to the psyche of the American male in *Why Are We in Vietnam?* (in which he suggests that the personal need for violence, usually stifled by society, has been turned by that society to the more socially acceptable arena of war).

Each of these issues is to be dealt with at length in *The Armies of the Night,* a book which comprises an informed and sophisticated analysis of the state of American society in 1968. The narrator/protagonist is Mailer himself, a voice who articulately clarifies national problems within the context of his own theories (of violence, freedom, totalitarianism) and a character who personally faces a series of crises which help him to grow dynamically. The Mailer of *The Armies of the Night* is not a hipster. Like Rojack, he lives by the code of the White Negro, but does so within a somewhat more mature and sophisticated life style. But unlike Rojack, he does not merely survive the experience of American society and then leave. Rather, he takes the step of personal involvement, in the desire to effect a change in that society. Recognizing as he felt the hipster might, that "if he would be free, then everyone must be free," Mailer continues to cerebrate and to act in his own behalf; but he chooses to act on behalf of his fellow citizens as well, and in so doing ties his own destiny to that of his society. It may be, then, that hope for the individual means hope for society as well.

"The White Negro" is a piece which is central to the abiding moral and intellectual values which inform all of Mailer's work. Its significance looms still larger when it is considered in conjunction with the works which follow it, especially *An American Dream* and *The Armies of the Night*. These books are important because they embody the structured morality by which one man lives. *An American Dream* does so in the experiences of a man who is one of Mailer's most successful creations; and *The Armies of the Night* goes beyond this to use Mailer's own experience without the shield of fictional distance. What is important is that this philosopher, Mailer, does not present a theory through abstractions which are reinforced only by generalized analogies to human life. Rather, he *realizes* his theories in his own life and performs the difficult and courageous feat of articulating both the act and the abstraction to his reader. The man of action and the philosopher become one.

"The White Negro" shows Mailer as a contemporary existential philosopher. *The Presidential Papers* is the application of his philosophy to topical situations. What is most immediately striking about this book is Mailer's repeated application of the term *existential* to aspects of the Kennedy administration. He writes of "existential legislation," and describes John F. Kennedy and his wife as existential hero and heroine. Mailer does not, in this book, express unqualified admiration for the Kennedys. What he does admire greatly is a dynamic quality in the personal style of President Kennedy and his wife.

The existential element which Mailer saw as a major hope for the nation in Kennedy's leadership was a capacity for dynamic action combined with humanistic compassion. Possibly the clearest expression of Mailer's view of John

F. Kennedy at its most hopeful is in a short story entitled "The Last Night," printed in *Cannibals and Christians*. The central character of the story is an American President, "perhaps not only the most brilliant but the most democratic of American Presidents," [20] faced with the massive moral responsibility of preserving a segment of humanity as the end of the world approaches. The story is one of courage and tormented decision, and finally of hope, for the President possesses the moral insight to make the right choice, the strength to act decisively, and the charisma to succeed "in engaging the imagination of the world's citizens with his project," [21] a project which calls for the cooperation of all of humanity in sacrificing themselves to save a small representative group of survivors.

In his introductory remarks to this story, Mailer explains that:

> The story was written in 1962, therefore was written with the idea of a President not altogether different from John F. Kennedy. L.B.J., needless to say, is altogether different.[22]

This difference is the central difference between Mailer's political writings in *The Presidential Papers* and those in *Cannibals and Christians*.

If Mailer was critical of certain aspects of the Kennedy administration in the former book, it was always criticism infused with the hope of helping to stimulate progressive action. But the more hostile tone of Mailer's attitude toward the Johnson administration in *Cannibals and Christians* is set as early as the dedication to that book, which reads:

> To Lyndon B. Johnson whose name inspired young men to cheer for me in public.[23]

The sardonic reference is to a speech Mailer made in Berkeley, California in May, 1965, opposing Johnson's Vietnam policy.

The President in "The Last Night" (and, by implication, John F. Kennedy) is portrayed by Mailer as a man constantly concerned with the question of whether his decisions and actions are good or evil. Mailer's treatment makes it obvious that the former is true, but it is significant that the fictional President cares deeply about such moral considerations. Although it is the capacity to act existentially and to capture the people's imagination with his style which Mailer sees as the most essential quality for a President, the commitment to humanistic ideals adds to the man's greatness as a leader. This order of priorities established by Mailer is central to an understanding of the several stages in his attitude towards President Johnson.

Early in *Cannibals and Christians,* Mailer presents us with a review (written in 1964) of Lyndon B. Johnson's book, *My Hope for America.* After a brief but incisive discussion of the content and prose style of Johnson's book, Mailer seizes the opportunity to make certain observations on Johnson's suitability for the Presidency. Simply stated, Mailer's opinion at that time was that although Johnson was certainly better than Goldwater, beyond that he was less than might be desired, since his personal style and his vision of contemporary American problems were rather colorless and simplistic in comparison to those of his immediate predecessor. Feeling that Johnson might be unequal to meeting the challenge of the twentieth century and making America a truly great nation, Mailer makes a specific comparison of Presidential styles. He suggests that since John F. Kennedy's death we may have:

> . . . lost the clue that a democracy could become equable only if it became great, that the world would

continue to exist only by an act of courage and a
search for style. Democracy flowers with style; without
it, there is a rot of wet weeds. Which is why we love
the memory so of F.D.R. and J.F.K. For they offered
high style to the poor. And that is worth more than
a housing project.[24]

With the passage of time, and the escalation of American participation in Vietnam, Mailer's view of the Johnson administration shifted from disappointment to active
opposition. By May, 1965, Mailer could say:

> Silently, without a word, the photograph of you,
> Lyndon Johnson, will start appearing everywhere,
> upside down. Your head will speak out—even to the
> peasant in Asia—it will say that not all Americans are
> unaware of your monstrous vanity, overweening piety,
> and doubtful motive. It will tell them that we trust
> our President so little, and think so little of him, that
> we see his picture everywhere upside down.
>
> •   •   •
>
> And those little pictures will tell the world what
> we think of you and your war in Vietnam.[25]

Mailer's attitude towards Lyndon B. Johnson underwent,
in 1968, another shift, one which is easily understood in
terms of the importance Mailer assigns to a President's
ability to act dynamically and imaginatively. After President Johnson's dramatic announcement in March, 1968,
that he would not seek reelection and that he would
immediately call a partial bombing halt, Mailer stated:

> Johnson, if he does nothing else, reveals to us that
> he's a man of incredible political imagination.
> Even if his resignation from the Presidency was
> done for Machiavellian reasons, at least he's a Machia-

vellian, which you couldn't say before. And I work on the firm theory that a democracy depends upon having extraordinary people at the helm—even if they're villains, because an extraordinary villain can sometimes create an extraordinary hero.[26]

This theory, elaborated upon in *The Armies of the Night,* becomes part of a highly sophisticated and comprehensive examination of the state of American society under the Johnson administration in that book.

Neither *The Presidential Papers* nor *Cannibals and Christians* deals exclusively with political issues. Both include some poetry, most of it published earlier in *Deaths for the Ladies.* Both include, as does *Advertisements for Myself,* reprinted interviews with Mailer, in which he goes over many of the ideas developed in his books. *Cannibals and Christians,* like *Advertisements,* includes several short stories. The two areas of Mailer's interest represented in these books which remain to be mentioned are literary criticism and sports writing.

The most interesting examples of Mailer's views on contemporary literature appear in two essays: "Evaluations —Quick and Expensive Comments on the Talent in the Room," printed in *Advertisements for Myself;* and "Some Children of the Goddess," in *Cannibals and Christians.*[27] Mailer's literary criticism is more intelligent and readable work than are most of the novels written by literary critics. Not only does he discuss his own fiction with perception and candor throughout *Advertisements,* he applies these qualities equally well to the work of his contemporaries. Mailer discusses the nature of criticism as much as he does the books he treats. In "Some Children of the Goddess," he disarmingly admits his own subjectivity:

One cannot expect an objective performance therefore when one novelist criticizes the work of other novel-

ists. . . . But the reader is at least given the opportunity to compare the lies, a gratuity he cannot always get from a good critic writing about a novelist, for critics implant into their style the fiction of disinterested passion when indeed *their* vested interest, while less obvious, is often more rabid, since they have usually fixed their aim into the direction they would like the novel to travel, whereas the novelist by the nature of his endeavor is more ready to change. One need not defend the procedure used here any further than to say it is preferable to warn a reader of one's prejudices than to believe the verdict of a review which is godly in its authority and psychologically unsigned.[28]

Mailer is always putting forth his own idea of what a novelist should be as a man. In his discussions of contemporary novels, he deals always with the writer as much as with the book under consideration. He is sometimes admiring, often devastating, never charitable. Thus, he can say of James Jones in *Advertisements:*

> The only one of my contemporaries who I felt had more talent than myself was James Jones. And he has also been the one writer of my time for whom I felt any love. . . . I felt then and can still say now that *From Here to Eternity* has been the best American novel since the war. . . .[29]

But Mailer goes on to say that he feels Jones has dwindled in his writing because he has imprisoned his anger against society. Of Truman Capote, Mailer writes:

> Truman Capote I do not know well, but I like him. He is tart as a grand aunt, but in his way he is a ballsy little guy, and he is the best writer of my

generation, he writes the best sentences word for word, rhythm upon rhythm.[30]

And here, too, Mailer feels that Capote's major fault as a novelist is that he caters to society. In both of these cases, Mailer ends his remarks with the hope that Jones and Capote will fulfill the potential of their talent by combating the falsity of society.

Mailer draws upon the past to illuminate the problems of the present in literature, and he writes with surprising sophistication and perception of Dostoevsky, Tolstoy, Melville, James. But he writes of them with a very real personal understanding of their anguish, rejecting what he feels are the bloodlessly cerebral reactions of the academy:

> There is a kind of critic who writes only about the dead. He sees the great writers of the past as simple men. They are born with a great talent, they exercise it, and they die. Such critics see the mastery in the work; they neglect the subtle failures of the most courageous intent, and the dramatic hours when the man took the leap to become a great writer. They do not understand that for every great writer, there are a hundred who could have been equally great but lacked the courage.[31]

It is this concept of courage which motivates Mailer's own writing and his evaluation of the writing of others. Thus, he can say of Philip Roth's performance in *Letting Go,* "He was too careful not to get hurt on his trip and so he does not reveal himself: he does not dig." [32]

Mailer's belief that a novelist must be a brave man, willing to bare himself to a hostile society, is clear in his own books and in his comments on the state of American letters. But the nature of the battle has shifted somewhat

in the past decade, with the changing of some societal restrictions in publishing. A comparison of two statements, written almost ten years apart, reflects the change in Mailer's view of what problems primarily beset the novelist in America. In *Advertisements for Myself* he lays much responsibility for the stifling of talent at the feet of society, represented by the publishing houses:

> I will cease with the comment that the novelists will grow when the publishers improve. Five brave publishing houses (a miracle) would wear away a drop of nausea in the cancerous American conscience, and give to the thousand of us or more with real talent, the lone-wolf hope that we can begin to explore a little more of that murderous and cowardly world which will burst into madness if it does not dare a new art of the brave.[33]

In *Cannibals and Christians,* Mailer is still aware of much that could be improved in the literary establishment and the society it represents. But he also suggests that much of the battle for artistic freedom, particularly in the realm of sexual description, has been won:

> A war has been fought by some of us over the last fifteen years to open the sexual badlands to our writing, and that war is in the act of being won.[34]

Mailer realizes here that the responsibility for an advance in American letters rests upon the novelist and not upon society. The writer is now limited more by what he is or is not brave enough to dare than by publishers' restrictions. And the territory which must be dared, as Mailer sees it, is that of the writer's own psyche. As early as *Advertisements for Myself,* Mailer was willing to brave ridicule in airing his personal fears and hopes. In *An American*

Dream he dared the existential journey into his own psyche and maintained fictional control, structuring his own preoccupations within the credible character of Rojack. In *The Armies of the Night,* Mailer will go on to take an even greater risk, presenting his personality to the reader without the protective shield of fiction.

The last piece I will mention before concluding this discussion of Mailer's three nonfiction collections is a long article in *The Presidential Papers,* entitled "Death." It is a report on the first Patterson-Liston fight, but it is much more as well. Mailer gives an exciting and informed account of the fight, and he develops his subject logically and persuasively into a series of perceptive statements about the current temper of the American people. He sees this championship bout as symptomatic of the psychic problems of the people, particularly the Negroes. From this he proceeds to a discussion of boxing itself as an index of our national personality. And then, with no clumsiness in the transition, he moves to detailed discussions of violence, the Mob, voodoo, and various aspects of the human condition. Here is an example of the connections of which Mailer's brain is capable:

> But the deepest reason that Negroes in Chicago had for preferring Patterson was that they did not want to enter again the logic of Liston's world. The Negro had lived in violence, had grown in violence. . . . The demand for courage may have been exorbitant. Now as the Negro was beginning to come into the white man's world, he wanted the logic of the white man's world: annuities, mental hygiene, sociological jargon. . . . He was sick of a whore's logic and a pimp's logic. . . . The Negro wanted Patterson, because Floyd was the proof a man could be successful and yet be secure. If Liston won, the old torment

was open again. A man could be successful *or* he could be secure. He could not have both.[35]

The most striking aspect of this fascinating article, simultaneously so cerebral and so concrete in its subject matter, is the constant presence of Mailer himself. From his arguments over the fight with friends and strangers in the Playboy Club, to his conversations with James Baldwin at ringside, to his climactic confrontation with Sonny Liston himself, Mailer the reporter is physically present as a character. He is brash, witty, foolish by turns, but always interesting. And it is this personal presence, developed to its peak of effectiveness, which will be seen to spark and support the narrative success of *The Armies of the Night*.

Notes

[1] *Advertisements for Myself*, p. 22.
[2] *Ibid.*, p. 17.
[3] *Ibid.*, p. 8.
[4] *Ibid.*, p. 92.
[5] *Ibid.*, p. 265. It should be clear that while Mailer admires much in Hemingway, this admiration is highly qualified. A more precise evaluation of Hemingway's successes and failures as Mailer sees them appears on pp. 20–21 of *Advertisements for Myself*.
[6] *Ibid.*, pp. 331–332.
[7] *Ibid.*, p. 335.
[8] *Ibid.*, pp. 339–340.
[9] *Ibid.*, p. 340.
[10] *Ibid.*, p. 342.
[11] See *Advertisements for Myself*, p. 234.
[12] *Advertisements for Myself*, p. 343.
[13] *Ibid.*, p. 347.
[14] *Ibid.*, pp. 349–50.
[15] This issue has been treated in my chapter on *An American Dream*.
[16] *Advertisements for Myself*, p. 347.
[17] *Ibid.*, p. 351.
[18] *Ibid.*, p. 355.

[19] *Ibid.*, p. 355.

[20] *Cannibals and Christians*, p. 384.

[21] *Ibid.*

[22] *Ibid.*, p. 380.

[23] *Ibid.*, p. vii. The drastic difference between Mailer's views of the Kennedy and Johnson administrations is even more clearly emphasized in a recent paperback made up of essays about the two reprinted from *The Presidential Papers* and *Cannibals and Christians: The Idol and the Octopus* (New York: Dell Publishing Co., 1968).

[24] *Ibid.*, p. 52.

[25] This passage is the conclusion of "A Speech at Berkeley on Vietnam Day," published in *Cannibals and Christians*, p. 82. For a more complete view of Mailer's position regarding American involvement in Vietnam in 1965, see *Cannibals and Christians*, pp. 67–90.

[26] In a panel discussion held by The Theater for Ideas, printed in *The New York Times Magazine*, May 26, 1968, p. 30.

[27] Originally published in *Esquire* in 1964.

[28] *Cannibals and Christians*, p. 109.

[29] *Advertisements for Myself*, p. 463.

[30] *Ibid.*, p. 465.

[31] *Cannibals and Christians*, p. 108.

[32] *Ibid.*, p. 122.

[33] *Advertisements for Myself*, p. 473.

[34] *Cannibals and Christians*, p. 130.

[35] *The Presidential Papers*, pp. 241.

8

The Armies of the Night and *Miami and the Siege of Chicago*

In Mailer's nonfiction prose, whether the subject be literature, politics, or existential psychology, there is never an attempt to mute or disguise the voice of the man, Mailer. He is always frankly subjective, and it is this quality upon which rests the success of Mailer's two most recent books, *The Armies of the Night* and *Miami and the Siege of Chicago* (both 1968). I must state at the outset that I regard *Armies* as the superior of the two books, in structure, style and content.[1] The first of the two to appear, it is a firsthand account of the October, 1967 march on the Pentagon, presented in a successful synthesis of the journalistic and novelistic forms. *Miami and Chicago*, Mailer's account of the Republican and Democratic national conventions of 1968, is itself a very worthwhile and readable book, employing much the same personal narrative stance used in *Armies*. But it is *The Armies of the Night* which represents the significant innovation in form and the more successful execution of it, and since the books are similar in tone and message, it is *Armies* with which I am primarily concerned in this chapter.

The Armies of the Night is as much an outgrowth of Mailer's fiction as of his journalism. The subtitle of the book is "History as a Novel/the Novel as History," and it is a successful combination of the two forms. Mailer recounts historical events here, but he presents them through a plot and structure and a participating narrator which belong to the novel.

In all of Mailer's work, his preoccupation with contemporary politics has been evident. But the most explicitly polemical of his earlier books is *Barbary Shore,* which failed largely because it disintegrated in its later chapters into a series of boring political essays. An indication of the enormous distance Mailer has come in his artistic development while maintaining his commitment to liberal political values may best be gained by a brief comparison between *Barbary Shore* and *The Armies of the Night.*

In *Barbary Shore,* Mailer wrote perceptively of the break between the prewar and postwar Left. In *The Armies of the Night,* he is once again concerned with a precise rendering of the essential differences between the old and the New Left. In both books, Mailer deals with the potential totalitarianism represented by the reactionary elements in America. But where the earlier book ends on a note of isolated resistance to a vague and decidedly pessimistic future, the later work finds Mailer more *personally* involved than ever before, hopeful that totalitarianism may be averted through the courage of a large minority of the citizenry. Today as twenty years ago, Mailer is aware of what the present portends; but now he is even more a man for the future.

The enormous discrepancy in the artistic success of

the two books lies primarily in form. Both represent conscious attempts to break away from old literary forms in the search for a nonderivative art. But in *Barbary Shore,* the combination of a new narrative voice, an experimental fictional form, and a polemical message are not integral to one another. *The Armies of the Night,* by contrast, is the effective culmination of Mailer's perceptible movement towards an assimilation of the best of his perceptions within a clear and compelling prose voice. The book is rife with digressions on a multitude of subjects. Yet none of these are superfluous, none unassimilated into the smooth, eminently readable narrative.

As his own narrator/protagonist, Mailer is free to present any perception or attitude without fictional disguise. And because *Armies* is a novel as well as a history, the author is freed from the obligation to create the ostensible mood of objectivity sought by most "factual" reporting. He begins with the assumption that the account is a subjective one.

The combination of subject and form is well chosen. What better subject could Mailer choose to deal with his abiding preoccupation with the problems of American society than an event which concerns the entire population and lies at the heart of the nation's illness? What better way to deal with the fears and hopes of the individual in that society than by choosing as his narrator a participant in that event, a concerned eyewitness who elaborates articulately and imaginatively upon his own reactions and those of such other participants as U.S. Marshals, American Nazis, and hippies?

What of this narrator/participant, then? To begin with, the book is written in the third person. Mailer refers to himself by name, and by such other designations as the Novelist or the Participant. Rather than rendering the narrative stilted, this device proves in execution far less clumsy than a straight first-person narrative might have been. The writing is eminently palatable.

The most striking thing about Mailer as protagonist is a new sense of modesty and personal limitation. He is often frightened and weak, uncertain of how he will react in the face of moral confrontation or physical danger (as when he worries about being clubbed or dosed with Mace; or when he stares down a young American Nazi and prepares for a fist fight). Although the public airing of his own defiances and defeats has been a part of Mailer's nonfiction writing since *Advertisements for Myself,* there is something new here: his willingness to present himself in a humorous light. If Mailer is often deadly serious in this book, he is also his own comic figure. If he examines the motives of others, from hippies to literary peers to governmental figures, he is equally honest, painstakingly so, about the validity of his own.

Mailer's understanding of what is comic about himself is presented with wit, but it also rises to great poignance, as when, leaving the stage of the Thursday night theater rally after delivering a particularly flamboyant performance, the author meets the disapproving stare of Robert Lowell. Incensed at what he considers the poet's intolerance, Mailer frames in his mind a reply which is never voiced:

> You, Lowell, beloved poet of many, what do you know of the dirt and the dark deliveries of the necessary? What do you know of dignity hard-achieved, and dignity lost through innocence, and dignity lost by sacrifice for a cause one cannot name. What do you know about getting fat against your will, and turning into a clown of an arriviste baron when you would rather be an eagle or a count. . . . How dare you condemn me! [2]

Even more central to an understanding of the new conception of self which Mailer reveals in this most mature of his books is his recogition that not every aspect of the life of the revolutionary is still open to him at age forty-four. Confessing that he had for years entertained the possibility that he would some day be an armed guerilla leader, Mailer now comes to the realization that "he would be too old by then, and too incompetent, yes, too incompetent said the new modesty. . . ." [3]

Mailer has, then, realized in himself a new version of the psychic outlaw, one step beyond that represented by Rojack. As did Hemingway in *The Old Man and the Sea,* Mailer announces in this book his arrival at a new sense of personal identity commensurate with his age. Another parallel to Hemingway is relevant here. The need to clarify one's identity and masculinity through repeated confrontations with danger informs the fiction and the life of both writers. But the dangers Mailer is concerned with are often internalized, their significance apparent only to him. That is, the objects of his fears are not as concrete, not as universally granted to be real dangers. Any reader can understand a fear of lions, or of Franco's soldiers. Mailer presents us with apprehensions about police brutality, Mace in one's eyes, or even concentration camps in a potentially totalitarian America. These dangers are very real to Mailer, but to a reader who does not share his political views they may seem chimerical.

This is a problem which is central to any understanding of Mailer's uneven public reputation. The reader who cannot accept the basic axiomatic assumptions with which Mailer begins can find little validity in a book like *The Armies of the Night.* If, for example, one finds unacceptable the idea that the war in Vietnam is an obscene war, he will be unable to accept the argument of *The Armies of the Night,* which rests in part upon that assumption.

Thus, the possibility of the internally generated totalitarianism which Mailer fears will seem to such a reader a ridiculous or offensive or even subversive idea; and the moral conflicts which Mailer undergoes in mustering the courage to commit civil disobedience will appear foolish and inconsequential.

Mailer's ideas and the art and actions which they inform are consistent and valid within the structure of his personal philosophy. Their validity to each reader is dependent upon the number of assumptions he shares with Mailer. But they are *totally* valid, of course, only to Mailer himself. Because Mailer is aggressively opinionated on every subject, his ideas coincide only at certain points with those of any other individual or any group. Thus, although Mailer describes the hippie youth at the Pentagon in largely sympathetic terms, admiring their courage and personal *style,* he is very much opposed to their abuse of such dangerous drugs as LSD. He considers them foolish and irresponsible for their use of that "devil's drug," [4] and thus inadvertantly aligns himself with what they would consider the establishment. Although he admires their youthful idealism, Mailer is all too aware that these youngsters are confused in their personal motives and ideas. This confusion is particularly evident, he feels, in their jargon, which employs such sloppy and imprecise terms as "do your thing." Late in the book, he refers to them sympathetically as "tender drug-vitiated jargon-mired children." [5]

Perhaps the most fascinating example of an uneasy alliance which is often shaken by Mailer's personal opinions is that between the author and the liberal intellectual community, among which are his greatest allies and enemies. Although most of these people find themselves more sympathetic to Mailer, more receptive to his words than ever before, because he shares their opposition to the war in Vietnam,[6] many of them are unable to countenance his exhibitionism (as at the Thursday night rally in *Armies*) or to share his fervent belief that obscenity is necessary and healthy. More important, they cannot take seriously a belief which Mailer advances in dead earnest: that violence is a necessary part of man's existence, on both personal and national levels. He sees it not merely as a necessary evil, but often a positive source of benefit, as in his cancer theories.[7] Mailer does not follow the liberal line which assumes that man is an inherently peaceful creature perverted by economic and political systems. He has shown as early as *The Naked and the Dead* that the common man often *elects* to be brutal and selfish. In *Why Are We in Vietnam?* he charges that the American male psyche is presently in need of violent action in order to survive intact, and that this situation as much as political considerations is responsible for American presence in Vietnam.

This division between Mailer and his liberal peers (he calls himself a "Left Conservative")[8] is clearer to him than it is to them. On the way to the rally in *Armies*, "Mailer could feel no sense of belonging to these people. They were much too nice and much too principled for him."[9] And in *Miami and the Siege of Chicago* he declines to join a silent protest march for the private reason that he would prefer not to face police in the company of people who cannot fight physically. The division becomes most clear when Mailer discusses his favorite remedy for this and all wars: a limited war in the Amazon between small groups of American and Red Chinese volunteers to be held and televised for several weeks each year.[10] Although Mailer makes it clear in *The Armies of the Night* that he feels the idea has real merit, he also remarks that few people are willing to take it as more than a joke. Such lapses in communication are characteristic of Mailer's relation to his public. He is so committed to being a dynamic personality and to airing his personal views in public that there is virtually no one, no matter how sensitive to his ideas, who is not occasionally repelled or mystified by one or another of his avowals or his methods.

The structure of *The Armies of the Night* is novelistic.[11] As in a novel, the action is not always recounted in a simple chronological order. Rather, Mailer constructs a plot which presents each incident at the point in the narrative where it is most relevant and dramatically effective. He uses flashbacks, authorial intrusion, and suspense as no history text or journalistic account would dare. The structure of the plot revolves about the protagonist Mailer, who is no passive observer. Like Rojack, Mailer undergoes in this book a series of confrontations which frighten him and test the strength of his commitment to a set of personal moral values. But these crises are not embellished by the greater drama which colors *An American Dream* (as, for example, the Romeo Romalozzo showdown), nor are the immediate stakes as high (Mailer risks five days in jail while Rojack risks electrocution) or the periods of respite as exciting. Mailer himself remarks humorously on this aspect of *Armies* at the end of the Thursday evening activity:

> Of course if this were a novel, Mailer would spend the rest of the night with a lady. But it is History, and so the Novelist is for once blissfully removed from any description of the hump-your-backs of sex. Rather he can leave such matters to the happy or unhappy imagination of the reader.[12]

This book, then, is a more obviously mature presentation of Mailer's perceptions than is *An American Dream,* partially because the protagonist here is treated with more humor.

The nature of the moral choices which plague men of conscience and the necessity of defining oneself existentially through courage in one's choice is a recurring theme throughout the book. Mailer deals at length with the moral dilemma of every man who carries a draft card and with the uncompromising idealism of a group of Quakers on a hunger strike in jail.[13] But the clearest articulation of Mailer's personal sense of conscience occurs when he is about to appear before a judge, and hopefully to be released. Another defendant, Tuli Kupferberg, elects to serve a five day jail sentence rather than promise to stay away from the Pentagon for six months. This action calls into question Mailer's intention to make such a promise (as have all previous defendants that day) in return for a suspended sentence. Cerebrating at length about this new, unwelcome challenge, Mailer sees "an endless ladder of moral challenges."[14] He elaborates further, structuring a theory which stipulates that each step up such a ladder purges some personal guilt, but that to step down at any stage leads to the negation of one's moral gains, and to "moral nausea." After a compromise courtroom situation in which Mailer does receive a suspended sentence, but in which he feels he has acquitted himself reasonably well, he comes to the conclusion that even a partial ascent up the ladder can leave one cleaner and braver.

It is interesting that in *Miami and the Siege of Chicago,* too, Mailer comes into conflict with authority and with violence and with his own fear. Attending the Democratic convention in Chicago, he is arrested and released twice within a few minutes, gets into a fist fight with a supposed delegate whom he feels is a disguised policeman, and several times wrestles with doubts of his own courage. More amusingly, at the Republican convention in Miami, he gains entrance to an exclusive reception by brashly pretending to be a secret serviceman. But in *Miami and*

Chicago these confrontations are not woven strategically into a taut plot structure as they are in *The Armies of the Night,* and one feels that in the convention pieces they are merely standard Mailer equipment.

The confrontations which Mailer experiences in *The Armies of the Night* are parallel to the innumerable similar experiences of other protesters, and symptomatic of the overall confrontation between the antiwar forces and the military establishment. In this sense, the book is thematically structured much like the *Iliad,* proceeding simultaneously on an individual and a national level. *The Armies of the Night* is about Mailer, but his personal story is an integral part of the larger conflict of which he tells. The comparison to Homer's epic of war is not an idle one, for Mailer states several times in the speeches he makes to the protesters (both in *Armies* and *Miami and Chicago*) that they are in the first battle of a war which may last many years. The title, *The Armies of the Night,* suggests this idea still further.[15]

The most frightening conflict to take place at the Pentagon, one which Mailer reserves for the dramatic climax of his book, is that between the relatively small (several hundred) group of remaining youth and a contingent of troops all through the night at the Pentagon. Refusing to leave as ordered, the young men and women are beaten and arrested. In what is perhaps the most effective combination of the novelistic and journalistic forms in the entire book, Mailer documents a series of factual incidents from eyewitness accounts in the news media, and molds the bare factual situation into a powerful and poignant piece of literature by the skillful use of authorial comment. He sees the confrontation as an archetypal rite of passage, in which the protesters overcome their own fear and become battle-proved veterans.

I must emphasize here what I have suggested earlier

about Mailer's sympathies. He is very much in accord with
the political aims of the New Left, and particularly of
these youth; but he does not romanticize them to the point
that he admires all of them and all of their methods without qualification. Although he makes a point of describing
certain individuals whom he feels are particularly dynamic in style or exceptionally brave, he does find fault
with numerous young protesters who appear selfish or
morally weak to him. Although he describes the panoramic
March on the Pentagon in stirring martial terms (civil
war metaphors particularly abound) and admires the flamboyant battle clothing of many participants (whom he describes without irony as "Crusaders" [16]), he sees the carrying of a Viet Cong flag by one group as foolish and purposeless.

Perhaps the clearest issue by which to illustrate the
precision of Mailer's perception of the national situation
as represented by the March, and the care he takes to
articulate the nice distinctions of his position as it differs
from that of any large group, is his treatment of the Negro
problem here. It might be well not to avoid a statement
Mailer makes in *Miami and the Siege of Chicago* which
may bring some public wrath upon him yet. After he and
other reporters are kept waiting for a scheduled press con-
ference with the Reverend Ralph D. Abernathy, Mailer
discovers in himself a new and very unpleasant feeling:
"he was getting tired of Negroes and their rights." [17] Although it is the product of a momentary irritation, the
reaction disturbs Mailer, for he sees it as an indication of
how much more unsympathetic to the Negro cause the
conservative elements in America must be today. Although
Mailer may be attacked for this remark by those who wish
to see bigots everywhere, my reaction is that Mailer, concerned always with the nuances of every situation, and of
his own reactions, is being characteristically candid here.

258 *The Structured Vision of Norman Mailer*

The statement must not be taken out of context. Mailer has been a consistent and vocal advocate of civil rights throughout his career, and elsewhere in *Miami and Chicago* he writes sympathetically of the Negro's problem. In *The Armies of the Night,* he writes perceptively and with some sadness of the general breakdown of the erstwhile Black/White liberal alliance,[18] finding particular poignance in the momentary feeling of reunion which is generated when the protesters sing "We Shall Overcome." And he recognizes validity in the decision of a group of Negro protesters to disassociate themselves from the March and demonstrate separately in another part of Washington. But he is not afraid to remark on his irritation even towards the movements he considers most valid and just.

Mailer always says what he thinks, and he is rarely silenced by considerations of tact or blind group loyalty. Thus, in *The Armies of the Night* he precipitates conflict not only with those individuals who represent everything he is opposed to, such as the American Nazi, the U.S. Marshals, and a *Time* magazine reporter, but with his allies as well when they diverge from his views, as in the case of Robert Lowell, Dwight Macdonald and Ed de-Grazia on the stage at the theater rally. Mailer reacts strongly and honestly to each individual he meets, regardless of political affiliation or color. Thus, he finds most of the U.S. Marshals and troops frightening or unpleasant, but he describes one Marshal and one young Negro MP in sympathetic terms. On the March, he particularly admires a young Negro leader named Harris,[19] but violently dislikes an officious Negro monitor.[20] And in jail, the worst cellmates he has are a "sly" octaroon [21] and a whining white boy, both of whom try to exploit him.

The metaphorical texture of *The Armies of the Night* (and of *Miami and Chicago* as well) is, as might be ex-

pected of Mailer, lush and diverse. We find many familiar
Mailer ideas and images, among them his theories of obscenity, cancer, excretion, witches, the Devil, God, and
the soul. More than in most of his books, he draws metaphors from sports: football, baseball, boxing, bullfighting.
But the dominating image of the book is that of war.
Returning the microphone to Dwight Macdonald at the
theater rally, Mailer muses on his own actions: "Under
the military circumstances, it was a decent cleanup operation." [22] The more precise comparison to the Civil War
has already been mentioned. Mailer uses it repeatedly,
and in the present political situation, with the nation
more violently divided than it has been for a century, the
comparison is apt. But for Mailer, the analogy has another
dimension as well. In this new struggle he sees a romantic
spirit surrounding the motives and actions of the more
sincere elements of the New Left; and on this day of battle
he gladly senses "a ghost of Gettysburg." [23] The sense of
romantic nostalgia which Mailer associates with the Civil
War is most obvious when, having won his release from
jail after a taut and exciting exchange of legal wit between
his lawyer and a fair federal judge, Mailer exchanges
words of mutual respect with the judge: "Mailer, prompted
by some shade in the late afternoon air of lost Civil War
protocols in Virginia, spoke to the Commissioner." [24] The
implication here, as elsewhere in the book, is that there
are good men in America, and that the old ideals of
courage and honesty may prevail yet. In this light, Mailer
is able to see a "sweetness" in the war between the Right
and the New Left: "the sweetness of war came back."
Mailer is not a pacifist. He considers most wars bad, and
the war in Vietnam particularly so. But he feels that there
are some wars which are just; and in this March on the
Pentagon, which he sees as the "first major battle of a war

which may go on for twenty years," [25] there is for him a romantic sweetness.

The central political statement of *The Armies of the Night* is set forth cogently and simply enough for the edification of the most naive reader, then elaborated upon with a sophistication which can teach something to the most politically aware. Mailer draws distinctions between the old and the new Left and between external and internal threats of totalitarianism, which seem self-evident to the liberal community but which are incomprehensible to much of the rest of the population. The oversimplified view of the patriotic right wing is best illustrated in a long passage in which Mailer describes a tough, sincerely patriotic U.S. Marshal who can barely control his rage at the protesters, whom he feels are "Communists," helping to weaken America for a Communist invasion. Mailer knows that the depth of this man's enraged commitment to this rigid preconception obviates any possibility of communicating logically with him:

> . . . in this Marshal's mind . . . the evil was with-
> out, America was threatened by a foreign disease, and
> the Marshal was threatened to the core of his sanity
> by any one of the first fifty of Mailer's ideas which
> would insist that the evil was within. . . .[26]

The simplistic fears of such men as the Marshal are misguided, as Mailer shows in the distinction he draws between the old and the new Left, since the people on the Pentagon March, with the exception of a few diehard Communists, have no allegiance to any international left-wing movement. The Communist party in America, as Mailer wryly notes, is dead but still being beaten; and its few remaining adherents are boring and ineffectual and closed-minded. The New Left, on the other hand, both student militants and moderate middle-class liberals, are interested not in any international movement, but in improving America by redressing social injustices, increasing individual freedom and opposing any movement toward a totalitarianism of the Right.

Throughout *The Armies of the Night*, Mailer criticizes much in America; but again and again, he affirms his deep love for her.[27] The clearest and most beautiful articulation of Mailer's feelings about America in 1968 is the powerful concluding paragraph of the book:

> Brood on that country who expresses our will. She is America, once a beauty of magnificence unparalleled, now a beauty with a leprous skin. She is heavy with child—no one knows if legitimate—and languishes in a dungeon whose walls are never seen. Now the first contractions of her fearsome labor begin—it will go on: no doctor exists to tell the hour. It is only known that false labor is not likely on her now, no, she will probably give birth, and to what?— the most fearsome totalitarianism the world has ever known? or can she, poor giant, tormented lovely girl, deliver a babe of a new world brave and tender, artful and wild? Rush to the locks. God writhes in his bonds. Rush to the locks. Deliver us from our curse. For we must end on the road to that mystery where courage, death, and the dream of love give promise of sleep.[28]

Mailer sees a frightening situation, but there is hope here as well. Unlike Rojack, Mailer remains tied to America, committed to ride out the battle and to work for a better future. Unlike D.J., the more courageous of today's youth can reject the outworn values of the past and still do their fighting here at home, working constructively for freedom. Finally, in *The Armies of the Night,* as in no other piece Mailer has previously written (except the short story, "The Last Night," which in this sense prefigures it), hope is societal as well as individual. In this thematic resolution, as in the masterful control of form and subject matter, *The Armies of the Night* is evidence that Mailer has progressed enormously, both artistically and personally, in the twenty years since the publication of *The Naked and the Dead.*

The Armies of the Night lends itself conveniently to a symmetrical conclusion of this study of Mailer. The book ties together virtually every line of development with which I have been concerned throughout his work. The theme of increasing hope for the individual and his society; the development in both fiction and nonfiction of a unique, highly controlled narrative voice and of a nonderivative prose art; the assimilation of Mailer's personal image and of his carefully structured philosophical and political theories into a literary form which presents them clearly to a large reading public; the consequent rise in his popular and critical reputation: all of these are here. The significance of *The Armies of the Night* is dramatically emphasized by the fact that it has won the 1968 National Book Award for Arts and Letters and the Pulitzer Prize for general nonfiction.

But one question remains unanswerable today. Mailer is still a novelist, and an ambitious one. Will he ever succeed in writing that major work of fiction to which he has always aspired? The exciting thing about studying Mailer's career is that one comes to realize how foolhardy it is to put anything past him. Mailer has yet to hit the longest ball in American letters. But more than ever, it seems today that if anyone alive can do it, it is he. I'm still rooting for him.

Notes

1 Mailer himself draws a comparison between the protest in Chicago and the far more symbolically significant one at the Pentagon. See *Miami and the Siege of Chicago* (New York: Signet [The New American Library], 1968), p. 144.

2 *The Armies of the Night*, p. 41.

3 *Ibid.*, p. 78.

4 *Ibid.*, p. 34 and pp. 92–93. Although Mailer feels marijuana is relatively harmless, he is opposed to the use of LSD because he feels it can destroy future generations by harming the user's chromosomes.

5 *The Armies of the Night*, p. 280.

6 I have mentioned in Chapter 5 above, that such sympathies with the political position of *Why Are We in Vietnam?* seem to have stimulated favorable evaluations by some liberal critics (and conversely, unfavorable ones by conservative critics). *The Armies of the Night*, a far better book in its own right, has received a more objective critical response.

7 See chapters 3 and 4, above, or *Cannibals and Christians*, p. 91, Also, see Mailer's definition of the hip psychopath in "The White Negro."

8 *The Armies of the Night*, p. 124, p. 180, p. 185.

9 *Ibid.*, p. 68.

10 See *The Armies of the Night*, p. 189. The germ of this idea may be found as early as *The Presidential Papers*, p. 248. Mailer has also expressed this idea in public on a number of occasions. I happened to be present at a speech Mailer made as part of an antiwar rally. When he mentioned this Amazon War Game remedy, the audience laughed uproariously (intent on showing that they were on his side and understood the absurdity of all violence). I doubt that anyone understood that he was serious.

11 For a more precise statement of Mailer's structural intentions here, see *The Armies of the Night*, pp. 254–255, where he draws a fine distinction between "History as a Novel" and "The Novel as History."

12 *The Armies of the Night*, p. 52. Another particularly amusing reference by Mailer to novelistic practices as they bear on the narrative form of *Armies* appears on p. 133, where he consciously adopts the Victorian practice of authorial intrusion.

13 *The Armies of the Night*, p. 270, pp. 286–287.

14 *Ibid.*, p. 195.

[15] The dust jacket remarks that the title was suggested by Matthew Arnold's "Dover Beach."

[16] *The Armies of the Night*, p. 92.

[17] *Miami and the Siege of Chicago*, p. 51.

[18] See especially *The Armies of the Night*, pp. 101–102.

[19] *Ibid.*, pp. 61–62.

[20] *Ibid.*, p. 109.

[21] *Ibid.*, p. 164.

[22] *Ibid.*, p. 40.

[23] *Ibid.*, p. 97.

[24] *Ibid.*, p. 211.

[25] *Ibid.*, p. 88.

[26] *Ibid.*, pp. 144–145.

[27] See especially *The Armies of the Night*, p. 47 and p. 113.

[28] *Ibid.*, p. 288.

Selected Bibliography

Works by Norman Mailer:

Advertisements for Myself. New York: G. P. Putnam's Sons, 1959.

An American Dream. New York: Dial Press, 1965. Paperback edition published by Dell Publishing Company: New York, 1966.

The Armies of the Night. New York: The New American Library, Inc., 1968.

Barbary Shore. New York: Rinehart and Company, 1951. Paperback edition published by Signet (New American Library of World Literature): New York, 1953.

Cannibals and Christians. New York: Dial Press, 1966.

Deaths for the Ladies and Other Disasters. New York: G. P. Putnam's Sons, 1962.

The Deer Park. New York: G. P. Putnam's Sons, 1955. Paperback edition published by Signet (New American Library of World Literature): New York, 1957.

The Deer Park: A Play. New York: Dell Publishing Company, 1967.

The Idol and the Octopus. New York: Dell Publishing Co., 1968.

Miami and the Siege of Chicago. New York: Signet (New American Library of World Literature), 1968.

The Naked and the Dead. New York: Holt, Rinehart and Winston, 1948. Paperback edition published by Signet (New American Library of World Literature): New York, 1951.
The Presidential Papers. New York: G. P. Putnam's Sons, 1963.
The Short Fiction of Norman Mailer. New York: Dell Publishing Company, 1967.
The White Negro. San Francisco: City Lights Book Shop, 1958.
Why Are We in Vietnam? New York: G. P. Putnam's Sons, 1967.

Secondary Material:

Aldridge, John W. "From Vietnam to Obscenity," *Harper's Magazine,* 236 (February, 1968), 91–97.
Foster, Richard. *Norman Mailer.* University of Minnesota Pamphlets on American Writers, 1968.
Fremont-Smith, Eliot. "Norman Mailer's Cherry Pie," *The New York Times,* CXVI (September 8, 1967), 37.
Geismar, Maxwell. *American Moderns: From Rebellion to Conformity.* New York: Hill and Wang, 1966.
Hicks, Granville. "Lark in Race for Presidency," *Saturday Review,* L (September 16, 1967), 39–40.
Hux, Samuel Holland. "American Myth and Existential Vision: The Indigenous Existentialism of Mailer, Bellow, Styron and Ellison." Unpublished doctoral dissertation, University of Connecticut, 1965.
Kaufmann, Donald Louis. "Norman Mailer from 1948 to 1963: The Sixth Mission." Unpublished doctoral dissertation, University of Iowa, 1966.
Kroll, Jack. "The Scrambler," *Newsweek,* LXX (September 18, 1967), 100–101.
"Mr. Mailer Interviews Himself," *The New York Times Book Review,* CXVI (September 17, 1967), 4–5, 40.

"Playboy Interview: Norman Mailer," *Playboy,* XV (January, 1968), 69–84.

Scott, James Burton. "The Individual and Society: Norman Mailer versus William Styron." Unpublished doctoral dissertation, Syracuse University, 1964.

Sokolov, Raymond A. "Flying High with Mailer," *Newsweek,* LXXII (December 9, 1968), 84–88.

Spicehandler, Daniel. "The American War Novel." Unpublished doctoral dissertation, Columbia University, 1960.

Toback, James. "At Play in the Fields of the Bored," *Esquire,* LXX (December, 1968), 150–155.

Index

| -